THE UNITED STATES
VERSUS
PORFIRIO DÍAZ

"It is an axiom in Texas history that when a Texan fights a Mexican he can win; but when he parleys he is doomed."
Walter Prescott Webb, *The Texas Rangers*

THE UNITED STATES
VERSUS
PORFIRIO DÍAZ

By Daniel Cosío Villegas

Translated by Nettie Lee Benson

UNIVERSITY OF NEBRASKA PRESS 1963

Publishers on the Plains

UNP

Copyright © 1963 by the University of Nebraska Press

All rights reserved

Library of Congress Catalog card number 63-15929

Passages up to 500 words may be quoted without permission in writing from the publisher.

Estados Unidos contra Porfirio Díaz was first published in 1956 by Editorial Hermes, Mexico, D.F.

First printing April 1964
Second printing June 1965

PREFACE:
EL HOMBRE Y LA OBRA
(The Man and the Work)

It is the responsibility of the writer of the preface to a translated work to introduce the readers in the new language to the author and work in question. Daniel Cosío Villegas, the author of *The United States versus Porfirio Díaz,* is a most exceptional subject since he has had not one career, but several and his achievements in each have been noteworthy. Cosío Villegas has made his mark as an educator, publisher, and diplomatist; and his writing in the fields of history, economics, sociology, and international affairs have won for him recognition as one of the intellectual giants of the Americas.

Educated in Mexico, the United States, England, and France, Cosío Villegas has served as professor and Director of the National School of Economics. From 1958 to 1963 he was President of El Colegio de México, a research and teaching institution emphasizing the fields of history, international relations, and philology. Under his leadership El Colegio has become a leading scholarly center and a model for institutions of its kind throughout Latin America. In 1950 Dr. Cosío was elected to El Colegio Nacional, an institution modeled on the French Academy and composed of the persons recognized as the outstanding representatives of each discipline.

The Fondo de Cultura Económica justly enjoys the reputation as the outstanding publication house for cultural and intellectual works in Latin America. Dr. Cosío was not only its

[v]

founder, but for fifteen years its principal force. He founded and for a dozen years directed *El Trimestre Económico,* the leading Mexican scholarly journal in the field of economics. For a decade he also directed *Historia Mexicana,* scholarly journal in the field of history, which he initiated at El Colegio de México.

As an economist he has served as advisor to the Mexican Secretary of the Treasury, the National Bank of Mexico, and the Mexican delegation to the United Nations. He has attended various international conferences with the rank of Minister Plenipotentiary. During Mexico's tenure on the United Nations' Economic and Social Council, Dr. Cosío was his country's permanent delegate and in 1959 served as president of the international organization.

Unquestionably, Dr. Cosío is best known by his writings. In 1949 he published a volume of essays entitled *Extremos de América.* One critic noted that the author of the volume "had converted himself into one of the most notable and most lucid Mexican essayists and into one of the most penetrating diagnosticians of the problems of Mexico and of America." As a historian Dr. Cosío currently is engaged in the most ambitious project of historical scholarship in Latin America. He is the initiator, director, and editor of the multi-volume *Historia Moderna de México,* to which he is also a major contributor. Five massive volumes of this monumental study of Mexican history from 1867 to 1910 already have been published and three volumes are in various stages of preparation. Upon completion of this project, Dr. Cosío and his colleagues plan at least four additional volumes on Mexico's history during the three decades since the initiation of the Revolution of 1910.

The *Historia Moderna* treats of the political, social, economic, and diplomatic history of Mexico from the restoration of the Republic in 1867 through the dictatorship of Porfirio Díaz (1876-1880, 1884-1911) to the beginning of the revolutionary movement which toppled Díaz and initiated the currents of contemporary Mexico. Dr. Cosío has undertaken to write several of the volumes, including two on the foreign relations of the period.

The volume offered here in translation might be called a dividend of the larger effort.

Dr. Cosío is concerned with the relations between the United States and Mexico from the revolt of Tuxtepec, which brought Díaz to power, through the end of the Mexican leader's first administration, with emphasis on the diplomatic episodes which developed over a year and a half and concluded with the recognition of the Díaz government by the neighboring government to the north. Dr. Cosío's volume stands as a model for case studies in diplomatic history. The book is distinguished by the author's excellence of method, by the good use made of materials obtained from archival investigations both in Mexico and the United States, by the scrupulousness of his judgments, and by his perceptive understanding of the period involved.

The book's second great virtue is a matter of its structure and form. Focusing attention on a single subject, Dr. Cosío scrutinizes it in all its variations, employing a praiseworthy economy of means while preserving unity and dramatic liveliness. From condensed diplomatic notes and reports, the author has skillfully reconstructed the conversations between able American diplomat John W. Foster and the man who proved to be more than his match, Mexican Foreign Minister Ignacio Luis Vallarta. Dr. Cosío provides the reader with a concise, effective picture of the historical setting and then develops the dramatic chancellery struggle to obtain recognition, which was accompanied, at times, by racking tension and the implicit possibility of armed conflict. Backed by the strong-willed Díaz, Vallarta, employing legalistic arguments and dilatory tactics, achieved his goal while avoiding a showdown.

There also is provided a corrective to stereotyped views which consider dominant characteristics of Díaz and his regime as applicable throughout the long years of his tenure in power. Latin America's longest term dictatorship received not only the diplomatic recognition, but also the plaudits of the international community. It came to be known for its order, stability, and financial soundness. The Díaz regime came to be known—

and subsequently criticized—for its good relations with foreign powers and its favored treatment of foreign nationals.

However, this picture was not true in 1876. Díaz, as the military leader of one more successful rebellion, was not firmly entrenched, the nation was in a state of financial misery, and the recognition of his regime did not come easily. Nevertheless the Díaz regime refused to agree to a prior treaty covering special concessions to the United States which would have given recognition a conditional character. When recognition was accorded, it was without exceptional conditions.

Dr. Cosío's case study involves consideration of problems which appear and reappear in the subsequent diplomatic relations between the two countries: claims, recognition, border raids, and the treatment of foreign investors. It is useful to see these problems, as well as a significant diplomatic episode, from the Mexican point of view. All too often our literature affords us a unilateral view and interpretation of diplomatic history. Here for all to see is the sensitive pride and nationalistic feeling of the Mexican; here portrayed much better than a foreign scholar could do it the attitudes and motives of the Mexican negotiators. While Dr. Cosío obviously takes pride in what he concluded was an important Mexican diplomatic victory, his spirit is objective and his account is well balanced and fair.

The many attributes of this study were recognized by Dr. Nettie Lee Benson who applied her talent and energy to the preparation of the English translation of Dr. Cosío's monograph. Dr. Benson, who is in charge of the Latin American Collection of the Library of the University of Texas, is a prominent Mexicanist in her own right, having made significant contributions with her writings to the understanding of Mexican historical development.

STANLEY ROBERT ROSS

State University of New York at Stony Brook
March, 1963.

CONTENTS

Preface: *El Hombre y la Obra* by Stanley Robert Ross   v

Introduction   xi

I.   A Good and Bad Beginning   3

II.   He Who Wins Pays   13

III.   Jealous as Can Be   22

IV.   The Other Side of the Intrigue   37

V.   More Adverse Signs   50

VI.   Blind Alley   65

VII.   On the Mexican Side   81

VIII.   The Exit from the Alley   98

IX.   Another Blind Alley   110

X.   A Bad Balance   129

XI.   Frontier Street   139

XII.   And Who Will Carry the Corpse?   158

XIII.   For My Race Mars Will Speak   178

XIV.   The Last Chat   189

XV.   Relevance and Moral   216

Notes   239

Bibliography and Key to Abbreviations   245

Index   251

INTRODUCTION

There can be no question but that Porfirio Díaz in his revolutionary days was what the press today would call a pink: a fierce anticlericalist and a Jacobin Liberal who was both xenophobic and anti-imperialist. In 1876, when he was in Oaxaca, organizing the armies which would carry him to military victory and political power, he issued a decree which declared null and void all contracts made under the government of Sebastián Lerdo de Tejada. By this means he intended to cancel the concessions made to foreign companies for the construction of public works—railroads, telegraph lines, highways—and especially to annul any arrangements for the settlement of Mexico's foreign debt. The decree was aimed at discrediting Lerdo politically, but it also expressed a conviction. To dispel any idea that the measure had been merely one of political expediency—of fortuitous origin, determined purely by circumstances—once he was victorious, Díaz caused it to be published anew in the capital of the Republic. Moreover, a short while later he decided to annul a concession given by the Lerdo government (and of course approved by the Congreso de la Unión) to the English firm of Barron and Forbes for the construction of a railroad. Despite the declaration of the United States minister, John W. Foster, to Ignacio L. Vallarta, the Secretary of Foreign Relations, that his government could not consent to the arbitrary annulment of contracts made by United States citizens with a legitimate constitutional government, Díaz maintained the validity of his decree; and he carried out his resolve to annul the concession even though Foster, who was then in charge of British interests in Mexico, interceded in behalf of the English firm of Barron and Forbes.

The doctrinaire anti-imperialism of Porfirio Díaz' rebel days and the anti-imperialism he practiced in his initial period as President of Mexico are plain upon the record. Nonetheless, by 1870 he had come to favor unreservedly the investment of foreign capital in Mexico and to consent to such a degree of outside intervention in internal affairs that there was a presidential campaign run entirely by foreigners without any ostensible participation by the Mexicans.

Is this another case of a man who preaches one thing and practices another? If—as I believe—it is not, then it is necessary to account for the change. But important historical mutations seldom, if ever, lend themselves to a single, direct, simple, and exact explanation. This book, therefore, attempts to explain only in part that notable transformation—a transformation which affected not only Porfirio Díaz personally but also the group then in power and the fate of the whole country. Its effects were felt in the United States as well, for after the episode studied in these pages United States diplomacy in Mexico changed radically.

I am indebted to Dr. Nettie Lee Benson for valuable suggestions in the composition of Chapter 4 and to Dr. John P. Harrison for having facilitated the use of the papers of the United States Department of State and the former War Department, now a branch of the Department of Defense, which are kept in the National Archives in Washington, D.C.

DANIEL COSÍO VILLEGAS

THE UNITED STATES
VERSUS
PORFIRIO DÍAZ

I
A GOOD AND BAD
BEGINNING

Long before the victory of the Mexican Republic over the Empire, while the duration of the struggle was yet unknown; at the moment when Maximilian, faced with the withdrawal of French aid, had already resolved to play his card of final resistance—for which he was certainly not lacking in forces; when, in a word, the end of the military campaign was very distant and uncertain, Matías Romero, Mexican minister in Washington, transmitted on March 28, 1867, to the Secretary of Foreign Relations, Sebastián Lerdo de Tejada, an urgent request from the government of the United States.

It was true that the departure of Carlota for Europe in July, 1866, was the first public demonstration that French support was being withdrawn from Maximilian, and that from that time it was doubtful that the Empress would succeed in regaining it. And so it was, in fact, that the French troops began embarking for their homeward voyage in the middle of December, 1866, the last ones doing so on March 12, 1867. Maximilian, however, decided to organize his own army, at the head of which he placed his two best generals, Miguel Miramón and Leonardo Márquez; and as a result some French, Belgian, and Austrian leaders and officers, and even troops, remained to serve under the imperial flag.

It was also true that the initial withdrawal of the invading armies made it possible for the republican forces to begin in

June, 1866, the spectacular accomplishments of occupying Monterrey, Saltillo, and later San Luis Potosi, Hermosillo, and Guaymas. But when Benito Juárez, confident that the tide was definitely turning, installed his symbolic government in Zacatecas, Miramón had more than enough resources and strength to recapture the city in January, 1867, almost apprehending the President himself. On March 14 of that year the republican forces of Mariano Escobedo and of Ramón Corona began the siege of Querétaro; but Miramón attacked the besiegers on April 1, broke through and sailed past their lines and defeated Corona's forces in the action at Cimatario Hill. Finally on that same day, April 27, Márquez arrived with his forces at Mexico City, and his orders were to hurry to Querétaro to break the blockade which was diminishing the main, though not the only, offensive force of the imperial army. In any case only on April 2 did Puebla fall to the republicans; only on May 15 did Querétaro actually fall; and not until June 15 was the capital surrendered.

William H. Seward, Secretary of State of the United States, based his optimism for the immediate triumph of the republican cause not on the direct information of diplomatic, consular, or military agents of the United States and not even on information from within his country, but solely on one fact: the "friendly and explicit" agreement between the United States and Napoleon III. According to it the French expeditionary forces would abandon Mexico in three sections: the first in November, 1866, the second in March and the third in November, 1867. Once the total evacuation was completed, France would announce its agreement with the United States not to intervene further in Mexico's internal affairs.

Seward knew that various United States groups doubted that the French government would faithfully fulfill its commitment, even though neither he nor Andrew Johnson, the President of the United States, shared that doubt. For that reason he expected that the first, or perhaps even all, of the forces would embark in November, 1866. His confidence wavered only slightly and temporarily when at the end of that month he received news directly from Paris of the postponement of the promised evacuation, but he regained it fully when France shortly thereafter offered to conclude the withdrawal in March, 1867. Not even the news of an eyewitness reporting that on December 11, 1866, he had seen two hundred soldiers of the French Foreign Legion disembark in Veracruz was able to shake Seward's faith; nor could the news that the Catholic church offered to raise fifteen million pesos and an army of thirty-six thousand men to place under the command of Miramón and Márquez.*

It is difficult to imagine a greater crisis in diplomatic relations between the United States and Mexico than that of the last months of 1866 and all of 1867. In the capital there remained only the consul general, Marcus Otterbourg, whom Henry Thompson, *New York Herald Tribune* correspondent who accompanied Maximilian during the siege of Querétaro, accused of sympathizing with the imperialist cause and even of receiving from the Emperor seven thousand pesos to go to Washington to induce the Department of State to take a more benevolent attitude toward the imperial cause. Liberals as eminent as Juan José Baz confirmed the reactionary bias of Otterbourg, in addition accusing him of swindling and of abusing his consular position by charging high prices to the merchants of the capital interested in seeing that their correspondence would arrive safely in Veracruz by protecting it with the seal of the United States consul.

Lewis D. Campbell, named United States Minister to Mexico in October, 1866, reached the Bay of Veracruz on the battleship *Susquehanna,* but upon seeing the port occupied by the imperialists he did not disembark. Instead he installed himself in a luxurious hotel in New Orleans from whence he refused to stir, offering at times the excuse of his own illness or that of his

---

*Seward's trusting nature can be seen very clearly in J. M. Callahan, *The Evolution of Seward's Mexican Policy* (Morgantown: West Virginia University Studies in American History, Series I, Nos. 1-6), a work which was certainly not written to reveal it. It actually caused Seward's diplomacy to be dubbed one "of rose water."

family, at other times the quarantine for going from Havana to Veracruz or that he would have to make the journey in English ships, a repugnant thing, for he considered it an evil omen to his diplomatic duties for him to arrive on Mexican soil under the flag of an enemy. Campbell was not interested in his mission. He was searching for a way to live unconventionally and perhaps he feared he would not be able to control his dipsomaniacal inclinations, which in New Orleans overcame him to the extent that he drank continually for entire weeks. Edward Lee Plumb, named secretary to Campbell, also lived in New Orleans, isolated from and boycotted by his minister, who hid official papers from him, as well as his own negotiations and intentions. Plumb eventually denounced Campbell, telling the Department of State of his scandalous conduct. The result was that the Department discharged Plumb, hastened to accept the resignation of Campbell, and named Otterbourg minister, only to have to relieve him of his duties a short while later.

MATÍAS ROMERO transmitted to his government the essence of a conversation which he had with Seward on March 26, 1867. Seward, under obvious pressure, had called Romero to confide his fears that the then President of the United States would be replaced by another who might consent to being dragged into a war with Mexico. This grave and tangible risk could be avoided if Mexico would do "one single thing" for which Seward would be "personally grateful." There were a "multitude" of claims against Mexico for damages to United States citizens and interests during the War of Intervention. Seward had been able to withstand until then the tremendous pressure of interested parties by alleging the weak position and nomadic character of the Mexican republican government; but now that the latter was on the verge of re-establishing itself, his argument lost its validity and his resistance its foundation. Therefore he proposed to conclude immediately a treaty by which Mexico would obligate itself to pay those claims and to exempt United States citizens from forced loans and from military service.

Romero, not a bad judge of public affairs in the United States, felt that if indeed the danger so darkly painted by Seward existed, nothing would be avoided by his proposed remedy because while a treaty of this type might certainly prevent future claims, it would not overcome already existing difficulties. On the other hand, if all the danger, or the greater part of it, could be attributed to the change in the personnel of the executive branch of the United States—a change that would not take place until after the election of 1868—the probabilities were greater that General Ulysses S. Grant would gain the Presidency, and in that case, "we [Mexico], instead of losing, would gain much." At any rate, Romero attached a memorandum prepared by the legal adviser of the Department of State, but advanced the belief that it seemed to him "very weak on various points."

Seward was right in fearing in March, 1867, that United States President Andrew Johnson would not be re-elected and that Seward himself would leave the office of Secretary of State. When Congress reconvened in December, 1866, it was clear that Johnson's enemies, the "Radicals," had obtained a majority in the House of Representatives and in the Senate; and at the opening of its first formal session on March 4, 1867, it was clear that the Fortieth Congress was resolved to destroy the reconstruction program of President Johnson and to impose radical treatment on the Southern question. Johnson, following Lincoln, thought that the Confederate States of the South should be reincorporated as soon as possible into the national life. According to the radicals, on the contrary, the rebellion had stripped the South of its category of independent states and lowered them to that of territories whose direct government would be by the federal executive, who would commit it to the care of military commanders for as long a time as necessary.

Mixed with these grave political issues were the crudest and most aggressive economic interests. The industrialists of the North, whose prosperity during the Civil War was associated with the predominance of the radical group, feared that a quick return of the South to the national political scene would renew the alliance of the agricultural interests of that region with those of the West, an alliance which would be adverse to the interests of the North: the abandonment of the protective tariff policy, the repudiation of the debt of the Civil War or its payment in depreciated paper money, etc. President Johnson, aware that he would pass the rest of his term of office under a congressional dictatorship opposed to his program and to that of his party, threw himself resolutely into the election campaign. And even though at first the outcome seemed to be in his favor, it ended by his being soundly defeated, with the results that the radical group imposed a program contrary to his own for dealing with the problem of the South, and that he was prosecuted and saved from impeachment by one scant vote. One of the most alarming manifestations of this deep cleavage between the Congress and President Johnson, and the one that influenced Seward, was the conspicuous predominance of the military in the government of the Southern states. General Sheridan, for example, charged with the military command of Louisiana and Texas, dismissed the civil authorities in order to replace them with a military government.

Time confirmed Matías Romero's prediction, for in the presidential elections that followed all these events, General Ulysses S. Grant won; but neither during the campaign did the victory appear certain, nor when the electoral count was made was it decisive. Grant's majority was 300,000 in a popular vote of six million, that is to say, scarcely 5 per cent. Juárez and Lerdo, in spite of Grant's election, decided on May 7, 1868, that Romero, on going to Washington to present his letters of recall—he had been named Secretary of the Treasury on January 15—should negotiate with Seward an agreement according to the wary and uncertain instructions that Lerdo would compose.

IT WAS HOPED that in the agreement the claims of Mexico against the United States might be included, unless the United States government should be opposed to considering the claims of both countries simultaneously. The investigation of the claims would be entrusted to a mixed commission of representatives of the two nations, whose seat would be either in Mexico or in Washington, and to an arbiter who would act as judge when the commissioners might disagree, with the nomination of the arbiter being made beforehand. If an insolvable disagreement should occur, the designation of an arbiter should be left to a friendly minister among those resident in Washington if the commission's seat was in that city, or, if on the contrary, from those resident in Mexico. The mixed commission would initiate its labors three or four months after the exchange of ratifications and would function continuously for a year and a half. Claims had to be presented within the time agreed upon to receive them in order to be eligible for settlement; and those that either the commissioners or the arbiter denied would be permanently rejected. An attempt would be made to define the type of claims to be accepted. As far as Mexico was concerned, only those originating in acts of the republican government would be imputable; in no way whatever would it consider those of the imperial authorities or of citizens resident in the territory of the United States who might have broken the laws of neutrality. The principal sum of the claims would be fixed and at the most an interest of 5 or 6 per cent computed annually from the date of the original damage would be admitted. For the payment of the claims the legal procedure of public auctions would be authorized, and a minimum period of ten years for their payment would be negotiated.

Lerdo's very detailed instructions, not an uncommon practice in Mexican diplomacy, did not reach Washington before June 22, the date on which Romero was to initiate his negotiations. Thus Romero began them with delaying tactics, which were helped when Seward proposed to him as a model the treaty concluded between the United States and England on February 8, 1853. Romero asked for time to read and study it, since he was unfamiliar with the treaty. Even so, Romero was able to send some good news home immediately. Seward seemed disposed to use the agreement in order to avoid the danger of demanding of

Mexico an immediate payment; also he was amenable to admitting Mexico's claims against the United States. On the other hand, he resisted the immediate elimination of the claims originating from acts of the imperial authorities.

Romero, nonetheless, was scarcely able to gain five days between the first and second meetings, and at the close of the second meeting he had to entrust the drafting of the treaty to the legal adviser of the United States Department of State. Meanwhile Seward showed himself entirely opposed to defining in the agreement the type of claims admissible, because this would arouse the mistrust of public opinion and the resistance of the United States Senate. He suggested, therefore, that this task be left to the commissioners and to the arbiter, who, on the other hand, would find it extremely difficult to avoid. Nor ought the treaty to disallow claims of imperial origin in its main text but rather in some clause of its preamble. Finally Seward urged, because he judged it most necessary, that the agreement be signed as soon as possible. Romero, confident that the United States was as interested in throwing out "spurious" claims of those who received damages from the civil and military authorities of the Confederacy as Mexico was to disavow claims from the Empire, agreed to go from the conversation about principles to the examination of a concrete draft of the treaty. This was done, in only two more sessions, during which Seward read it, Romero discussed it, and along the way they both incorporated into it the changes which Seward agreed to of those suggested by Romero. The final text was arrived at on July 1, 1868. Many of Lerdo's aspirations expressed in his instructions were incorporated into the final text of the agreement; but those he considered the principal ones were not accepted in as clear and explicit form as he desired.

Matías Romero and William H. Seward signed the agreement in Washington on July 4, 1868, and thus Mexico was protected from the most immediate dangers which so preoccupied the Secretary of State. In reality, however, Mexico gained much time. The United States Senate promptly approved the agreement three weeks after it had been signed by the plenipotentiaries. The Mexican Congress, on the other hand, did not do so until December 22. President Juárez ratified it immediately, four days after congressional approval; but President Grant did not do so until January 25, 1869, until which date the treaty was not considered in force. To this must be added the fact that the agreement itself was to be prorogued two times: first on April 19, 1871, and again on August 12, 1873; and the fact that as late as April 9, 1876, the period was extended until November 20 of that year in order for the arbiter to finish judging all the pending cases. As a result almost ten years elapsed between Seward's initial demand and the time of Mexico's first payment.

THE PURPOSE OF THE CONVENTION was to liquidate reciprocal claims for damages done to citizens of each country since the treaty of Guadalupe Hidalgo of February 2, 1848. Thus the idea was admitted that the claims both of the United States against Mexico and of the latter against the former should be examined, judged, and paid. Seward was faithful to his promise to Romero to write the convention in such terms that, without expressly so stating it, those claims attributable to the imperial authorities could be disallowed. In fact, Article I stated that "all" claims originating in damages caused by the authorities of the Mexican *Republic* would be examined, thus providing grounds for dismissal of those originating from official acts of the Mexican *Empire*. The Mexican government so understood it, and operated tacitly on that basis. Only in an official document of February, 1871, does that idea appear explicitly expressed. In delineating a series of rules for gathering evidence for limiting or disallowing United States claims, the document refers to ascertaining if the acts from which the claims proceeded occurred in places whose authorities recognized the "legitimate" government, the "reaction," or that of the "so-called Empire." In addition, some interpretative margin was given by another article that empowered the commissioners and the arbiter to decide in each case whether a claim "has been duly made, communicated, and submitted . . . according to the *true spirit* and the letter of the convention."

The receipt, study, and adjudication was entrusted to a mixed commission, constituted of two commissioners, two agents, and two secretaries, one a citizen of each country, who would be designated by the respective governments. The function of the commissioners was to judge; that of the agents, to plead the cases; and that of the secretaries, to certify. If the commissioners could not agree on a decision, the arbiter, who would have been designated by the commissioners before they began their work, would decide. If they could not agree on one, each commissioner would nominate a man, and the arbiter would be selected by lot from the two nominees for each concrete case. The decision of the commissioners or of the arbiter would be considered "as absolutely final and definitive," and the governments were committed to comply with it "without any objections, evasion, or delay." The period for receiving the claims was fixed at eight months beginning with the first meeting of the commissioners, and that for the judging of the claims at two and one half years.

As for payment, it was prearranged that when all of the claims were judged, the lesser amount would be subtracted from the larger and the difference up to the sum of 300,000 pesos in gold would be paid in favor of the government which had been judged to have the largest amount due, the remainder to be paid in annual installments of not more than 300,000 pesos. The convention did not say that the amount due would bear interest, much less from what date; but neither did it say that it would not earn any. Instead, it authorized the deduction of final expenses, such as salaries of the commissioners and secretaries and the compensation of the arbiter, if they did not exceed 5 per cent of the total amount owed.

II

HE WHO WINS, PAYS

Porfirio Díaz entered Mexico City triumphantly on November 23, 1876, and found that the political and military advantage, to all appearances decisive, which gave him possession of the capital could be lost completely if he could not rapidly obtain from it the economic resources necessary to maintain himself in power and to conquer his enemies, Sebastián Lerdo de Tejada and José María Iglesias. Therefore, four days later he convoked a meeting of wealthy people in order to ask them for an "entirely voluntary" loan. At ten thirty on the morning of November 27 "all the moneyed aristocracy" met in one of the salons of the National Palace. General Díaz himself explained the object of the meeting. He was asking a loan of 500,000 pesos with such guarantees as the group might deem necessary. He, for his part, solemnly offered to repay it as soon as possible, and to pay an interest of 1 per cent monthly. "The circumstances were of such urgency" that he had to have their decision in that very meeting. Those attending passed into an adjoining salon, deliberated briefly, and announced that they had agreed to hand over that same afternoon 135,000 pesos apportioned among forty-five persons at the rate of 3,000 each. They named Pedro Valle and Antonio Escalante to collect from the Mexicans; Antonio Mijares, representative of the house of Barron and Forbes, from the English; Vicente Sobrino and Juan Martínez Zorrilla, from the Spaniards; Martin Daran, from the French; and Esteban Beneke, from the Germans.

"Juvenal," a journalist of the day who had a burning hatred of Lerdo, commented enthusiastically:

What a difference! A very few days ago Lerdo held a meeting in his [sic] palace of the same capitalists to ask them for money and he received the most resounding negative, the most frightful rebuff: today the chief of the revolution realized a loan without any guarantee other than his word. Permit us to congratulate General Díaz for the show of confidence he has received on the part of the capitalists; his government has been inaugurated under the very best auspices; in his hand he holds the future of the country: . . . Long live Porfirio Díaz!

The United States minister, John W. Foster, himself endorsed the admiring reaction that these journalistic commentaries created, for he informed his government on the same day on which he read them:

His ability [that of Díaz] to maintain his present position was illustrated in a conference which he held yesterday with a number of capitalists of the city who responded forthwith to his application for a temporary loan of 500,000 pesos.*

"Juvenal," above all an honest man, deplored the fact that the execution of Díaz' Plan of Tuxtepec would throw out into the street, without discrimination or any wisdom whatever, a great mass of public employees because they were held to be partisans of the deposed President. But as Díaz also ordered the salaries of the new servants of the nation cut in half and only a third of the vacant positions filled, he ended by praising the austerity of all these measures and with the sententious reflection of Vallarta on the meeting of the capitalists: "the problem of calming our social misfortunes is not in politics but in administration."

Porfirio Díaz had obtained that prompt reply from the na-

---

*Naturally Hubert Howe Bancroft, *Vida de Porfirio Díaz* (San Francisco: The History Co., 1887), p. 515, caught and disseminated the error. See for instance José López Portillo y Rojas, *Elevación y caída de Porfirio Díaz* (Mexico City: Librería Española, s.f.), p. 153.

tional and foreign capitalists because he had the reputation, cultivated by spectacular deeds, of rigorously fulfilling his economic promises, and also because the city had scarcely recovered from the anxiety of having lived for three days on the brink of anarchy without any authority whatever. In other words, Díaz entered Mexico City as a victorious warrior at the front of an army glutted with triumph but starving for food and shelter.

The main argument of Díaz before the capitalists was not, however, the boorish and disputable one of the economic aggrandizement of a political and military faction but the necessity of fulfilling a sacred promise to pay the first installment of the "American debt," or rather, the claims as judged by the Joint Claims Commission created in 1868. Díaz anticipated his inability to make the first reimbursement before March 15, 1877, although on January 31 he was supposed to pay 300,000 pesos, the amount of the first annual payment of that debt. In fact the Joint Claims Commission concluded its work on November 20 awarding in the United States' favor claims to the amount of $4,225,622.20, and in Mexico's favor, $150,498.41. That meant that Mexico had against her a net remainder of $4,075,123.79, which was to be paid in annual installments of 300,000 pesos beginning on January 31, 1877.

On the same day that Porfirio Díaz appealed to the Mexican and foreign capitalists, and on the day following, thirty persons instead of the forty-five expected each contributed 3000 pesos, making thus a total of 90,000. Then eight foreign houses and twelve Mexicans of the former aristocracy—José María Iturbe, Nicolás de Teresa, Antonio Mier y Celis, Ramón S. de Lascuráin, Jesús Bringas among them—also contributed. Another of Díaz' supporters was a seductive lady whose fortune had been started in a brothel, which came to be the most famous one in the capital, and whose Porfirista affiliation proceeded from the fact that she was the mother-in-law of an important personage. Between December 2 and 27 very modest sums were added by other Mexican aristocrats—Faustino de Goríbar, Fernando Pimentel, Rafael Ortiz de la Huerta—and some of the first con-

[15]

tributors made a second offering, like the Iturbe brothers and Antonio Mier y Celis, who then gave totals of 5000 pesos each. Some foreign houses, like those of Barron and Forbes, also contributed sums not exceeding 5000 pesos.

In reality, with the passing of each day the contributions became fewer and less important, and some seemed like donations to a charitable cause. The great stagecoach firm of Casimiro Collado and the estate of Félix Béistegui lent 1000 pesos each; Manuel C. de Cervantes, 600; Sebastián Camacho, 500; and the firm of J. Aubert et Cie., only 250. Only the intriguing lady repeated her first contribution of 3000 pesos, and José Ives Limantour initiated his political career by spectacularly contributing on the last day and at the final hour, the largest sum of all: 12,000 pesos. At the close of the subscription of the loan exactly one month from its opening, sixty-four contributions from forty contributors had been received, and the final total came to only 189,100 pesos. The failure of the "entirely voluntary" loan was a carefully guarded secret; but it was not possible to keep it from reaching United States Minister Foster, who immediately informed his government.

As a matter of fact, anyone could have guessed it and with good reason, since on the very day that the period for receiving the "entirely voluntary" loan closed, Juan N. Méndez, acting in those days as the head of the executive power, issued a decree creating an extraordinary tax "for once only" on all capital of over 100 pesos. The decree stated that from the collection preference would be given to the part "necessary to cover the payment that had to be made during the coming January." That confession was enough to awaken the supposition of the failure of the loan; and besides, the immediate antecedents of that decree and the nature of the tax revealed the magnitude of the failure, which was such that one could consider it a very nearly complete one.

The resolution to resort to such an extraordinary measure must have required no little courage and determination. In fact, it is appealing to think that if Porfirio Díaz had been in the capital then, and if Justo Benítez and his colleagues of the cabinet had consulted him, he would have opposed the measure— he, who had more acute political acumen than all of them, and who like no one else would receive the abuse of comparisons and contradictions. In fact, Díaz in his statement of the Plan of Tuxtepec had accused President Lerdo of killing trade, of asphyxiating industry, of paralyzing agriculture, and of impoverishing labor with extremely high and arbitrary taxes. Lerdo, precisely in order to defend himself from the revolt of Tuxtepec, had levied on July 19, 1876, an extraordinary tax on capital that drew the liveliest and most explosive reply from Díaz. Upon learning of it, he denounced it in passionate terms from Oaxaca, warning of its black and irreparable consequences. It "would end by destroying all individual activity."

Díaz went even further. He made Lerdo and "his accomplices and agents" personally and financially responsible; and for that reason he authorized his military commanders as soon as the opportunity arose to imprison Lerdo, his accomplices or agents, and confiscate their property. Furthermore, he announced that all who had anything to do with collecting that tax and applying the remittances of any coercive economic measure would be tried by military courts. Finally he said that the injured would have the right to demand the necessary reparations; declared null all acts relating to the collection of the tax; and urged the whole country "to resist the payment of the tax," saying that all had "full right" to do so. Despite all these antecedents, the Díaz revolutionary government, scarcely a month after establishing itself in the capital and only four months after that furious condemnation, imposed the same tax with the burden of higher quotas and much shorter periods of payment, and descended even to the irony of using the same rolls prepared for the payment of Lerdo's tax.

But even so Díaz' advisers were not sure of being able to pay the claims. Trusting in the success of the loan, among other reasons, they had decided on the solution of the special tax too late. When the decree which created it was handed down on

December 27, 1876, a levy in three parts was planned, the first of which was due between January 1 and 5, 1877, and the last between February 19 and 24. The first was before but too near to the payment of the claims, and the last, after it. Therefore, even considering that in time the special tax would bring in one million pesos, rather than use it for the payment of the first installment of the "American debt," it was now offered as a guarantee for a loan that Díaz attempted to obtain on more commercial terms; and from that time Díaz abandoned the tone of a call to patriotism and the system of meetings.

Ignacio L. Vallarta, in charge of the Department of Foreign Relations, was the one commissioned to do the negotiating, which did not bring easy results. He inquired immediately of the Bank of London and South America as to the possibility of a loan of 200,000 pesos, the amount needed to make the payment; but the bank refused to even consider the operation because its statutes expressly prohibited it. He then approached the firm of Darven y Cía., which asked 15 per cent interest to make the loan in New York and exemption from the import tax of the 200,000 pesos of the loan and from the interest and the commission of the lender. Then he decided to approach the rich Mexicans. He talked extensively with Antonio Mier y Celis, to whom Vallarta offered the guarantee of the second and third levies of the special tax and the export duties that would be produced by the next shipment of silver from Guanajuato; but Mier y Celis did not even examine the guarantees and the proposed conditions, because neither he nor his closest friends could quickly raise so large a sum. Vallarta went finally to Antonio Escalante, who offered to obtain and turn over in Mexico City 200,000 Mexican pesos at a charge of 16,000 pesos for interest and commission, but without committing himself to delivering them in New York. After a study of Escalante's proposals by a council of ministers, presided over by General Juan N. Méndez, they were accepted, though Escalante was asked to agree to the reduction of the interest and commission to 12,000 pesos, which he finally accepted.

AN INTELLIGENT, educated, thoughtful, sound-thinking man like Ignacio L. Vallarta, upon whom weighed in addition the responsibility of advising Díaz on the most delicate matters, even internal ones, must have been deeply worried by the proximity of the first payment of the claims and by all the circumstances under which he initiated his work as acting Secretary of Foreign Affairs. The Díaz government carried on its shoulders the stigma of revolution, of having overthrown by force a legitimate constitutional government, and even though in the less recent history of Mexico that was not an unusual occurrence, it was unusual in the immediate history of the Restored Republic.

This last circumstance necessarily posed the delicate problem of the recognition of a *de facto* government, whose dominion over the country, furthermore, was then far from clear. Added to this, the Plan of Tuxtepec and several of Díaz' decrees and proclamations had a militant anti-imperialistic tone. Then too, Vallarta did not know what was going to be the reaction of Mexican diplomatic and consular representatives abroad toward the dispute between Díaz, Lerdo, and Iglesias. His greatest worry, of course, was the attitude of Ignacio Mariscal, head of the legation in Washington, D.C., because he was a serious, distinguished person knowing well the atmosphere of the United States and having good connections in it, and also because of his rectitude and even because of his separation from active political life. Finally, Sebastián Lerdo de Tejada, the deposed President, and the larger part of his ministry would soon be in New York, and José María Iglesias with his, in New Orleans.

The very fact that the final settlement of the Joint Claims Commission had coincided with the date on which the Lerdo government had abandoned the capital and with the unfortunate negotiations for an understanding between Díaz and Iglesias complicated the situation even more. The Department of Foreign Relations lacked information concerning the awards of the commission on the amounts of the claims favorable to both countries, the kind of money in which the payments were to be made, the amount of the expenses of the commission, and the portion that Mexico was committed to pay.

The Porfirista press took as an accomplished fact that "not only the United States Minister but all the diplomatic corps" was dealing with Díaz as the head of the national government. Their confidence was so great that when *El Federalista,* the only Lerdista daily in the capital, gave notice that the decision of that body was to the contrary, the Porfirista press declared imperiously:

> We have already said what there is to say on this subject. The administration of General Díaz has been recognized by the diplomatic corps.

Furthermore, rumors spread periodically that such and such government had made a formal recognition.

The truth was that John W. Foster, dean of the accredited diplomatic corps in Mexico, called a meeting in which he explained that "no step would be taken" toward the recognition of any other government than that of Lerdo, especially because the United States continued to recognize the Mexican minister in Washington. He believed, furthermore, that the triumph of the Porfirista revolutionaries was far from being a sure thing, that the possibility that Lerdo might raise a considerable army was not to be discounted, and that Díaz' differences with Iglesias might bring disastrous consequences upon Díaz. Prudence counseled therefore watching the course of events, informing the respective governments, and awaiting instructions. Meanwhile they might well maintain personal, not official, relations with any authority in the capital. That position was approved unanimously.

Foster hit the mark, for the Department of State also judged official recognition premature, although it recommended purely personal relations. Already on his own account, Foster had asked his government to send to the port of Veracruz a United States warship in view of the reigning confusion. Likewise, alarmed, he transmitted the news of there having been published in Mexico with the undoubted intention of confirming its validity a decree issued by Porfirio Díaz in Oaxaca as revolutionary chief, in which he annulled all contracts made by the Lerdo government, which if applied retroactively, Foster reflected, would be injurious to the interests of United States citizens.

Vallarta, in spite of everything, did not stop communicating to the heads of the diplomatic missions first, that Porfirio Díaz had taken charge of the executive power on November 28, 1876, and second, that he himself had been designated to handle the Department of Foreign Relations. But Foster answered, marking his communiqué with a very conspicuous "unofficial," that he was sending to the Department of State Vallarta's two notes "for its information and decision."

III
JEALOUS AS CAN BE

As recognition was not granted immediately, the punctual payment of the first part of the "American debt" gained singular importance as a means of advancing toward recognition and as proof that the Porfirista faction was solvent and responsible. Ignacio L. Vallarta resolved to take two somewhat impetuous steps on December 29, 1876: to write to Ignacio Mariscal and to talk to John W. Foster. He assured the former that "nothing remained of Lerdo's administration, that the one which Iglesias hoped to establish in Guanajuato was losing support every day, and in a few days would have disappeared also," and that Porfirio Díaz' was therefore the only viable government. He was greatly worried by the payment of the claims but was ignorant of the final amount agreed upon and of the expenses and deductions, and also of the "question of interests and the various moneys" in which the amounts were to be paid.

Vallarta, knowing that honesty was not a bad road to follow in approaching Mariscal, confided in him his state of mind: "I become increasingly frantic as the maturity of the first installment shortens the time in a cruel manner." Therefore, as a friend, he asked Mariscal to send him all the information he lacked, announcing to him that the Díaz government had decided to pay, and that it would do so if no grave and unforeseen events intervened. He asked if the 300,000 pesos happened not to arrive in Washington exactly on January 31, 1877, "Do you

[22]

think that this might be cause for difficulties afterwards? Would the delay in payment for a few days damage us?" Vallarta offered Mariscal his friendship and impatiently asked him for a reply by telegram and a report on the intentions of the United States government on the matter of recognition.

Mariscal had anticipated Vallarta's desires and fears. From New York, in January, 1877, he addressed him "as adviser in foreign relations" to Porfirio Díaz. He put forth his resignation from the position of minister to Washington: if the United States recognized Porfirio Díaz, a thing he did not think possible, he would want to retire from the diplomatic service. But a serious matter worried him to the point of his considering that "its favorable solution ranked above all considerations emanating from our domestic dissensions." It was the payment of the first installment of the claims, which apparently could not possibly be made on the day set. However he could assert that if "it should be fulfilled without a long delay, before the 4th of March, at which time there would be a change in the administration of this country, serious dangers to our independence would be avoided, or at least to the integrity of our territory."

The United States, he explained, was passing through a disturbing political crisis which had been revealed by the presidential election, and one of the easiest means of looking for a way out of the disastrous situation would be "to call attention to Mexico." A proposal had already been presented to Congress to authorize the President of the United States to pay at once all the claims of its citizens; in this way the United States government would have the right to collect them all directly from Mexico at once and for cash. Mariscal thought therefore that if Porfirio Díaz made the first payment, "He would render the nation a service of incalculable importance, saving it from very real dangers, which I do not exaggerate." Finally Mariscal offered to make the payment "in the name of the Mexican government," because he did not believe that the United States would permit Foster to do it, or a commissioner of Porfirio Díaz' to do it in Washington.

Vallarta, on the same date of his letter to Mariscal, visited Foster in the United States Legation to talk with him and to ask him that the conclusions of their conversation be transmitted confidentially to the Department of State, because "he did not wish to offend the patriotism and the sense of duty" of Mariscal by stating that in Mexico there was doubt concerning his conduct. It happened that Vallarta was ignorant of whether Mariscal and Eleuterio Ávila, the Mexican agent on the Joint Claims Commission, wanted to act as representatives of the Díaz government. The change in the political situation in Mexico had been communicated to them opportunely; but since the telegraph lines to Matamoros had been destroyed during the revolt of Tuxtepec, the government had to make use of the extremely slow mail service. Therefore in order to take advantage of the steamboat that would leave in two days, he desired to communicate to Foster the opinions of the Mexican government on the payment of the claims.

The last news which the Department of Foreign Relations had was that the Mexican agent had presented a note asking for a determination of the final amount of the claims and the particulars regarding them; but the decision relative to the expenses of the commission and what had happened to some of the claims already decided upon but whose fraudulent nature had been denounced by new proofs and testimonies was unknown. All these questions seemingly were pending because news of the political changes occurring in Mexico had then reached Washington. Nevertheless, Porfirio Díaz was disposed to pay; but the special conditions of the country and the uncertainty of whether its agents in the United States were willing to act in accord with the new government might cause some delay. Vallarta wanted to anticipate that fear by explaining to Foster the reasons for the possible delay and asking him if he had received any instructions on the matter.

Foster had not received any, doubtless because such a sudden change had surprised the United States government; but he offered to communicate to the Department of State all that

Vallarta had told him, although he hoped that all the questions suggested by the latter would not affect "the practical aspect" of the business, that is, the payment of the installment on January 31. A delay of only a few days would have little significance. The important thing was "the spirit in which the government of Mexico accepted the awards and the now concluded work of the Commission." Vallarta then declared that his government "accepted and recognized them in their full validity" and that Foster could assure his government that Porfirio Díaz was well disposed to "fulfill faithfully all his contractual obligations."

The Department of State informed Foster that it had been difficult to determine the exact amount of the first payment, for while some of the authorities were inclined to interpret the agreement in the sense that Mexico could deduct at once the surplus of the expenses of the commission already paid, others held that that deduction should be extended to the fifteen annual payments that were to be made. The Department of State left Mexico at complete liberty to decide if it should make all the deduction at one time, "for the pecuniary amount of the difference between the one course and the other is to us at least comparatively unimportant." Hamilton Fish, Secretary of State, did not know how they intended to make the payment, but the United States government would face the expenses and risks of its conveyance if it were made in dollars in Mexico City; therefore it would be better to realize it by means of documents on the United States or England. It did not seem that Foster would need formal authority to receive the payment; but he could show that communication to the Mexican government if they should question his authority for receiving it.

Not having received news from Mariscal or from Ávila, and now feeling the uncertainty of United States recognition, in spite of the possibility of a Lerdista resistance having vanished and the crumbling of the Iglesias faction being almost complete, Vallarta decided on January 15, 1877, to commission José María Mata and Ciro Tagle to go to Washington to make the first payment of the claims and to establish at the same time direct contact with the United States authorities which would permit better exploration of the problem of recognition in a less hostile climate. Vallarta must have been astonished and confused by the coded telegram that Porfirio Díaz sent from Guadalajara in reply to the one that Tagle sent him announcing his departure for Washington:

Telegram to the Minister of Foreign Relations repeating the question asked of him if the United States government recognized ours or not, or if that is the purpose of the Commissioner who is carrying the 300,000 pesos.

The head of the commission was Mata; the nomination of Tagle must be interpreted as a concession to his brother Protasio, a representative in the cabinet of the "pure" Tuxtepecanism. Mata was, therefore, the one who received the official instructions. Before doing anything else, he was to go to the Mexican Legation in Washington to obtain from it the information which the Department of Foreign Relations lacked: namely, the final result of the general settlement, the exact amount of the expenses of the commission and if the total of these could be deducted entirely from the first payment, the resolution on the fraudulent claims denounced by Mexico and the agreement on the payment of interests in the cases judged against it.

If Mata encountered a good reception in the legation he was to make use of its personnel in order to facilitate his task; if to the contrary, he would make the payment alone, for which purpose he was given a formal appointment which he should present to the United States authorities. If the latter refused to receive him, because of not wishing to deal with him or for any other motive, he should consign the payment judicially. He should offer it "in the name of the Mexican government, who was making it in faithful and due fulfillment of the Convention, and as jealous as can be of the national honor." Mata would try to explain that the revolt of Tuxtepec had not been another explosion of anarchism in Mexico but a necessity in order to end an "immoral system of government." General Díaz enjoyed

complete popular sympathy. Congress would be installed in
March and it was probable that he would triumph in the presidential elections. Mata would have to explain all of this "not
only to secure the honor and prestige of Mexico but in order to
deal with the matter of recognition." He, nonetheless, should
prudently make clear that the motive of his government in making the payment "is not the desire for its recognition nor does
it seek this in a humiliating manner."

THE MILITARY DEFECTIONS which weakened the Iglesias faction,
and particularly the defeat of General Florencio Antillón at
the hands of Ignacio Martínez, as well as the disintegration of
the resistance of José Ceballos in Jalisco, had become known
by this time in the United States. The interpretation of the
Department of State was that Porfirio Díaz no longer had a
rival and that he would be the true ruler of Mexico. It therefore concluded:

. . . since we cannot receive from a Government which we do not
acknowledge the installment of indemnity payable by Mexico on the
31st instant, especially it would be justified that you [Foster] would be
warranted in recognizing the government of Porfirio Díaz, unless before
this reaches you, such a step should be made inexpedient by events
which are not now foreseen.

"You will exercise your best judgment in these matters," Foster
was told. Furthermore, the Department of State did not want
to make an international question of the decree of Porfirio Díaz
which annulled all the contracts made by the Lerdo government.
It did not understand the reasons for the measure since it would
not contribute to creating confidence in the persons disposed to
enter into contracts that could help to fortify Díaz' power.
Besides, those who should decide to make them would try to
obtain from the Mexican government more advantageous conditions as compensation for a possible repudiation.

Foster, nevertheless, had other ideas. Vallarta visited him to
inform him of the appointment of Mata and Tagle and to tell

him in advance that as the Mexican man of war in which the 300,000 pesos would be transported could not sail at once, Mata and Tagle might be obliged to resort to the mail ship to New Orleans. They would sail then from Veracruz on January 23 and could barely get to Washington by January 31. Vallarta wanted Foster, furthermore, to announce to his government Mata's appointment and the object of his mission. Foster promised to do so, but he asked if the envoy had any diplomatic character. He had none, Vallarta replied; his only mission was to pay. Foster, suspicious, asked what would be the official Mexican interpretation if the United States should receive the payment and give the corresponding receipt, that is to say, if such an act would signify recognition. "To which," said Foster, "Vallarta unhesitatingly replied that he did not understand that the payment and the receipt of the 300,000 pesos involved the question of recognition," since this payment would be made "in the name of the Republic of Mexico and not of a particular government." Recognition was a different matter, although Vallarta trusted that the United States, desirous of maintaining friendly relations, would act on this point "on a liberal and just basis."

Pursuing this line, Foster asked him if he would be interested in knowing what points the United States government would consider in studying the recognition of Díaz. Vallarta, of course, was interested. The principal problem was the situation on the northern frontier. In the Mexican part of it incursions were frequently organized to introduce contraband foreign goods into Texas or to steal cattle that were afterwards brought into Mexican territory. Likewise, criminals from Texas frequently escaped to Mexican territory, where they found a safe refuge. Foster had made various appeals to José María Lafragua for the Lerdo government to remedy this situation; but actually it was getting worse. General Juan N. Cortina, a partisan of Díaz in the past revolt, a man "whom the Texas courts had sentenced for murder, robbery and other crimes," had returned to Tamaulipas, where he was exercising his nefarious influence.

Foster announced to Vallarta that he had already sent to the Department of State a copy of the decree by which Díaz had annulled all the contracts made by the Lerdo government. Even without having special instructions, he doubted that his government would admit the principle that Mexico could annul contracts made by citizens of the United States with a previous government which the United States recognized as legitimate. Other pending questions remained; but for the moment he did not consider it opportune to refer to them. Vallarta admitted that the frontier question was grave. He was sure that the Díaz government would do everything possible to resolve it, although he did not feel authorized as yet to talk about it, considering the very little time that the Díaz government had been in power and the circumstances under which it had come into it.

MATA AND TAGLE left Mexico City by the Mexican Railway carrying the heavy package of the 300,000 pesos. They proposed to embark immediately on the warship *Independencia* to go to New Orleans; but on arriving at Veracruz they found that the ship needed extensive repairs if they were to have any safety on so long a voyage. To Mata's anguished call, Vallarta replied authorizing him to contract and pay for the repairs from the funds he carried, even if it left them incomplete. Fortunately, by this date Foster had received the dispatch from the Department of State authorizing Mexico to deduct in advance all the expenses of the Joint Claims Commission that had been made in advance. Foster communicated this at once to Vallarta; the latter in turn, and with great relief, forwarded the information to Mata.

But the latter mistrusted even such help from fortune; he telegraphed Vallarta expressing his fear that Foster might have been mistaken on the possibility of the deductions, for Eleuterio Ávila, the Mexican agent with whom he talked upon disembarking at the port, denied that it was so. Therefore, Mata announced that he would carry with him more than enough money, for with some aid from the collector's office of the Veracruz customs he had at his disposal 325,000 pesos. Vallarta reiterated that Foster had communicated to him "without the least doubt" that he would be able to make all deductions from the first payment, and he announced that Foster would leave on a special train for Veracruz on the same day to convince Mata of it.* Mata was satisfied at last, and he put to sea on board the *Independencia* on January 21, carrying with him only 269,000 pesos.

But fortune, it seems, was determined to complicate things, devising a complete comedy of errors. On January 15, the same day on which Vallarta, unsure because of the lack of news from Mariscal, resolved to entrust the payment to the special commissioners Mata and Tagle, Mariscal answered Vallarta's letter of December 29, declaring above all his joy on learning that Vallarta also accorded great importance to making the first payment of the claims punctually. He reiterated that it could be made without danger in February, even though by then there would be "clamor" in the United States. "Therefore it is important that it arrive as soon as possible. If only by February 1st I could say that it is on its way!" Mariscal also answered the question of the possibility of recognition. He did not believe that it would be long delayed if Díaz ascended to the Presidency by means of popular elections.

It took Mata six long days to get to New Orleans in his warship; but once on land and to compensate for the tedious voyage, he entered into unbridled activity. He immediately exchanged his 269,000 Mexican pesos for $242,501 in gold and ordered it sold in London, where the price was better. He succeeded in arriving in Washington on the morning of January 31, and at an appointment previously made by Mariscal with Hamilton Fish, he made the payment in the afternoon, got the receipt and attached it to his very schematic report. He left immediately to

---

*It is true that Foster made that trip to Veracruz; but neither in his *Memoirs* nor in his diplomatic dispatches does he refer to it. Might his officiousness have appeared so excessive to him that he did not wish to let others know of it?

return to New York, and there learned that the steamship *Bavaria,* on which the 269,000 Mexican pesos were being shipped to London, had burned on the high seas, and the boat was lost along with all it carried. Fortunately, Mata added with pride, Lloyd's of London would have to pay the loss, since he had been careful to insure the shipment with that company.

Mata's report to Vallarta was extremely brief and he sent it from Veracruz upon disembarking, without waiting to deliver it personally in Mexico City. Perhaps it was human to proceed thus, for the completion of his mission, effective as it was insofar as making the payment on time, was not very successful or effective from a political standpoint. Mariscal accompanied Mata to the Department of State for the audience with the Secretary of State; but it was Mariscal who entered the office and talked with Fish, while Mata waited alone in the little waiting room. Mariscal showed Fish the money order that Mata carried; he asked if it seemed satisfactory to Fish and if he would give him a receipt for the money for the payment. Fish asked that the money order in the name of Mata be endorsed to Mariscal. He went to the waiting room to ask Mata to endorse it, and then explained that he would give Mariscal a receipt for the money order but not for the money that it represented. This operation concluded, Mariscal told Fish that Mata had brought with him a letter of introduction from Foster, and Fish then said he would receive it if Mariscal would bring Mata and would be present at the interview. After the briefest conversation, both bade farewell and Mata left the Department of State. Fish himself gave a decisive description of Mata's mission: "the payment was made by Mariscal as minister and in the name of the Republic of Mexico, and *no question of recognition of the Díaz authority was suggested.*"

Mata's reticence about the vicissitudes of his mission was, in the end, unnecessary. Some United States newspapers—like the New York *World*—reported that the United States government had refused to receive the payment from Mata, and that "it was not accepted until it was delivered by Mr. Mariscal." Far from recognizing Díaz, "it has recognized Mr. Lerdo in the person of his diplomatic agent." Mata was unfortunate not only in the deceptive air of his report, but also because it was believed that he and Tagle had received a splendid compensation for a mission that was pictured as purely patriotic. They had to declare publicly that they had not received the fifty-odd thousand pesos that the Mexican press supposed; on the contrary, they had paid from their private funds many of the smaller expenses left out of the account presented to the Secretary of Foreign Relations, to say nothing of what seemed the very modest sum of 768.95 pesos for the expenses of the official trip of two high ranking persons. Finally, to clear their honor of the slightest suspicion, Mata and Tagle resolved to cede to public charity the thousand pesos which the Department of Foreign Affairs persisted in paying them as compensation.

THE DEPARTMENT OF STATE felt by January, 1877, serious misgivings at receiving the claims payment from a government with which it had no official relations, and for that reason it authorized Foster to recognize it at once. Nevertheless, on learning that Vallarta did not understand that the acceptance of the payment and the extension of the receipt signified recognition, the Department of State approved Foster's conduct of not having extended it, and on February 12 it gave him new instructions. In them he was commissioned to impress strongly on the prominent men of the country with whom he conversed that, before recognizing Díaz, the United States government awaited the suppression of the Free Zone and effective measures to prevent the incursions on United States territory of cattle thieves and wild Indians. Nonetheless, Hamilton Fish was vacillating, since he added that even though the fundamental interest of his government in these questions was not to be doubted, the measures whose adoption was being asked "might not be deemed indispensable in the end" to the granting of recognition. Persons outside official United States circles also understood that the payment of the 300,00 pesos did not carry with it ready recognition, but they thought that this would come "if the country remained at peace and General Díaz was elected president according to legal formalities."

In fact, Foster was of the same opinion; he, who with the authority to recognize Díaz did not do so, and without it pretended henceforth to condition recognition on the solution of pending questions. Using the form of a personal and confidential letter to Secretary Fish, which permitted him to express his opinions with greater freedom, he explained that the government of Porfirio Díaz, although it had gained control of Mexico as the threat of Lerdo and Iglesias had now disappeared, carried with it the weakness of its origin. If, in order to gain power, it destroyed by force the legitimate government, any other group in turn could destroy it, and do so without the necessity of "bribery, intrigue or malevolence." Therefore he thought that "the Díaz government would be one of at least a year." Then, alarmed, he asked: "Are we able to postpone for so long a time the recognition of a government with whom we necessarily need to have so many relations and with whom our citizens ought to deal?"

He was so preoccupied with the problem that he dared to make a suggestion "not requested" by Fish. Since the Díaz government had overthrown a legitimate government by force, the United States could refuse to recognize it in "its provisional and revolutionary character"; but, if the presidential election was carried out "with some degree of popular participation," Díaz should then be recognized. In the meantime negotiations should be continued with the existing government on the problems presented to Vallarta; namely, the pacification of the frontier to the point where the incursions by wild Indians, malefactors, and cattle thieves would be wiped out; the lifting of the closure of the frontier ports in the hands of Díaz' enemies and the withdrawal of the threat that those who imported merchandise through the closed ports would have to pay customs tariffs; the revocation of the decree that declared null all contracts made between private individuals and the Lerdo government; and others.

Less than a month afterwards, on February 19, 1877, Foster seemed convinced that it would be better to recognize the Díaz government immediately, announcing it as follows in a clear and solemn form:

In view of the instructions contained in your dispatch No. 366 of the 19th last, I regard it as my duty to recognize the government of General Díaz as the *de facto* and only existing government in Mexico. I have therefore to notify you that I will proceed to do so.

But scarcely two weeks later he changed his mind: it was not advisable to make a public or written declaration on that matter. Prudence and one diplomatic precedent established by the Mexican government itself had caused him to reach that new decision. The counsel of prudence was obvious: it would cost nothing to wait a few weeks, which might well prove the strength and stability of the Díaz government. The elections for federal offices had already been called; soon Congress would be installed and the results of the elections would be known.

Then there was that famous diplomatic precedent: when King Alfonso ascended the Spanish throne in 1875, the Mexican government declined to accredit the Spanish chargé d'affaires until it had received the letter signed by Alfonso notifying it of the change of government. Therefore he, Foster, suggested to Vallarta a letter from Porfirio Díaz to the President of the United States informing him of his ascension to power "was a preliminary step to the formal and official recognition of his government." Meanwhile, he verbally informed Vallarta that he would consider the Díaz government as *de facto,* and that military expeditions hostile to it would not be permitted to organize in the territory of the United States. Vallarta took the suggestion and soon sent the letter; but W. Hunter, legal counselor of the Department of State, marked Foster's dispatch with an adverse opinion to the effect that the letter signed by Díaz should not be answered until the character and tendencies of the Mexican Congress were known.

Meanwhile Foster was carrying out the instructions to impress on the minds of Mexican notables the gravity with which his government viewed the border frictions. He conversed with Díaz himself and even suggested to him concrete measures: immediately to deprive General Juan N. Cortina, whom the United States authorities held as the principal cause of all the friction, of all military command and to remove him from the frontier; to nominate as commander-in-chief of the armies in the North a general of renown and experience and to place under his command sufficient forces of the regular army; and to have that general agree with the commanding officer of the United States on the best measures to secure the pacification of the zone.

VALLARTA quickly accepted Foster's suggestion of an official letter because its execution was simple. It had already been used and with very flattering results. Porfirio Díaz returned from Guadalajara to Mexico City on February 11, 1877, after his campaign against the Iglesias forces, which had deserted until all had been converted to partisans of Díaz. Vallarta at once informed the heads of the diplomatic missions of these facts and received replies of acknowledgment from the legations of Germany, Spain, El Salvador, and Guatemala. On February 20, he sent a letter signed by Porfirio Díaz to all the chiefs of state who had accredited representatives in the country, informing them that he had taken possession as "interim president." They all responded, declaring their intention to transmit it to their respective governments. Only Foster marked his reply with an almost aggressive "unofficial." On April 27, Emperor Wilhelm of Germany answered, recognizing thus the Mexican government before knowing the results of the election and the transformation of Díaz to constitutional president. And gradually the chiefs of state of El Salvador, Guatemala, Italy, and Spain did likewise. Two days after Díaz inaugurated his term as constitutional President, he again sent a personal letter, this time to all chiefs of state with whom Mexico maintained relations even without their having diplomatic missions in the country; and again one after another answered recognizing him.

Foster had persuaded the accredited diplomatic corps in Mexico to entrust to him, because of his seniority, the mission of advancing to Vallarta the fear that their governments might await the formal declaration of the Mexican Congress on the result of the presidential election before answering the personal letter from Díaz. Also Foster had found out that Vallarta showed himself "manifestly disillusioned" when he informed him at the end of April that he was still ignorant of the fate of the personal letter sent to the President of the United States. Vallarta, for his part, succeeded in preoccupying Foster to the extent that on May 8, three days after Díaz had been made constitutional President, he telegraphed the Department of State informing it of that fact and urging his superiors to give him "specific instructions." Vallarta succeeded also in worrying Foster enough for him to inform his government of the avalanche of recognitions that the Díaz government was receiving, until, when the last of them—that of Italy—was granted toward the end of July, Foster drew with dismay the conclusion that the United States "is now the only power represented in Mexico which has not acted upon the question." Ignacio L. Vallarta emphasized with dignity and force the position in which the United States remained, whose government

. . . has not found it convenient yet to recognize the one which the populace has chosen, and the government of the Republic believes that it is unbecoming to solicit as a gift a recognition which justice accords it. . . .

IV
THE OTHER SIDE OF
THE INTRIGUE

Along the Rio Grande, from Piedras Negras to Matamoros, and in a band whose width, from north to south, was usually around 125 miles and never less than 65 miles, lived a Mexican population which had not yet settled down either on the soil that still remained in Mexico or on the soil that it once owned, but now belonged to the United States, to the state of Texas. That population was made up of strong men, fighters, many of them bold adventurers, long accustomed to frugality and even privation, whose best friends seemed to be the horse and the six-shooter. The great length of this zone and its not insignificant width, its uncultivated and uninhabited character, the lack of any economic activity that would give a stable occupation to its inhabitants, the patent weakness of the central government to make its influence felt in the extremities of the country, the factious nature of the local authorities, the historic antecedent that that land had belonged for many years to the Mexicans, and the lack of a natural barrier which would easily identify it with the notion of an international boundary: all these things conspired to make of this area a turbulent zone, difficult to govern and even to subdue by force. The frequent political upheavals, local, regional and national, and more recently the Wars of the Reform and the Intervention heightened the disturbing action of all these factors.

The situation on the United States side was much worse. The

whole population was sparse in relation to the enormous territory of Texas. The population of Mexican origin, but now of United States nationality, comprised the oldest settlement; but neither its number nor its wealth gave it in the aggregate a weight equal to its feeling that that land had belonged to it ancestrally. The Mexican population was followed in time of settlement by the descendants of the old Texas colonists, who, in their turn, were only slightly more than a third of the total. The remainder, or the majority, did not form a homogeneous group, which would have served as a moderating and cohesive element among the other groups. On the contrary, it came from each of the United States and from foreign lands: Germany, Ireland, England, Scotland, and even Poland and France. Those from distant lands had come to Texas with the idea that there they would soon find recompense for their sacrifices, their needs and their ambitions, consequently creating a psychology of easy and direct conquest.

To ALL OF THIS should be added the action of several factors that aggravated the situation on the border to an incredible degree. The character of conquest that the Anglo-Saxon population of Texas had from the beginning lasted for many years: the trampling underfoot and the violence; the deceit and duplicity; the notion that force, as supreme necessity, justifies everything. Then, more recently, the tremendous effect of the Civil War, which even so profound and proudly Texan a writer as Walter Prescott Webb finds himself obliged to recognize:

> It cannot be denied that Texas was then a lawless land. The Civil War had wrecked the country financially and had left behind a social debris in the place of an organized and well-ordered society. When the armies were disbanded, the Confederates drifted back to their homes with a war psychology still on them. For four years or less they had used firearms and had become accustomed to bloodshed and to violent death.

Things began to change, with great slowness, during the period of Reconstruction; but there was the unfortunate coincidence of the appearance of new disturbing factors which counterbalanced those beneficial effects.

The political parties had degenerated in the United States South into factions, and the Democrats and the Republicans fought with singular violence and rancor: the former tried in every way possible to prevent the military defeat from bringing upon it a permanent political subordination; the latter wanted at all costs to convert the military victory into an unquestionable political supremacy. As a result each local authority belonged unfailingly to one or the other faction and used its political and administrative power to exterminate its rivals. All interest in public welfare was lost sight of and that of the faction predominated. In that strife and in that unmerciful battle the Mexicans resident in Texas played a very unenviable role, for they neither understood the forces at play nor did they learn how to gain from their attachment and knowledge of the land anything except the wrath of the Texas authority for their misdeeds.

To that political battle, truly feudal, must be added the economic one. It was evolving on much more complex and extensive levels, but it was much more cruel and ferocious. The Republicans used the Civil War to obtain the first protective tariff law for the industry of the Northeast, and they feared that if the South should recover its influence, Congress would return to the traditional politics of free international trade with cheap manufactured goods for the rich Southern farmer and cattleman. This single and limited battle was reflected in the border troubles between Mexico and the United States. In effect, the government of Mexico had created in 1851 a so-called "Free Zone" in Tamaulipas with the purpose of encouraging the settlement of the northern part of the state by permitting the duty-free importation of foreign merchandise which otherwise would have to come from Veracruz, with the added cost of land freight and import duties.

It inevitably occurred that under the cover of this well-meaning disposition there should develop a contraband trade toward the interior of Mexico, with damage to the merchants who imported their goods by way of Veracruz and who paid, naturally, the high duties which were imposed on them. Another current of contraband trade was aimed directly at Texas, where United States industrial products came high due to insufficient transportation from the Northeast, where it was usually manufactured, and because the industrial development of the United States had not reached sufficient maturity. The manufacturer of the Northeast, because he lost a market that he considered his nationally, and the Texas merchant, unable to compete with the European manufactured goods introduced by contraband, both complained bitterly until they induced the local and federal authorities of the United States to make of the Free Zone an international question whose easy solution was based on demanding that Mexico suppress it. Other factors which entered into the border situation were the spectacular development of the cattle industry in Texas and the renewal of the migrations to the West, with the battle for the extermination of the Indian which each one entailed.

The Civil War—two now classic United States historians have said—was a political revolution that brought with it an economic and a social revolution. The prime impulse was the Homestead Act, which gave 160 acres of government land to whoever wished to cultivate it; in the same year, the Morrill Act authorized subsidies to agriculture and to agricultural education using the same formula of gifts of national lands. The development of railroads was greatly dependent upon the settlement of land, since the official subsidies to stimulate its construction were given in government land, which the railroad companies disposed of in order to colonize settlers along their rights-of-way.

Then, the United States territory lying between 98 degrees longitude west and the Pacific Coast and from Texas to the Canadian border was practically uninhabited except by the "barbarous" Indians and a few Mormons. The permanent white settler did not reach the so-called plains or prairies, much less the western mountainous region, until the beginning of the

1870's; but once the movement was begun, the migratory wave advanced with such impetus that before 1890 it had reached the Pacific Coast, and the famous American "Frontier" ceased to exist.

The first condition of the colonization of the prairie was to subjugate the Indian who possessed it; then, as it was a region of scarce rainfall, irrigation and dry-farming were necessary, as well as the penetration of the railroad in order to be able to sell the new products in the Eastern markets. Also the invention of the barbed wire fence was a decisive factor, since as the Great Plains—as Webb calls it—lacked wood and stone, the boundaries of the new farm had to be made with some other material.

Until then, the white man had had to contend with a semi-civilized Indian, living an urban life and inhabiting the eastern forest region. Those three circumstances made his extermination much easier. The Plains Indian was not civilized, but "barbarous" or "savage," that is, he had the notion that the white man was his enemy. At the beginning of the struggle the Indian was stronger, since he was a consummate horseman who fell upon the enemy like a streak of lightning and magically disappeared. For the fight on horseback and without the protection of the trees but face to face on the prairie, on the Great Plains, the poisoned arrow was much more effective than the rifle, whose use caused the horse to lose direction, or the single-shot dueling pistol, the only one that the white man then had. The Comanches, the best horsemen among the barbarous Indians, began to steal horses from the Mexicans who lived in the southern part of Texas, and when it reached the extreme that one good thief possessed between 200 to 500 horses, each Indian became a horseman. Therefore Webb asserts that the horse made the Indian—and he might have added the same of the white man—"out-wanderers, raiders and splendid thieves."

The initial advantages of the Plains Indian soon disappeared, for the white man learned to live on the horse and to manage him with equal dexterity; he invented the repeating revolver, the famous six-shooter, an arm infinitely superior to the poisoned arrow of the Indian and the lance or saber of the Mexican. The white man began by pursuing and destroying the buffalo, from which the Indian obtained food and shelter; and afterwards he pursued and destroyed the Indian himself. The result of the struggle was that of the 225,000 Plains Indians which there were at the beginning, ten years later only a third of them remained.

It would be useless to trace in any detail the melancholy story of the Indian relations in the period from 1860 to 1887 . . . It is a tale of intermittent but barbarous warfare, of broken pacts and broken promises, of greed and selfishness, corruption and maladministration, of alternating aggression and vacillation on the part of the whites, and of courageous defense, despair, blind savagery, and inevitable defeat of the Indians.

In this dramatic hunt, Mexico was a miraculous refuge for the persecuted Indians, since in principle, the white man was stopped by the international boundary of the Rio Grande. The Indian did not long delay in using Mexican territory to organize his criminal expeditions into Texas, nor did the border Mexicans delay in making use of the Indian as an inciter and agent for stealing. But the underlying motive was the persecution by the white man of the Indian in Texas, whose proceedings are so well painted by one of the chiefs of the Bureau of Indian Affairs of the United States:

. . . despoiled, by irresistible forces, of the land of their fathers; with no country on earth to which they can emigrate; of a people with whom they cannot assimilate; they have no recognized claims upon the government and are compelled to become vagabonds to steal or to starve.

The fabulous growth of the cattle kingdom, whose principal seat was Texas, complicated still more the situation of the border by creating a traffic in stolen cattle in which Mexicans, Texans, and Indians soon participated.

The cattle kingdom was born in southeast Texas because it was sustained by the use of the horse for the rounding up, the guarding and the transporting of the herds to market. It was born where there were already horses and where the natural grasslands offered almost free and permanent food. It grew with the conquest by the white man of the Great Plains to extend itself in only ten years to west Texas and to the states of Oklahoma, Kansas, Nebraska, the Dakotas, Montana, Wyoming, Nevada, Utah, Colorado and New Mexico.

Such expansion was stimulated by the decline of the cattle industry in the East, the penetration of the railroads toward the West, the great demand created by the first large cities of the East and Middle West as well as technical inventions like the refrigerated freight car (whose first trials were made in 1873) which made it possible to preserve meat while it was transported great distances and by slow railroads, or like the appearance, above all in Chicago, of the great slaughtering and packing houses.

The origin of the cattle empire or kingdom, nevertheless, was a diamond-shaped domain with the main axis from north to south; the intersection of the coast of the Gulf of Mexico and the mouth of the Rio Grande on the south vertex and the city of San Antonio on the north vertex, the sides of the diamond being formed by lines uniting San Antonio with the Gulf Coast and San Antonio with Laredo. In this diamond, a region of natural grasslands and of a climate that permitted the cattle to be left out in the open even on winter nights, the Americans found not only the old Mexican horse, but also the long-horned cattle, descendants of the Andalusian bull and cow brought there by the Spaniards in the remote past. Cattle multiplied in the Nueces Valley without any care, as stray cattle, whose owners always had a doubtful title which could not even be based on brands frequently falsified or altered. The fact that the Republic of Texas declared all unbranded cattle as public property indicates the manner in which the cattle industry was run in that valley.

Even though several previous attempts had been made to sell cattle outside of Texas, heavy traffic did not commence until after the Civil War. From the 100,000 head of cattle registered in the census of 1830, the figure had reached over five millions by 1870. When an outside market was opened for Texas by the factors already mentioned, the cattle were rounded up in the spring for branding and for separating the different herds. Once this was accomplished, the long drives were begun, first to the West and afterwards to the North, until they reached the cow towns, like that of Abilene, Kansas, where the railroad that could carry them to the slaughtering and packing houses had already been put through. In the first great drives so made, 35,000 Texas longhorns arrived in Abilene; but two years afterwards not less than 350,000 made the trek. Thus developed the "drifting herd," as Webb, the great historian of the South, calls it; and as he himself concludes, "The drifting herds offered a splendid outlet for stolen cattle and stolen horses." To this panorama should be added the fact that the cattle thief stole Texas cattle not simply as an immediate food supply or to begin his own herd but also to export it by way of Matamoros or Tampico to Cuba, where at that time there was a great demand.

THE RESULT of such a complex, serious and confused situation was a wave of criminality which seemed to grow without anything or anyone being able to contain it and much less diminish it, plus a state of acrimony and of mutual reproach between the people and the authorities of Mexico and of the United States. The Texas press and politicians implored the help and protection of the United States government, above all of its army, describing the situation gloomily:

Throughout the Valley of the Rio Grande, from the mouth for a distance of two hundred miles up the river, and for one hundred and forty miles back from it, crops and herds had been abandoned, the people dared not travel except in armed parties; civil law outside the towns was suspended, and the sheriffs and judges reported to me that it was unsafe to attempt to execute processes' of law outside of towns unless the officers of the law were accompanied by soldiers to protect them.

[44]

The state of Texas, for its part, created in 1874 the Rangers, whose command was entrusted to the celebrated Civil War veteran, Captain L. H. McNelly. When McNelly began to patrol the frontier zone he found numerous groups of men, armed with the apparent purpose of mutual protection, but whose appearance indicated the profession of pillage and violence. An honest man, but stubborn and imprudent, he presented a little later to his superiors an official report which concurred with his final order not ever to take prisoners:

> The acts committed by Americans are horrible to relate. Many ranches have been plundered and burned, and the people murdered or driven away; one of these parties confessed to me in Corpus Christi as having killed eleven men on their last raid. I immediately issued an order . . . disbanding the minute companies. . . . Had I not disbanded these companies . . . it is possible and very probable that civil war would have ensued, as the Mexicans are very much exasperated.

But the damages were suffered by both the Mexican and the American populations of Texas. One hundred bandits proposed to take over the government of the county of Eagle Pass by terrorizing all the region. The Civil authorities considered themselves so impotent that the judge of Maverick County did not dare to sleep in his own house. And the band of King Fisher robbed in broad daylight cattle and arms from any ranch without the despoiled owners even daring to denounce them, preferring to declare to the authorities that the barbarous Indians or the Mexicans were the authors of the outrages. The evil was so extensive and seemed so deep rooted that the adjutant general of the Texan forces felt obliged to compile and publish *The Book of Crime,* which contained the names and descriptions of the principal malefactors. Among them figured prominently John Wesley Harding, who had assassinated twenty or twenty-five men, "not counting Mexicans or Negroes."

The civil struggles in Mexico alleviated or aggravated the situation less somberly but with equal effectiveness. When Porfirio Díaz organized in Brownsville his Tuxtepecan invading army, the cattle thieves and smugglers followed him, considerably bettering the situation on the Tamaulipecan frontier; on the contrary, when General Escobedo disbanded his forces after his revolutionary failure in the summer of 1877, "a band of bandits and cut-throats remained free" that caused intense fear in the region.

The Congress of the United States approved in May, 1872, a resolution by which the President was authorized to name a committee to investigate the nature and the extent of the crimes and robberies committed along the Rio Grande frontier. Apart from personal losses, the commission estimated material damage at about 28 million dollars. For its part, the Mexican government named the Investigating Committee of the Northern Frontier, whose report was published in 1874. Its effort was oriented more than anything else toward studying the depredations of the barbarous Indians within the national territory, and it concluded that Mexico had suffered more from them than had the United States. It also concluded that the venality of some American authorities, or their lack of cooperation in fighting the Indians and malefactors on each side of the river, was the principal cause of the depredations of which the Texans complained.

THE EXISTENCE of an international boundary was the major apparent obstacle to the pursuit and punishment of the Indians and the malefactors. And the obstacle appeared even greater in that these fugitives, far from respecting the boundary, used it to their advantage; the authorities, on the other hand, recognized the existence of it and they became helpless as soon as the bandits crossed it. Thus arose the idea that only through close and continual cooperation of the policing agents and the military forces of both countries could such a situation be terminated. The cooperation, nevertheless, was not as easy as it might seem. On the American side the military authority was divided, and the local authority always thought that the federal authority was insufficient and sluggish; the civil authority, divided into political factions, was far from being expeditious and honest. The situation was, if you please, worse on the Mexican side, since the federal military authority was frankly impotent in imposing itself on the rivalry of the local caciques, or political bosses, and the latter were usually interested in contraband and in rustling.

Therefore the Americans reached the conclusion that the Mexican authorities were not able and did not want to cooperate, and that consequently Americans should take on their shoulders the complete solution of the problem, but, of course, without respecting the international boundary. And it seemed inevitable that from there should sprout the idea that the most effective and complete remedy was to provoke an international war, conquer in it, and obtain from it a strip of territory that, besides enriching the United States, would facilitate guarding the new frontier. There seemed to be little doubt that McNelly, the head of the Texas Rangers, embraced those ideas and that in order to make them triumph, he tried either to gain the support of the federal officers or to coerce them in some manner. Besides, McNelly gave to the pursuit of the criminals and the crossing of the frontier a bellicose nationalistic tone. Before crossing it on November 19, 1875, he harangued his troops in Rio Grande City, telling them that they would give the Mexicans "a Texan lesson" which they had forgotten since the war of 1847. And his orders could not have been more definite: to kill all living beings, except old men, women and children. And so they did that time—only to discover that they had assassinated the residents of another ranch and not those of Las Cuevas, the one on which they actually sought to make that exemplary punishment.

The civil authorities of Texas supported the opinion of their military men. Governor Richard Coke affirmed in one of his letters written to President Ulysses S. Grant imploring the aid of the federal troops of the United States:

Peace can not be secured by confining the operation of troops to this side of the river. As long as the west bank of the river is the inviolable sanctuary for the marauders, they will depredate on us as heretofore . . .

Furthermore, the same Governor Coke had been ordering since 1875 that the state troops pursue the malefactors "as much on this side as on the other side of the river." Such an order vividly attracted the attention of Secretary of State Hamilton Fish, who asked the Attorney General of the United States to study juridically the subject to see if the United States government could counteract it. The conviction of the attorney general was so strong that he not only told Coke that his order would violate the international boundary of a country with which the United States maintained friendly relations but also that the very issuing of it exposed him to impeachment proceedings according to the laws of the country. But Coke was so sure of the necessity and justification of his order that he did not modify it, nor was he afraid of the prospect of being prosecuted. Rather, he argued angrily that if in 1873 Richard S. McKenzie, a colonel in the federal forces, invaded Mexican territory without meriting the disapproval of any of his superiors, he did not see why Texas troops could not do what federal troops had done earlier.

In fact, other federal authorities of the United States agreed with Coke. Among the military, Lieutenant Colonel W. R. Shafter, who later would gain some fame for his invasions of Mexican soil, expressed that opinion to his superiors in March of 1877:

Full authority to operate in Mexico as we choose is the only way in which life and property can be made secure on this frontier.

And he even came to affirm as an "incontrovertible fact" that all the intrusions of bandits proceeded from Mexico and none from the United States. Brigadier General Edward O. C. Ord, military commander of the Texas Military District, was of the same opinion. On one occasion, two Crow Indians (of whose nationality Ord was not even sure) who had served as guides for United States troops in the fight against a band of barbarous Indians, crossed into the Mexican territory as spies for the same troops and were apprehended by the civil authorities of Piedras Negras. On learning of it, Ord did not vacillate in telegraphing the nearest military commander ordering him that, using all his forces, he should enter Mexican territory and recover them. In fact the Secretary of State himself took the same position: in January, 1874, he wrote to the Secretary of War expressing his opinion that an incursion of American troops into Mexican territory was not a violation of the international law if it was indispensable to do it. And thus is explained the harsh tone of Foster to Lafragua in May, 1875: the Department of State "is reluctant to believe that the authorities in this Capital are insincere in their professions of good will, but it is hoped that they may have sufficient control over the local authorities and residents of the frontier" to pacify them.

V

MORE ADVERSE SIGNS

Each one of these numerous antecedents was bad in itself, and all together they created a very delicate situation; but still two new facts which filled the cup to the brim should be added. On November 23, 1876, the revolutionary group of Porfirio Díaz took over the government from Sebastián Lerdo de Tejada, and three months later, on March 4, 1877, Rutherford B. Hayes ascended to the Presidency of the United States.

Porfirio Díaz did not come to power by a single blow. His victory of Tecoac and the defection of the federal forces of Puebla allowed him to reach Mexico City, a fact that gave him a signal advantage over his two rivals; but Lerdo seemed to have abandoned the capital with the intention of strengthening himself in the interior, and José María Iglesias received the immediate support of strong military and political contingents of Lerdistas and Porfiristas, not only because being Vice President he was legally entitled to succeed President Lerdo, but also because at the moment he seemed to be a good compromise between Lerdo and Díaz. All of the month of December was for Díaz a period of great uncertainty, and even at the end of January of 1877, when the possibility of his rivals now forming a government or even offering real resistance was vanishing, Porfirio Díaz was far from dominating the country, and especially the northern frontier.

Servando Canales, the most influential Porfirista in Tamaulipas, had gone to the center of the country with his forces in order to assist in the final victory. That absence made it possible for Juan N. Cortina, his old rival, to arrive in the state with the intention of again gaining command and local influence. General Silvestre Revueltas, initially a supporter of Lerdo, afterwards of Iglesias, and later of Díaz, refused to deliver Matamoros to Cortina or to Canales, and strengthened himself in the plaza. In Nuevo León, Lázaro Garza Ayala, the former governor Narciso Dávila, Pedro Martínez and Julián Quiroga, local figures of renown and Lerdo's men, although momentarily isolated in Texas, did not cease to represent a threat for the Treviño hierarchy, Díaz' strongest regional support. The victory of Ignacio Martínez, another of the Nuevo León aspirants, over General Florencio Antillón, the largest force that the Iglesistas had in Guanajuato, was also a black question mark as far as the equilibrium of the conflicting local forces was concerned and above all as far as the ascendancy over them might be obtained by the caudillo of the Tuxtepecan revolt. The situation in Coahuila was still more uncertain because of its location at a distance from the center and its lack of communication with it, as well as its lack of an outstanding local leader. Besides, this state was the zone in which the Lerdista groups put up their most energetic and prolonged military resistence.

All this explains why Porfirio Díaz, with the danger of an immediate Lerdista or Iglesista reaction eliminated, did not try to intervene in the rivalry of his adherents and even less to superimpose himself upon them. Thus, when he did not obtain for his government the clear recognition of the United States, but found that this was conditioned on the pacification of the frontier, and later, when the United States attempted to dictate the effective measures to that end, he could hardly do otherwise than order General Rafael Benavides to survey the frontier in order to inform himself of the situation and in particular of the frictions among the local caciques. And when the pressure from the United States increased and Foster, in a personal conversation, pointed out to Díaz the necessity of designating as supreme chief of the federal forces on the frontiter a military man of high rank, of renown and of experience, Díaz finally resolved to name Jerónimo Treviño, regardless of his faults. The military prestige of the latter had declined much by then, even though it was superior to that of any other of the frontier chiefs. His adherence to Díaz in the Tuxtepecan revolt was not early and consistent as it had been in the revolt of La Noria; then, Treviño had been returned to the governorship of Nuevo León, a return in which figured his fondest hopes and a political position which he needed in order to promote his personal and group interests. Lastly, when Díaz decided to name him, he could scarcely give him 400 men, most of whom were ready to desert to Texas, tired of more than a year of forced military service, facing the unpleasant prospect of living in an inhospitable region and destined to associate with American forces in order to exterminate Mexicans, that is, brothers, or Indians, who were not their enemies.

WHAT CLAUDE G. BOWERS calls "the tragic era" of the United States was to culminate with the victory of Rutherford B. Hayes in the presidential election of 1876; but it was initiated in 1865, with the death of Abraham Lincoln and the ascension to power of Vice-President Andrew Johnson, whose government—courageous, even though sterile—ended with his trial by the Congress and his miraculous salvation from impeachment; and it continued with the two terms of General Ulysses S. Grant, of 1868 to 1876.

Grant, elected and re-elected because of his legendary prestige as victorious general in the Civil War, proved to be a poor President. Less prepared than either his predecessors or his successors, he always considered the Presidency as a personal prerogative, simple payment for all the great services he had rendered in the dark days for his country. The men with whom he surrounded himself were seldom any better. Most were either incompetent or corrupt if not both together; and few, intelligent and honest. Coinciding with this grave moral and intellectual crisis in the official sphere, the United States was passing through another crisis no less profound, that of an excessive economic development, with its attendant consequences: an inflamed siege to gain official favor and the use of the worst forms of bribery in order to obtain it; rampant attacks to obtain public favor by using the worst forms of deceit; fierce struggles among the warring economic groups in which all bounds, any scruples, the very notion of risk or of moral obligation became completely unknown.

It was inevitable that a series of frauds and bribes that scandalized the whole nation should flower. In those of the Union Pacific Railroad and of the Credit Mobilier even the Vice-President of the United States was involved, four or five members of the House of Representatives and a senator. In the famous resolution to make retroactive—against one of the fundamental principles of the Constitution—an increase in the salaries of congressmen and senators, Congress compromised its good judgment and integrity. The officials of the naval department received rewards for awarding jobs to their favorite contractors; those of the Department of the Interior were in collusion with the most unprincipled of speculators in public lands; those of the Treasury Department shared with the contributors the fruit of fiscal concealment, an affair in which President Grant's private secretary was found to be implicated; the head of the War Department hastened to resign before the Congress should try him for illegal selling of licenses for establishing stores on Indian reservations.

The corruption was not confined to the federal government; even the integrity of all the local legislatures was put in doubt. The two groups engaged in the struggle to gain control of the railroad lines subjected the New York state legislature to repeated bidding that ended with a favorable verdict for the one who offered the greater bribe. And the same occurred in the municipal governments, where the concessionaires for public services were buying off the authorities. Because of all this, two United States historians have said that "never before and only once since—after World War I—have public morals fallen so low."

The ineptitude and inconsistency of Grant, the unbridled greed of bankers, businessmen, industrialists, and speculators, that general and interminable series of bribes and frauds, created such an adverse political atmosphere toward the Republican party that its defeat seemed inevitable. The first aspirant for election from it was James G. Blaine, who tried to divert public attention from the theme of corruption to that of reconstruction in the South, with the hope of rekindling the passions of the Civil War, still not entirely extinguished. But he did not succeed, because Blaine himself was then denounced for his immoral ties with some of the railroad companies. So it happened that in the convention of the Republican party the "respectable but mediocre" candidate, Rutherford B. Hayes, former governor of the state of Ohio, was elected, on whom fell the hard task of "saving his party from disaster." The Democrats, determined to make corruption and the moral reform of the government the central point of the campaign, designated Samuel G. Tilden, a reformer, as candidate.

The first electoral returns seemed to give Tilden a sweeping victory. His supporters poured into the streets to celebrate tumultuously the very night of the election, and the Republican high command abandoned its offices in New York City early, sure that defeat was at hand and nothing remained to be done. A Democratic senator went, nevertheless, to the offices of a large New York City newspaper to ask for the count of the states of South Carolina, Florida and Louisiana. The report that the Democrats were doubting their triumph spread like a cloud of dust, and the Republicans then realized that with those three states Hayes would have 185 electoral votes, the necessary majority.

The popular elections now over, the fight to obtain the electoral votes of such states as these three became decisive. Grant's Secretary of War sent to the capital of Florida "a sufficient number" of troops "to protect" the committee charged with counting the votes cast in the state, announcing that soon "funds from Washington" would arrive in order "to sustain" all those favorable to Hayes and to annul those of Tilden. Even the Western Union Telegraph Company took part in the fight by transmitting in advance to the Republicans any communications that the Democrats were sending to one another.

The former tried to invalidate in Louisiana a sufficient number of Democratic votes by using the argument that they had been obtained through intimidation. Such argument was based on the major premise that, since the Republican party was the anti-slavery party, all the Negroes would have voted for its candidate; and as the Negro population in the state surpassed the white by more than 24,000, the fraudulent character of the Democratic victory was incontestable. Election return recount committees hence had to annul about 18,000 votes, a feat which was performed thanks to innumerable sworn declarations in which the original voters "confessed" to having voted for Tilden under pressure and not of their own will. In South Carolina similar proceedings were followed, and just for good measure the governor of Oregon annulled the credentials of a Democratic elector in order to substitute for him another favorable to the Republican candidate.

It is curious that a month earlier Hayes had written in his personal diary that the elections might end in armed conflict. And things seemed to be moving in that direction, for in spite of the frauds in Louisiana, Florida, and South Carolina, and of the arbitrary act of the governor of Oregon, it fell to Congress to say the last word; but in it little was to be gained, since the Republicans dominated in the Senate and the Democrats in the House of Representatives. The Constitution of the United States provided that "the President of the Senate shall, in the presence of the Senate and the House of Representatives, open all the certificates [of the electoral college], and the votes shall then be counted." But, who was to count them? If the Senate did it, Hayes won the election; if the House of Representatives, Tilden. The Democrats, in this situation and knowing the methods used in the "doubtful" states, were resolved to throw caution to the wind, and began to talk of organizing in Washington a concentration of 100,000 partisans to pressure Congress. On the other hand, it was certain that Grant and the army would go to any extreme to aid Hayes; in fact the President filled the Potomac with gunboats in reply to the announced Democratic concentration.

Congress, in the face of the obscurity of the constitutional text and the identical strength of the contenders, resolved that a special committee composed of seven Republicans, seven Democrats, and one independent Republican should count the votes. This special committee was composed of five senators (three Republicans and two Democrats), five representatives (two Republicans and three Democrats), and five magistrates of the Supreme Court (two Republicans, two Democrats and one independent Republican). Thus came about the fantastic situation by which only one man, that independent Republican justice, was the person who elected the President of the United States. In the four cases of doubtful election, he cast his vote in favor of the Republican party and in that manner Rutherford B. Hayes was elected by a majority of only one electoral vote, in the midst of the most scandalous fraud of all the political history of the United States and against an opponent who had won the popular vote by more than a quarter million votes.

Things did not degenerate into an armed conflict, as Hayes himself feared, because of Tilden's not being up to the crisis, the good sense of the people and its desire to forget as soon as possible so much nastiness; but, as had been said by a United States historian, "Hayes assumed office under a cloud from whose shadow he was never able to escape into the sunlight of popular approval." And, in fact, some of his actions relating to Mexico were to have that somber origin, and others the shining design of gaining the approval of his country.

THE FIRST SYMPTOM of such a state of affairs was an explosion of the United States press which, very curiously, coincided with the accession to power of President-elect Hayes on March 4, 1877.

The *Times,* the *Herald Tribune,* and the *World,* all of New York, as well as the *Republican* of Washington and *The Press* of Philadelphia, published news and commentaries on a visibly agreed-on theme: Mexico would never obtain by itself political stability and economic progress; it would only attain them in the beneficient shadow of the United States, by becoming one of its protectorates. This new relationship would cast aside a knotty problem whose solution became easy by separating oneself from the fiction of a nationality which ought to be treated with the kid gloves of international law. The explosion deeply wounded public sentiment in Mexico and created an attitude of great reserve in the government, in spite of the fact that moderate opinions like those of "Alcestes" and Anselmo de la Portilla succeeded in superimposing themselves.

The first declared that he did not share the surprise of many of his colleagues, since all ought to be accustomed by now to the "always hostile" inclination of the United States press; all were acquainted also with the existence of speculative and lazy Americans, determined to provoke conflicts between the two nations. In spite of it one should trust in the good sense of the United States government and in the conviction that none in Mexico believed the protectorate advantageous since "the electoral frauds", the lack of respect to institutions and the administrative corruption were common to both countries. "Alcestes" hoped that said press would come to admit that "the only invasion that Mexico would not resist" was that of the railroads from the United States. De la Portilla, with less good humor and very sententiously, tried to explain the impatience of the United States press with the wavering progress of Mexico in politics and economics: the country had not been so fortunate in enjoying a prolonged peace as the United States. Besides, the intervention of a nation could only be justified if the other placed peace, its liberty, or its independence in danger. That not being the case, the decisive point was Mexico's lack of appetite for the protectorate; and "the absurdity of its being imposed by force was not to be feared."

This campaign, which seemed to have surprised and even displeased Foster, may have been born from his initial opinions. In one of his dispatches that the Department of State classified as "illuminating," Foster caught the complete despair of the country when, Lerdo overthrown, it seemed that the civil war would be prolonged between the Díaz and Iglesias factions:

It is difficult to suggest the deplorable conditions of the country and the feeling of depression which prevails. Those who have hoped from the past ten continuous years of constitutional government that the Republic had at last entered upon an era, if not of absolute peace, at least of legitimate authorities, regard it as a sad fact in the history of Mexico, that when the parties have accomplished what both sought for in ridding the country of what they claim was a personal despotism and usurpation of power they would be unable to find a way to union and peace.

IT HAS ALREADY been pointed out that the first idea of President Ulysses S. Grant and his Secretary of State, Hamilton Fish, was to recognize Porfirio Díaz at once, among other things because it seemed embarrassing to them to accept payment from a government with whom it did not maintain official relations. John W. Foster's dispatches from Mexico concerning settlement of frontier frictions and the election of Díaz and his telegram about his establishment of unofficial relations with Díaz' government reached Washington when Rutherford B. Hayes was already President and when William M. Evarts had replaced Hamilton Fish in the Department of State. Evarts approved Foster's conduct, but explained that "it seemed advisable to await the progress of events" and the attitude of the Mexican Congress "before advancing toward a formal and official recognition." The second resolution—and it was taken three scant days afterwards—was not one of waiting and of caution, since by it a stand was taken. The United States Secretary of War had transmitted to the Department of State the opinion of Lieutenant Colonel W. R. Shafter that the only way to end the "atrocities" on the frontier was to pursue the delinquents within the Mexican territory and to attack them in the dens that they had there. The Department of State made the opinion of Shafter its own by instructing Foster to spread among the Mexicans the version that "as the authorities of that country seem to be unable or unwilling" to combat the frontier banditry, the President of the United States might come to accept Shafter's opinion as advice, although it "would be preferable, doubtless," to count on the official consent of Mexico to United States troops invading their territory in pursuit of these culprits.

Lieutenant Colonel Shafter was not the supreme chief of the federal forces in the state of Texas. He was hardly that of those stationed at Fort Clark. His report was not based, then, on general experience; nor in writing it did he pretend to appreciate the complete situation, much less to suggest a policy to be adopted by the United States. He simply related that from December 30, 1876 to March 9, 1877, a hundred head of horses and some three hundred head of cattle had been stolen in the vicinity of Fort Clark. With his troops he had followed the tracks of the first group of Indian cattle thieves some two hundred kilometers within Mexican territory until reaching their camp; in it he saw one hundred slaughtered cattle, whose meat was being dried under the rays of a benign sun. The Indians, nonetheless, warned of the proximity of their pursuers, fled to the environs of the nearest town, in which they would hide if an attempt was made to attack them. He roundly contended that the Mexican authorities did not make the least effort to control the barbarous Indians fleeing from Texas and, consequently, only an accident would permit his troops to catch them, because they were alert, especially after the surprise that Lieutenant John L. Bullis had given them the previous July in their Mexican encampment. He added that not one single Indian lived permanently on Texas soil; for that reason it was completely useless to go hunting for parties of four or five that were formed to commit their misdeeds. From this he concluded that the situation would improve when the government of the United States should concede full powers for United States soldiers to operate on Mexican soil as they might judge necessary.

But Shafter's superior officers judged otherwise. Brigadier General Ord thought in January, 1877, that the reports of the Texas authorities and of local newspaper stories on the frontier situation were always exaggerated and the offspring of partisan interests. The merchants and Texas ranchers knew "the customs" of Mexico and they ought to abide by them; because of it he refused to intervene in order to avoid the forced loans levied on the Americans of Matamoros by Generals Revueltas and Cortina. The commandant of Fort Brown had a different opinion: "Never before now have the robberies and assassinations ceased," and "the sensation of absolute security of life and property exists." Since May, 1876, there had not been known a single case of cattle thievery in his district. And in order to explain this new situation he entered into matters to a depth seldom found in a military man. When the commander of the United States Army in Missouri, under whom was the military department of Texas under the command of Ord, transmitted to the head of the United States Army some reports received from his subordinates, at the end of May, 1877, he said:

I believe that all reports of invading groups on the southern territory of Texas should be examined with great reserve. A revolutionary situation exists along the length of the Mexican frontier which to a certain degree Texas citizens encourage and if there is any incursion, it is very probable that their effects are exaggerated.

Foster, in any case, complied with Evarts' instructions by visiting Vallarta at once in order to transmit to him the facts contained in Lieutenant Colonel Shafter's report and the recommendation of the latter to the United States government. Neither dilatory or indolent, he reminded Vallarta that at the very beginning of his negotiation in the Department of Foreign Relations he had explained to him repeatedly the necessity of attempting some effective means of imposing peace and order on the frontier.

To President Díaz he had suggested the advantage of designating immediately an officer of high rank and prestige as commander of the federal forces in the north. Far from doing this, General Miguel Blanco had been sent on a purely political mission. Vallarta replied that General Díaz recognized without reserve the necessity of maintaining peace; and if the designation of that supreme official had not been made so far it was due to the inevitable readjustments that the situation in the country temporarily imposed. Vallarta thought, nonetheless, that complete cooperation among the military leaders would not be achieved if the relations between the two governments were not previously normalized, since all agreements made among the first would have to be approved by the second.

He pointed out also that the recent incursion into Piedras Negras of Lieutenant Colonel Shafter, whose purpose was not to pursue criminals but to recover by force two Mexicans held under custody by the legitimate authorities of the country, was a very poor endorsement of Shafter's own recommendation to his government; instead, it very justly alarmed Mexico. Foster thought that Vallarta wanted to impress on him the thesis that the solution of this and other pending problems depended upon recognition. Therefore he thought that, this granted, an agreement among the military leaders could be obtained, sanctioned by the government, that would permit the crossing of the border without considering such an act a violation of the territory. If his government would thus instruct and authorize him, he would direct his efforts in that way, "although the condition of affairs on the frontier and the indifference of the Mexican authorities might justify the issuance of instructions to the military forces" to pay no attention to the international boundary. And Foster condescendingly manifested his preference for not injuring the national pride "of this people" by means of the agreement which he suggested.

Foster must have not felt entirely sure that the possibility of reaching that agreement would succeed in inducing the Department of State to grant prior recognition. In fact, four days after he sent his note he was making efforts to evaluate the general situation in Mexico and his own personal one before the Díaz government, and, in order to express himself better, he decided on a long, personal, confidential letter to Evarts. It began by recalling that the tone of the dispatches of former Secretary Fish induced the belief of an immediate recognition, and that, in fact, Fish believed that the act of receiving from Mexico the first payment of the claims would be equivalent to conceding it; therefore he had left it to Foster's discretion to do so. Foster's first advice, however, was not to be precipitate; Vallarta had declared that the receiving of the payment and the granting of recognition were independent acts. Foster had believed it advisable to wait for the elections to transform the revolutionary government of Díaz into a constitutional one; such had now occurred and it seemed to him a propitious occasion to return to the question.

Almost complete peace had prevailed in Mexico during the period of waiting advised by him, and everywhere the authority of Díaz was recognized. Foster, within the limitations which his office imposed on him, always had manifested his preference for constitutional government. The government of Díaz now was constitutional, and thus the question arose: Had not the time arrived for officially recognizing it and of holding it to be the only one in the country? In order to judge to what point the criterion of stability was relative, it should be remembered that in the last fifty years Mexico had had sixty distinct governments, in spite of which the United States maintained relations with most of them. It was quite probable that Díaz would be dispossessed of power in the same manner in which he had obtained it, but at the moment he had the support of a large army and enjoyed military prestige and popularity. Foster did not consider the administrative capacity of Díaz to be great, thus his success would depend largely on those with whom he surrounded himself; but he believed him to be an upright, frank man of good habits, traits seldom found in the leaders of Mexico's government. There was little place for many illusions about his friendly attitude toward the United States, since the disparity of means and force between the two countries naturally created mistrust in the Mexican, although also a respect that restrained the hostility and impeded him from manifesting ill-will openly.

Foster did not know if the discussed project of a protectorate had the support of those around President Hayes. Ignorant as he was on this point, he thought that, for the present, the United States should not press for more than peace on the frontier and the protection of American lives and interests. Besides, the other accredited diplomatic representatives sought in him a guide and it was even probable that their governments instructed them to follow him. He had resolved to write such a frank and lengthy letter because he feared that his first opinions, expressed in his letters to Fish, might have caused the present doubts of the Department of State on recognition. Therefore he asked if President Hayes and Evarts did not wish to leave it to his discretion within the instructions that they had given him. That point solved, he believed negotiating the pending questions would be easy. In any case, if his present opinions did not coincide with the politics of his government, he felt obliged to ask that he be fully informed of the course that he should follow, stating that he would follow it with all his heart in so far as he knew how.

VALLARTA did not miss any discreet occasion to remind Foster of recognition and Foster, in turn, did not miss any in speaking to his own government about it. Ernest Burdel, in charge of the archives of the French legation, had already made some suggestions for opening negotiations directed to the establishment of diplomatic relations with France, Vallarta told Foster; but remembering that on former occasions the United States had offered its good offices on this subject, President Díaz had resolved to defer direct negotiations until relations should be normalized with the United States, whose friendly intercession between France and Mexico could then be made good use of. Foster immediately informed his government of this conversation with Vallarta and of Burdel's having asked him if he could count on his intercession, should the occasion arise. He nevertheless had decided to wait until his government resolved the question of the recognition of Díaz.

On May 7 Foster telegraphed Evarts to inform him that the Mexican Congress had now declared that Porfirio Díaz had been elected constitutional President for the four-year term 1877-1880, and that Díaz had taken the oath of office on May 5. On the following day he confirmed that information, adding that the judicial power had been duly·installed and that the call for the elections of senators had been made to complete the integration of the legislative power. Thus, all constitutional orders having been observed and in view of his confidential letter of April 28, he was awaiting "specific" instructions.

While he was awaiting them, Foster remained in contact with Vallarta and transmitted the news that the latter gave him which confirmed the good disposition of the Mexican government to settle its differences with the United States. Porfirio Díaz had removed General Vicente Jiménez from the military command of the state of Guerrero for having disobeyed his orders to set free the United States consul at Acapulco, whom he had arrested when he entered that port with his forces. Likewise, he had resolved to replace Mariscal with José María Mata, who was to carry instructions to negotiate a settlement of all pending problems.

Foster was able, therefore, to report with satisfaction that the Mexican government, finally aware of the pressing importance of the border problems, had resolved to put at the head of the federal forces a divisional head who would actively cooperate with Brigadier General Ord in pursuit of malefactors and barbarous Indians.

VI
BLIND ALLEY

Great must have been Foster's surprise when, in reply to his numerous dispatches and telegrams and so much news which he regarded as flattering, he received other "specific" instructions than he had been expecting; for evidently President Rutherford B. Hayes had a personal opinion of his own on the subject. It was not William M. Evarts, temporarily absent from the Department of State, who made the reply, but Frederick W. Seward, first undersecretary temporarily in charge of the office, who would not have taken a resolution without consulting with the President.

The United States government, Seward told Foster, had maintained with Mexico a just conduct, besides a generous and friendly one. It had not tried to intervene in its internal affairs and it was accustomed to accept the results of its elections without very close scrutiny of the methods by which its presidents reached power; but it would not recognize Porfirio Díaz until it was convinced that the Mexican people approved of his election, that his would be a stable and lasting government and that he wished to respect the norms of international law and its contractual obligations. Recognition from the United States was not merely a formal procedure; it also carried with it a high moral influence; it strengthened and prolonged the life of the government which received it and helped to preserve the internal and external peace of Mexico, because the conduct of the United

States guided that of other countries. Seward applauded Díaz for having made the first payment on the claims, but lamented his carelessness in fulfilling his other international duties and of having violated some. He could not, therefore, fail to take notice of those acts, particularly those of the frontier depredations. He decided to point out that Foster should not be surprised at the eagerness of President Díaz and Ignacio L. Vallarta to have friendly relations with the United States, or that they should insist on the theme that the re-opening of them would open the road to the settlement of pending problems; but also it was natural—he added with expressive force—that the United States, far from trusting in the eventuality of a settlement, should ask for this before recognition. For all this, he instructed him to make known these opinions informally, but

. . . to let it be clearly understood that while the Government of the United States seeks amity and cordial relations with its sister Republic, it prefers to await some evidence that its friendship will be reciprocated.

Evarts moved with great celerity upon returning to the Department of State. On May 27 he revived a report of the Secretary of War, dated March 16, on the robbery of two hundred head of cattle. He transmitted it to Foster and in a not at all conciliatory tone commented that as the Mexican government failed in its international agreement to cooperate in the pursuit of barbarous Indians, the United States, in legitimate defense, would have to do it alone, but without respect to international boundaries. Evarts, nonetheless, ended his boastful note with a hesitation; for instructing Foster to make known its contents "in the proper places," he asked him not to present an official protest to the Mexican government at once.

Whether this hesitation was real or feigned, the truth is that four days after Evarts wrote the note, the Secretary of War, George W. McCrary, made the resolution taken by President Hayes in regard to the border problems known to General W. T. Sherman, Commander of the United States Army, so that he in turn transmitted it to Brigadier General Edward O. C. Ord, head of the federal forces of the Military District of Texas. The President had examined Lieutenant Colonel W. R. Shafter's report and "numerous other documents"; he wanted the federal troops to exercise the greatest vigilance in order to suppress such transgressions, and in order to realize this he considered the cooperation of the local authorities of Mexico very desirable. Ord should be ordered to seek that cooperation and to inform those authorities that, although President Hayes did not wish to offend Mexico, he now found the incursions of malefactors into Texas intolerable. Ord should express "the great desire of President Hayes of joining them" in that task; but if they did not comply with their duties, the United States government would take charge of doing it even if the "occasional" crossing of the frontier by United States troops was necessary. Sherman's communication could not have ended more peremptorily:

> You will therefore direct General Ord that, in case the lawless incursions continue, he will be at liberty, in the use of his own discretion, when in pursuit of a band of the marauders, and when his troops are either in sight of them or upon a fresh trail to follow them across the Rio Grande, and to overtake and punish them, as well as retake stolen property taken from our citizens and found in their hands on the Mexican side of the line.

Seward's dispatch of May 16, that of Evarts of May 27 and the order to Brigadier General Ord of June 1 did not correspond to the reports, news and opinions that Foster was transmitting so clearly and frequently; but

> . . . certain gentlemen . . . conceived the idea that, in view of the tension . . . created by partisans of Mr. Tilden and of the disturbed condition of affairs in the Southern States, it would divert attention from pending issues and tend greatly to consolidate the new Administration, if a war could be brought on with Mexico and another slice of territory added to the Union.

Texas, furthermore, seemed to exercise a great influence on Hayes, since not only was Guy M. Bryan, his closest adviser, from that state but also the votes of the Texas representatives and senators were indispensable in Congress for combatting his enemies. For that reason alone it was to be expected that the Hayes government would adopt toward Mexico an energetic policy. It was not only energetic but turbulent. The order to Brigadier General Ord was not communicated to the Mexican minister in Washington, and President Díaz knew of it through the press before Foster received it and officially communicated it. Furthermore even when one gave heed to it, neither then nor afterward was Ord instructed to search for the understanding and cooperation of the local authorities on the border, thus brushing aside the local federal authorities and, in the last analysis, the President of Mexico. This seemed to eliminate government-to-government dealings and, consequently, diplomatic negotiation.

The interests that surrounded Hayes were so strong that even at the end of that year in his first message to Congress on December 3, the President gave official notice of the change in the traditional United States policy on matters of recognition:

It has been the custom of the United States, when such changes of government have heretofore occurred in Mexico to recognize and enter into official relations with the *de facto* government as soon as it should appear to have the approval of the Mexican people and should manifest a disposition to adhere to the obligations of treaties and international friendship. In the present case such official recognition has been deferred by the occurrences on the [Rio Grande] border.

Hayes in his message admitted having received from the Mexican government assurances of being able to control and desiring to punish the depredators on the frontier, but he sceptically limited himself to the desire that events would justify those assurances. In the meanwhile, although he was far from believing in a prolonged interruption of relations, he viewed with anxiety the persistence of the frontier disorders that were arousing popular feeling and were exposing unfortunate acts not very propitious to full friendship.

IGNACIO L. VALLARTA found himself each day in a more uncomfortable position since, in spite of the fact that Ignacio Mariscal agreed with him throughout the negotiation of the first payment of the claims, Mariscal did not manifest his support of Díaz; nor did Vallarta think that Mariscal had made a loyal effort to obtain the recognition of a government that he was not representing nor would represent. Now that Díaz was constitutional President after the elections, the fiction that he as revolutionary chief could not accredit a diplomatic agent in Washington had ended, while Mariscal continued representing the nonexistent government of Sebastián Lerdo de Tejada. The possibility of using Mariscal was made even more doubtful when recognition was based on the negotiation of various treaties or agreements. Finally, there remained what Vallarta and Díaz himself could expect from Foster. Without knowing, as was natural, the initial opposition of the latter to an immediate recognition, they had to suppose that Foster would be and could not fail to be a loyal and active representative of his government; and it, evidently, was resisting giving full and clear recognition. All of this induced Vallarta to send with José T. de Cuellar, the secretary of the Mexican legation in Washington, Mariscal's letters of recall.

Vallarta, in effect, on May 27, 1877, gave Cuellar secret instructions ordering him as soon as he arrived in Washington to deliver those letters to Mariscal, and to remain as chargé d'affaires ad interim until José María Mata, to be named minister plenipotentiary arrived, under whose orders Cuellar would remain "without any limitations." Cuellar was to abstain from treating any subject whatever with the United States government. Only Mata could do so, directly if the Department of State accepted him as minister, or through him if otherwise. Mariscal, without delay, notified the Department of State on June 26 that he was retiring from his position because of his health and accredited Cuellar; and the latter, on his first official visit, heard Undersecretary Seward tell him that the United States government had not recognized Díaz because it was waiting to see if he was consolidated in power, since at the beginning it feared

[69]

that he would fall within a few weeks; on the other hand it was gratified for what Díaz had done in favor of the United States.

Without any difficulty whatever Vallarta thus obtained his first objective, that of eliminating the unsure aid of Mariscal. Next he would try his luck with the second, to replace him with a loyal element. On May 25, 1877, Porfirio Díaz named José María Mata special envoy and minister plenipotentiary of Mexico to the United States government and gave him a personal letter of introduction to President Hayes, six months' pay in advance and 10,000 pesos for expenses of installation; and Vallarta, days later, gave him the necessary instructions.

Mata was to have a "confidential" interview with the Secretary of State, and if he found it favorable to recognition he was to present his credentials; if not, he was to reserve them. In the latter case, Cuellar was to continue as chargé d'affaires and as official representative, but for the government of Mexico Mata would be the responsible minister and Cuellar's superior. To obtain recognition would be, of course, his principal mission; but "by means which would in no way compromise the national decorum and interest"; and what was more, he was to make known "prudently" that such an act was not nor could be one of grace, "but rather one required by international law and already executed by several European and American governments." He should make it known that Mexico rejected the order given to Brigadier General Ord, and that it would dictate the measures necessary to obtain peace and order on the frontier, besides being "disposed to hear propositions which might be made to it in order to adjust a treaty" to this effect.

Even though his instructions said that he should be ready *only* to hear what the United States government might wish to propose, Mata carried with him a complete project of a treaty to put an end to the border frictions, the most important element of which was to throw out as inadmissable the idea that the forces of one nation could pass into the territory of the other to pursue, apprehend and punish malefactors. With this as a starting point, the project offered norms for securing close cooperation between the military forces of both nations, by each one operating within its territory, and a series of juridical reforms to facilitate the trial and punishment of the delinquents. It established, for example, the obligation of maintaining along the length of the boundary line enough forces to make effective pursuit of the thieves, Indians and rustlers, and that of placing these forces under the orders of highly qualified leaders, who would spread them out in an advantageous manner according to plans agreed on by them. These obligations would be extended to the leaders directly in charge of the detachments among which the troops were divided.

It was hoped to obtain thus a coordinated vigilance on both sides of the river, a vigilance that would be all the greater if the military chiefs fixed by common agreement the fords for the passing of cattle which were legal traffic between the two countries, it being presumed that stolen stock would be that which passed at other places. The proposal, considering that the frontier had come to disturb the good relations between Mexico and the United States, proposed to treat rustling as a crime of federal concern; consequently, federal judges would be required to handle trials for rustling and for the extradition of culprits. Also it proposed a reform of the current treaty of extradition to make it obligatory on the part of each country to turn over its nationals accused of rustling, regardless of the size of the theft, although specifying the guarantee that, once extradited, they could not be tried in the other country except for that precise crime. In fact, the treaty proposed that the federal and local authorities of the two countries facilitate in every way possible the identification and recuperation of the stolen property.

The proposal was good in principle, for except for rejecting the reciprocal passing of troops from one country to the territory of the other, it contained preventive measures directed to impeding the commission of the crimes, and executive dispositions to facilitate the punishment of the crime and the recovery of stolen property.

VALLARTA of course did not fail to make known to Foster his decision to replace Mariscal by Mata. He even explained to him that the departure of the latter was delayed with the hope that the United States minister would receive definitive news on the recognition. And Foster, expecting it momentarily, suggested to the Department of State that if at last he was to be authorized to concede it, it would be much more convenient for Mata to remain in Mexico to participate in the negotiations that he, Foster, would soon undertake with Vallarta. As the good news did not arrive, Mata resolved to leave for Washington on June 18, and on that same day Foster received Seward's instructions conditioning recognition on the guarantee of prior settlement of pending problems.

It is very possible that Vallarta, in the face of such bad news, should have resolved to detain Mata. The truth is that the latter, trusting in the aid of time, made a slow trip that brought him to Washington on July 1. Five days later he had his first "confidential" interview with Evarts, to whom he explained the object of his mission and his intention of sending him a copy of his credentials "for the usual purposes." "You may send them," Evarts responded, "and all the papers which you may believe useful, for they will be given due consideration." Mata then communicated to the Department of Foreign Relations that he had been privately informed that in a cabinet meeting it was agreed to submit them to the judgment of the Department of State; likewise that in a second meeting comment was made of the anomalous state of the Mexican diplomatic representation in Washington, since Mariscal had not officially notified them of the change of government in Mexico or presented his letter of recall. But Mata was optimistic, for he added: "It seems that the recognition of the administration of General Díaz will be decided."

On July 12 Mata again had an interview with Evarts, from whom he received assurances of continuing to consider the questions of recognition and the frontier. Mata tried to press him into receiving a prompt reply, alleging that he wanted to transmit it to his government on the next boat. Evarts did not think he would be able to accommodate him, and Mata commented philosophically: "This is the state of things at the moment, and if something unusual occurs, I shall communicate it by telegraph." Vallarta did not wish to dishearten him, for on commenting on these communications, he told him that the government "recognized his strong efforts in discharging his commission."

In reality it was condemned to failure. On the one hand, Mata was received only "informally" and there never was the intention of treating him as a regularly accredited diplomatic agent, because he represented a government with whom there were no official relations. On the other hand, he did not comply with Vallarta's instructions of ascertaining if there was "a favorable disposition to receive him as an official representative" before leaving a copy of his credentials. And neither did he fulfill them by limiting himself to expressing his willingness to listen to suggestions for resolving the frontier problems, for among the papers that he left in Evarts' hands was the proposal of a treaty annexed to his instructions, and the judgment on it was what decided the fate of his mission.

Evarts, apart from recognizing a very creditable willingness of the Mexican government to cooperate with the United States, found the treaty proposal insufficient: first, because it referred only to the depredations on the frontier and not to other pending problems such as the Free Zone and forced loans; then, because even though limited thus, it did not refer "explicitly and clearly" to the use of military force in order to pursue criminals and recover the stolen property "outside the territorial limits of the United States." Lastly, the Department of State was determined to hold in Mexico the conversations on the matters that "should necessarily precede the recognition of Díaz." Therefore, Foster was instructed to renew his conversations with the Secretary of Foreign Relations, by announcing that until new information from him was received, the United States government was reserving its decision on recognition. And in order to give its minister a clearer idea of the importance that the Department of State attributed to the matter, Evarts added:

While the President is desirous of terminating as early as may be, the present period of suspended diplomatic relations with Mexico, he nevertheless deems it essential that those relations when restored shall be placed upon a just and amicable basis. It is only upon such a basis that they could be permanent; and their interruption, if it should again occur, would probably menace the stability of the one Government and the peace of both.

Evarts, in fact, was telling Foster that Mata had been informed of the "nature" of the instructions contained in this note.

The concept of the "nature" of these instructions must have been very vague, for Mata remained in Washington six weeks more without gaining intimate contact with the United States authorities, until on September 12, convinced of the uselessness of waiting and fearful that winter would renew an old lung ailment, he resigned his mission and gave prior warning that he would remain in Washington only one more month. Vallarta, with the idea of using him in some way, sent him a protest against a new invasion into Mexican territory, adding, however, that if when he received it he had not been yet officially recognized, he should have it delivered by Cuellar. And this, of course, raised the real problem: if on receiving these instructions —Vallarta told him—he had not been accredited or had no immediate hopes of it, he should return to Mexico, but not without first manifesting to the Secretary of State that with Mata's mission the Mexican government had wished to give one further proof of its desire to resolve the problems pending between the two countries, but that since so much time had elapsed without his being accredited, a difficult situation that "affected the honor of the nation" was being prolonged. Mata should, nonetheless, add that even though he was resigning, the Mexican legation, in charge of Cuellar, would remain open and in contact with the United States authorities. Vallarta, still not having lost complete hope for a reversal of opinion, told him he should abandon Washington only if the Secretary of State "did not give satisfactory explanations."

Vallarta salvaged one advantage from the failure of this mission: that was, the approval of the congressional circles of his country. In some manner the rumor circulated that Mata was sent to Washington to obtain recognition at any cost; and as the Mexican Senate was aware that he had the rank of minister plenipotentiary, and that the nomination was never sent for ratification, it asked for explanations. Vallarta gave them in a secret session. The Executive had not sent the nomination for its ratification for the very valid reason that the Senate did not then exist. Condemned by the Plan of Tuxtepec as a "creature" of Lerdo, Juan N. Méndez, on issuing the call, limited the elections to the Chamber of Deputies. He showed, furthermore, the instructions given Mata which said that he should procure recognition without compromising the national decorum and interests and that Mexico thought that it should be extended not as a gift but as an act required under international law. The Senate found nothing censurable in Vallarta's conduct or in the official documents which were made known to it; it concluded with the opinion that the reading of these "was enough to satisfy the most worried spirit." Furthermore, he was authorized to publish them when he judged it convenient.

FREDERICK W. SEWARD's instructions to Foster, repeated afterward by Evarts, the order of June 1 to Brigadier General Ord and the failure of Mata's mission quickly embittered the relations of Vallarta with Foster, those of both governments and even those of the lesser functionaries who had any connection with this affair. The tension on the frontier reached such a point that any insignificant act might have caused open hostility between the forces of the two countries without anyone being able to predict that a mere local incident might not be converted into a general war. In the case of the invasion of Piedras Negras, for example, Lieutenant Colonel Shafter stood for several minutes with his pistol drawn in front of the political chief of the district, who was also with his gun ready to fire. And not only they but the three hundred men with Shafter and the armed citizens of that place were mutually on guard for one anguished hour, wishing for and fearing to hear the first shot that would initiate an attack of everyone against everyone else. The relations between the local chiefs of the United States and Mexican forces became uncivil, and the communications which they had occasionally with one another acquired a tone of distrust.

So it happened also with those communications that Vallarta ordered Mariscal to present to the United States Department of State and with those that Vallarta and Foster exchanged in Mexico. Vallarta assured Mariscal that Shafter's deliberate contempt of Mexico's territory was "unquestionable." And Mariscal, in his note to Evarts, pointed out that, besides that violation, the authorities of the country were insulted by being threatened with guns in hand. When Foster visited Vallarta to give him Shafter's report on his invasion of Piedras Negras, and Vallarta told him that he would never be able to consider it as a justification, Foster grossly answered that he had come not to defend Shafter but to deliver the document. In that same conversation Vallarta commented that the authorities seemed to be allowing the Lerdistas to organize a counterrevolution with impunity on Texas soil; Foster replied that Porfirio Díaz had done the same when in 1876 he was organizing the Tuxtepec revolt in Brownsville. Vallarta commented that the situation was different, since the Lerdistas were not organizing open warfare but rapine; Foster replied that Porfirio Díaz' partisans were criminals of such renown as General Cortina in Tamaulipas and General Trías in Coahuila.

The gravest manifestation that this embroilment produced was, nevertheless, the reply of the Mexican government to the instructions to Brigadier General Ord. The Secretary of War, Pedro Ogazón, wrote to Jerónimo Treviño, commander in chief of the Northern Division, informing him that Ord had been given discretionary authority by his government to pursue malefactors, apprehend them, punish them and recover the stolen property within Mexico's territory. Even though the United States Department of State had given some reassuring explanation to the Mexican minister in Washington, President Díaz believed that the national honor would be in danger so long as that order was not made compatible with existing treaties between the two nations, the international norm and the practices of civilized nations.

The instructions that Treviño already had to spread out his forces and to move them so as to prevent malefactors from crossing the Rio Grande and remaining unpunished were reiterated; besides, he should seek the cooperation of United States leaders so as to combine the operation of each in their respective territory and to obtain thus the best results. But he was told also that the agreements made could not include the authorization of crossing the dividing line, for not even the President himself could concede this; it was the exclusive power of the Senate. He was asked to transmit those instructions to Ord and to make him understand that President Díaz' desire for collaboration was limited only by that of the national dignity and the rules of international law. But Ogazón added:

You will make known to him that, the national government not being able to permit foreign troops to enter Mexican territory, nor much less carry out jurisdictional acts, you will repel force with force in case an invasion takes place . . . Working with the prudence that this grave business demands in order to avoid motives for conflict between the two countries, you shall proceed, nevertheless, with all energy by repelling by force the insult to Mexico of invading its territory.

Mexico's official protest against the United States order was more menacing, more insistent, and more vehement than the United States' instructions for Treviño; but both were in large measure useless. Mariscal was instructed to make Mexico's protest known to the United States. He presented it verbally, first to Evarts and afterwards to Undersecretary Seward. On protesting Mariscal's in "the most serious but respectful manner," Evarts limited himself to asking, "in an informal manner," why

Mexico did not restrain the barbarous Indians. Mexico was trying to do it, he was told, although the task, as the experience of the United States superabundantly indicated, was not as easy as it seemed. Seward, in turn, gave an assurance: the order was not intended to provoke Mexico, but "simply" to appease public opinion in the United States and in particular that of Texas. Besides, his government felt that the government of Porfirio Díaz was incapable of making its presence felt in zones far from the capital; thus, the United States, taking advantage of the interruption of relations, felt itself at liberty to safeguard its frontier by itself. In any case, Seward assured Mariscal, the United States was not attempting to attack Mexico but to force it to give the necessary aid in putting an end to frontier frictions.

Foster, for his part, maintained that the Mexican government interpreted mistakenly the instructions given Ord, for they did not authorize him unconditionally to go beyond the dividing line, but only after giving the local Mexican authorities notice, inviting them to cooperate in the suppression of the invasions, and verifying the fact that that aid was denied him. The statement of the Mexican Secretary of War that such an order was in contradiction to existing treaties between the United States and Mexico, the rules of international law and common practice of civilized nations, hence was unjustifiable. Furthermore, he considered that those charges, made in an official document, were sufficiently serious "to excite apprehensions for the maintenance of cordial relations" between the two countries.

Foster, on learning that the Department of State was resolving to condition recognition on a guarantee of the settlement pending, announced his intention to talk immediately with Vallarta on the border frictions, the suppression of the Free Zone and the measures for containing the Indians, leaving to one side momentarily the question of the forced loans and the claims for damages and grievances caused during the revolts of La Noria and Tuxtepec. In spite of everything he felt so optimistic that he announced that in the next mail he would be able to send good news about the progress realized through his efforts. In his first interview he obtained the acquiescence of Vallarta to initiate a systematic examination of all of these issues and to take as a point of departure a memorandum that Foster offered to present; but the tone of the conversation and what was said in it foretold that Foster would not be able to transmit good news to his government in the next mail or in the following one.

Foster began his negotiation by reading almost the entire text of Seward's instructions; thus Vallarta learned that the United States, cuttingly and repeatedly, refused to believe that a prior recognition would open the road to settlement of the pending questions; inversely it wanted first to obtain the settlement and renew relations afterwards. Vallarta then felt the need of appraising the whole situation. The Mexican government met the requirements demanded by international custom and law for being recognized, and proof of this was that all the other countries had done so. It was evident that the United States had varied its traditional policy in this matter, and that that change should be attributed to the hostile disposition of President Hayes, to the influence exerted on him by the Lerdista exiles in New York, and to the consequent ease with which he accepted the suggestion of Brigadier General Ord, a well-known annexationist, pledged to bring about war between the two countries.

Vallarta, with a vehemence that impressed Foster, referred to the order of June 1, asserting that no member of the Mexican government had believed in its authenticity on reading it in the newspapers, for it was impossible to understand why the United States government would have such an aggressive and hostile attitude. Mexico did not want war, as was indicated clearly by the tone and language of the instructions sent to Treviño; but if Ord made use of the powers given by his government, "the consequences could be of the most serious nature." That order indicated that the United States wanted to treat Mexico like a country of barbarians or savages; an open declaration of war would have been a hundred times more preferable. If the United States had presented an ultimatum and Mexico had refused to give due satisfaction, the order might make some sense. Vallarta concluded his long speech by assuring Foster that "no Mexican government would survive popular indignation" if it took an attitude different from that of Porfirio Díaz.

Foster withstood Vallarta's tirade calmly. He affirmed that each country decided by itself if it would bestow or deny recognition; in the case of the United States, nevertheless, the existence of a very extensive mutual land frontier made its situation very different from that of the governments that had already recognized Díaz. It had not done so yet because Mexico had neglected the fulfillment of its international obligations. He asserted that no change whatever existed in the policy of recognition of his country, judged the declaration about President Hayes' hostile attitude rash and urged Vallarta to tell him where he had obtained the idea that Ord was an annexationist.

It is not known whether Vallarta's last declaration impressed Foster immediately; but it is known that the latter reported two days afterward that the order received by Ord had provoked a passionate reaction in Mexico and that it had aggravated the instructions given Treviño. A little later Foster qualified as "universal" that reaction, because everybody judged it uncalled for and inspired by Hayes' necessity of making his power secure by turning to the expedient of a war with Mexico and by the combined action of Lerdistas and speculators who saw in the war a source of easy wealth. And on the following day, Foster, remembering that the United States battleship *Plymouth* had abandoned Veracruz without being replaced, counseled the sending of another, "in view of the present condition of our relations with Mexico and of the feeling of intense excitement and hostility manifested in the country." "It is not necessary that a large vessel be sent," he concluded, "but the display of the flag at Veracruz and other ports will have a salutory effect."

VII
ON THE MEXICAN SIDE

The Mexican government, as was logical and inevitable, conducted its negotiation with great reserve, so that the public was hardly aware of important developments, such as the resignation of José María Mata as magistrate of the Supreme Court and his nomination for a mission to the United States, or of those news accounts in the United States press that the Mexican press reproduced. Reports from both sources were, nevertheless, so sporadic and confused that there were angry protests attenuated only by the circumstance that, after all, each nation was thus free to interpret the situation more to its liking.

Few were those who kept cool enough heads to allow themselves to joke about a matter that seemed so serious to all. Someone, however, invented a letter from Rutherford B. Hayes approaching Porfirio Díaz, and another of the latter's repulse of the former. In the first, Hayes addressed Díaz by using the hallowed formula of "great and dear friend," and told him that they should embrace one another and swear eternal friendship, since Díaz had won power by force of arms and Hayes by fraud and perjury. In the second, the one from Mexico addressed itself to "his excellency R. B. H." as the "fraudulent President of the United States" to protest against the indiscriminate mixture, since the presidential title of Hayes was "entirely another"; that of Díaz was legitimatized by the fact of his having obtained it by risking his skin, fortune and good name; therefore he rejected

[81]

the "undue familiarity" with which Hayes pretended to treat him.

Few also were those who tried to study objectively the problem of recognition and the incidents that it gave rise to, since they had at their disposal very little information for doing so. One newspaper supposed, for example, that there were three conditions imposed by the United States for recognition of "the situation of Tuxtepec": the settlement of the frontier problems; the abstention by federal and local authorities from imposing forced loan on United States citizens; and the punishment, "according to the laws of Mexico," of those who offended these. Nothing objectionable was found in the first and last of such conditions; but to agree to the second would create "a serious precedent," the reason why it should be qualified as "inadmissible."

In the opinion of others, recognition had not been given because the United States, "a rather turbulent companion and almost never disposed to concede reason to the weak," could and would understand only legal appearances. Sebastián Lerdo de Tejado was still constitutional President of Mexico when he was driven from power by the military victory of Porfirio Díaz; the first was the victim and the second was the offender. This was in direct contrast with the vision that the Mexicans themselves had of the situation, since for them Lerdo's government, in spite of its legitimacy, was a bad government and they expected of Díaz a good one despite its spurious origin. Furthermore, the conduct of the United States was incongruent, since on this occasion it gave the "vice of origin" as reason for denying recognition when others granted it to governments corrupt both in their origins and in their purposes. This same argument, however, served the most exacting partisans of Díaz for commenting, remorsefully, that if an imperfect constitutionality was the cause of international danger to which the country was exposed, all the more reason for making it disappear immediately.

Some thought of Vallarta as the source of the evil, since recognition of other countries, achieved automatically, without any effort of his, filled his head with pipedreams:

> . . . now he is drowning himself in his private parlour to whose space he is extending his foreign relations. He absorbed with eager lungs the consoling gusts of winds that blew from the Escalerillas; he believed in those feigned horizons formed by a positivist imagination; he anticipated the hour of his morning ablutions; he required the charger and, making himself fast in the stirrups, he directed his vision to his image reproduced by the sun: and it seemed gallant to him, and of handsome mien, and it is well-known that he exclaimed: "A minister of the proportions that his shadow paints cannot do less than realize the prodigies that one of his most disinterested admirers attributes to him."*

In truth, the "congenial and able" Vallarta had only collected the trophies of disdain, humiliation and invasions of Mexican territory.

One who had lost the right track thought that the mission entrusted to Mata was that of "soliciting" the United States to prevent the invasions of the Lerdista freebooters into Mexico; and taking off from this so mistaken premise, the conclusion could not be any less:

> . . . and why instead of soliciting and begging is not a respectable army force stationed on the frontier? Or is it that the numerous Tuxtepecan army serves only for sham battles?

Another, befuddled with the somber side of an international war, counseled respecting the imperious need of economizing by doing away completely with the army, although "inventing" a way of bringing it back again when it was necessary.

More than once the sensation of danger was the general trend of the Mexican press. It was said on one occasion that, meeting precipitately, the cabinet had entrusted to President Díaz in person the "campaign" on the frontier. In another, that a Joe

*The reference is to the daily *La Epoca,* published in Escalerillas Street, and to Carlos Olaguíbel y Arista, its director.

Shelby, a United States Civil War general, had 300 men ready to initiate a barefaced conquest of Mexican territory. Shelby had already been assigned the government of Sonora, about 16,800 acres of the best lands of the state and some 720 for each one of his men.

The more irresponsible Díaz supporters seemed unaware of the facts; they were accustomed to maintain that, in spite of the threats and Lerdista lies, the Díaz government was consolidating itself more and more, as was demonstrated by the fact that President Hayes and his foreign minister would officially "receive" Mata. His most vicious enemies, on the other hand, cast aside as cause of denying recognition technical discrepancies or antagonistic interests; the true motive was the holy horror of the United States of the ecclesiastical-military regime of Díaz, since long tradition demonstrated, in fact, that the militaristic and conservative parties always were enemies of the United States democracy.

THE FIRST TO PROTEST against the instructions given Brigadier General Ord were José María Iglesias and Sebastián Lerdo de Tejada, since both read it in the New York dailies of June 1, 1877. On the following day, Iglesias noted in his protest that it was customary in the United States to exaggerate the frequency and the magnitude of the damages of the frontier depredations, and that both countries suffered from them. Mexicans should trust, in any case, that the people of the United States would repudiate "the tricks of the Hayes cabinet, of his party or of his speculators of the law"; but if it was not so, Iglesias and all of his followers would be on the side of any Mexican government, "*de facto* or legal," in the defense of national independence.

Lerdo, knowing better the problems of the frontier than Lafragua himself, his Secretary of Foreign Relations, made in his protest a brief reference to the two inquiry commissions named by him at the end of 1872, the first to study conditions in Tamaulipas, Nuevo León and Coahuila, and the second in Chihuahua and Sonora. Both commissions recognized the damages caused to the United States, but they also demonstrated that Mexico had suffered them also, and to a greater degree. This circumstance, together with its own impotence to exterminate those raiding bands organized in its own territory, took from the United States all foundation for its complaint. The Secretary of State therefore had suggested confidentially to the Minister from Mexico in Washington the conclusion of a treaty agreeing to the reciprocal passage of the military forces of one country into the territory of the other in order to carry out a more effec-tive pursuit of the criminals. But Lerdo had rejected the proposal on the basis that "the government of Mexico was not authorized" to enter into such a treaty, besides the fact that it would easily give place to complaints and difficulties of another order.

Lerdo was invoking an argument that Vallarta never used for obvious reasons, that is, the United States House of Representatives had disapproved in 1876 a bill in which the President was authorized to permit United States military forces to enter Mexican territory; and the reason for disapproval was that such authorization would be contrary to international law, since both countries were maintaining normal diplomatic relations.

Lerdo concluded by stating that neither he nor his followers, although desiring and searching for the re-establishment of his own government, would fail to comply with their duty in the face of any danger to the autonomy or the rights of the country. That re-establishment would have to be the exclusive act of the Mexicans, and he and his supporters considered sacred "the honor, integrity, and independence of the homeland."

Lerdo's protest, dated, like that of Iglesias, in New York on June 2, was not known in Mexico until a month and a half later;* therefore, before and even afterwards, the current version

---

*José María Iglesias asserted that the protest of Lerdo was written and published on a much later date (*La questión presidencial en 1876* [Mexico: Tipografía literaria de Filomena Mata, 1892], pp. 331-336) ; likewise that its terms were not very energetic and his conclusion vague. All seems to be a reply, through tardiness not fair, to the charge (also notoriously unjust) that

was that part at least of the reticence to recognizing Díaz was due to Lerdo. Favored by his prestige, by United States interests created during his government and by his government being considered as the legitimate one, he was influencing that of Hayes to deny Díaz the accolade of recognition. To this should be added the unquestionable fact that various of his partisans, like Paulino Machorro in Coahuila, Lázaro Garza Ayala, Pedro Martínez and Narciso Dávila on the frontier of Nuevo León, and Pedro W. Valdés, alias "Winkar," on that of Tamaulipas, were organizing revolutionary expeditions on Texas soil; and others, like General Mariano Escobedo, an old Lerdo supporter and his Secretary of War when he fell from power, were organizing them with the knowledge and with the financial backing of their leader.

Not only was it believed that Lerdo continued political activity from his exile in New York but that his agents were organizing a complete freebooting army in the United States— they to overthrow Porfirio Díaz and the United States to take possession of the country, either with the ultimate purpose of taking away its territory or with that of establishing a protectorate. And as in the case of Díaz in 1876, when he was accused of turning to foreign soldiers to put himself in power, Lerdo supporters labored now in vain to impugn an accusation whose political effect was fatal. At times they tried to do it by resorting to vague, poetic declarations:

If constitutional restoration should be effected supported by free-booting bayonets; if President Lerdo should stain the prestige of his banner and his name by putting them in the hands of foreign legions; if General Escobedo should lay down the laurels he has harvested by defending independence; if now there were no virility and energy in the supporters of the Constitution so that they must entrust to foreigners the struggles in which principles fought usurpation; then we

the Lerdista press made against Iglesias that he attempted to buy his return to the country with his protest. In any case, it is a fact that Lerdo's protest was published in the New York *Herald* on June 2 and that of Iglesias in the *World* on the same date.

should be the first to desert our lines to join with those who carried the Mexican flag.

They also resorted to more concrete statements. Lerdo, interviewed by a reporter of the New York *Herald*, declared that he would never participate in a matter of that kind; and his friends and allies, General Mariano Escobedo and Manuel Romero Rubio, manifested the same public attitude.

The Porfiristas, of course, gloried in rejecting the lyric cries and even the explicit declarations of their enemies. The government itself, as has been seen, blamed Lerdo for the difficulties it had encountered in obtaining recognition. The official accusations could not be clearer nor more apparently probable, since by Lerdo's side—it was said—was working Edward Lee Plumb, former first secretary of the United States Legation in Mexico, and now representative of United States companies interested in obtaining railroad concessions in Mexico. Both, with tempting offers of public lands made to men close to President Hayes, had won the will of the latter to deny recognition to Díaz and to put him, with the instruction to Brigadier General Ord, in the most annoying dilemma: either he would submit to them and the Mexican people would indignantly repudiate him or he would defy them, and, besides exposing himself to the danger of a war whose inevitable end would be his downfall, he would create the feeling of being an imprudent man, incapable of overcoming the dangers which he himself had brought on the country. The *Diario Oficial*, in which this story appeared, gave nothing more as proof of Lerdo's culpability than his not having publicly protested against the instructions to Ord, insinuating that that silence was natural since by it he expected his cause to triumph.

The *Diario,* seeing not so much the protest of Lerdo supporters as that of Foster, justified itself by saying that those were not its appraisements but the United States press's, which were reproduced in it simply under the label of journalistic information. The curious thing is that *El Federalista*, attributing to itself and not to Foster the unexpected self-correction of the *Diario,* congratulated itself on such a great victory and allowed itself to comment that the declaration of the director of the official daily (in the sense of the comments first published being his own) was a sacrifice that the government had imposed on him in order to free itself from its own responsibility.

The *Diario* yielded, but not the Porfirista press: the organ of the pure Tuxtepecans, for example, published information as peremptory as this:

> The disposition [Ord's instructions] of the American government is more serious than seemed at first. Lerdo is conspiring with his men in the United States. Escobedo has decoyed people into military service and is working eagerly to organize an expedition.

The conclusion was unavoidable: "Here is manifest the crime of treason attempted by Lerdo and his followers." The entire Lerdista group was working at full steam: the leaders in Mexico City and agents in each one of the states of the Republic, "all are doing everything they can to destroy the dignity and the autonomy of Mexico." In vain the Lerdista supporters tried to protect themselves from that flood of maledictions or from inconstancy by declaring that, in case of conflict, "we would not be Porfiristas, we would be Mexicans . . . [and] in the presence of dangers to the country, we would not recognize any other insignia than its"; it seemed useless for them to recall that Lerdo had been the leader of the resistance to foreign oppression since the repeal of the Wyke-Zamacona treaty. And, nevertheless, even within the Porfirista camp voices were not lacking that exonerated Lerdo from what they considered a base slander.

THE TRUTH IS that the instructions given to Ord provoked much less public protest than was to be expected in the face of its unquestionable seriousness, and certainly less than that which Foster made his government believe, a sign that it impressed him more than usual. The cause of such an apparently strange phenomenon can be found in the fact that the Porfiristas, desperate in the face of the danger that the order represented for them and for Mexico, tried to explain their misfortune by vilifying Lerdo. The situation thus became confused, and risky the opinion of he who was ignorant of the battle of factions. And it is quite possible that the Porfiristas did not fail to feel the embarrassing position of the government, for if it was convenient to it that the danger of a foreign intervention might attract public opinion to its support, it was very possible that the latter might be raised to such a pitch that it would become another obstacle to an understanding with the United States.

There were, of course, those who on learning of the order would speak of the national horizon being clouded, of a black storm brewing "on the other side of the Bravo" that would implacably fall upon the country. The order was humiliating for Mexico, impolitic for the United States, and the consequence of a President elected through fraud and intrigue. In it was seen also the first step toward an invasion decided beforehand; the threat could not be more imminent or more colossal, and proved what all Mexicans should then have known: Mexico was a truly unfortunate country, for after the civil wars and the deep social decadence that resulted from them followed the threat of a country powerful like few on earth.

The orders sent to Jerónimo Treviño were worthy and energetic replies. But, even so, on the Díaz government rested the "terrible" responsibility of gracefully eluding such pitfalls. In order to do so, Díaz should before anything else unite all Mexicans, an easy goal if the law was absolutely respected. The United States order, according to Díaz' supporters, was "just a pretext" for placing their leader in the dilemma of backing down before the invasion and returning the power to Lerdo, or of resisting it only to be overcome in an unequal contest. The United States, furthermore, was artfully taking advantage of a country sapped by civil wars and partisan disunity.

Although badly informed, the reaction was stronger—and on occasion much livelier—in regard to other events. Mata's mission engendered for a moment an optimistic feeling in the newspapers supporting Díaz, in spite of the fact that it was founded on news from the United States press, little inclined as it was to opening a road to agreement between the two countries. While the New York *World* said that the United States government should be cautious in its decision of receiving a new Mexican minister, *La Patria* of Ireneo Paz believed in the probability that the Díaz government would be quickly recognized, for the newspapers of the United States were so announcing. Lerdo's followers, on the other hand, from exactly the same *World* news accounts, concluded that that mission had had "no success," and was cause for the "discomforting" conviction that nothing had been changed. The fact that Evarts accepted from Mata "some papers" had filled the Porfiristas with glee, though the only meaning of the gesture was the curiosity of the Department of State to know and study the calligraphic abilities of the new Mexican chancellery. The only certainty was that Mexican national officials in Washington had presented a sad spectacle:

> The Palo Blanco enterprise contracted the actors with the greatest reputation: Mata, Treviño, General Rafael Benavides, Charles, Canales and even Don Bibiano,* of Monterrey, appeared in the cast. It served for nothing to realize the designs of the Tapatian Minister of Foreign Relations, because the American public, little impressed by phantasmagoric revelations, has turned its back on us, not without making us feel the most bitter humiliations.

The country needed to know in good time that the dignity of the nation, its interests, its laws, the violation of its territory—all were being given in exchange for the fleeting recognition of an usurping government. And this because Vallarta was accused of having declared before Foster that "Mexico accepts all the infamous conditions that are being proposed" in order to obtain it. Mata was accused of having carried "his flexibility to an unexampled extremity." He had consented to United States troops crossing the international boundary and to the exempting of United States citizens from all extraordinary taxes. This as a

*Bibiano Villarreal, Treviño's private secretary.

[90]

consequence would cause Mexican agricultural, industrial or mining enterprises to become foreign, which, in turn, was going to create a "pleasing prospect" for the nation:

Handcuffed, sold to the foreigner by the passage of troops, national capital and production ruined by the freedom of American citizens from extraordinary taxes.

Mata not only had failed, but

. . . while he was getting a backache in the waiting rooms of Mr. Evarts, the tread of American horsemen were raising the dust on the Mexican soil . . . a new violation was repeated to honor Señor Díaz' envoy.

Not even was the Díaz partisan press wholly with Mata. It declared, it was true, that perhaps the real cause of the denied recognition was the fault of the times or the will to give it while the United States government "does not have the necessary information," or because "it does not work very fast"; but also that it may have been contemplating the possibility of an international war, even though, in this sphere of action, some help from errant phenomena could not fail to be expected: if the United States government wanted to provoke war, the American people would not consent to it, "and it is already known that the people are the ones that decide everything" there; Mexico being weak and the United States strong, it should not be deduced that "it would heedlessly throw itself upon it."

THE VIOLATIONS of Mexican soil, on the other hand, elicited general comments of indignation, sometimes adverse to the United States and other times to Lerdo and his followers, by attributing to Lerdo their provocation, or to the Díaz government for its incapacity to prevent them. What had actually happened was that on June 16 there had arrived in Mexico City United States newspapers of the first of that month with the text of the order sent to Brigadier General Ord. On the following day the cabinet examined the situation created by it, and on the day after that,

[91]

"dictated the resolutions required by the country's honor," giving to Jerónimo Treviño the orders then published. The telegrams received from the chief of the Mexican forces at the boundary line after June 18 said nothing of invasions.

The New York *Herald* presented its readers on July 17 with a map of Mexico with the modifications that it should suffer to the benefit of the United States, by adding to its "already immense territory" Lower California, Sonora, Sinaloa, Durango, Chihuahua, Coahuila and part of Nuevo León. It was said in Mexico that the immediate precursor of that idea was the border frictions whose instantaneous disappearance would occur, it was believed, by moving the dividing line as proposed by the New York daily. Nonetheless, aside from the fact that Hayes had on his hands "thorny enough tasks," the United States—it was said— would find a Mexico which in this peril would not fail to have the support of other nations; and a united Mexico, as revealed by the protests of Lerdo and Iglesias, irreconcilable rivals of Porfirio Díaz:

> The Mexican nation will not be today what the Americans trampled underfoot in 1846. Taught by experience, it will not permit the foreigners to proceed illegally against the integrity of its territory nor allow it to limit its autonomy as a free nation.

"Few times" had occurred when United States troops had boldly crossed the dividing line. That was worse than an international conflict and immediately gave room for charging the "Washington cabinet" with the crimes provoked by those invasions. Besides, the inhabitants on both sides of the Rio Grande hated each other; therefore they were arming and waiting, with the consequent danger that any local incident might be converted into a general conflagration. War—who could doubt it?—would hurt both countries, although Mexico more; there was good cause, therefore, for being cautious "up to the last minute" and thus at least avoiding the blame that giving rise to it would fall on her. Even the newspapers supporting the government demanded explanations for the invasions and details about the excuses that had been given and what had been achieved, "for in spite of all our impotence, there was no authority for treading underfoot our rights."

And one newspaper was pained that the Mexicans were not united during the supreme moment of danger:

> At the moment when every Mexican shouts angrily at the insult the soldiers of the North have done to our national dignity; now when we would wish that all the inhabitants of the Republic should be like one single heart filled with patriotism to return aggression by aggression, force by force, to the Texas dragoons,

was occurring the dissension of the Roman Catholics, engaged in blaming Díaz for involving the country in such an entanglement. The government, as if without seeming to want to, explained that the problem of the frontier was complex enough. Some of its facets, by "pertaining to the realm of international law and to that of diplomacy, required absolute silence"; and others were the incursions of freebooters and "above all" of wild Indians, serious because of the damages caused to the inhabitants of that zone. Besides its own resources, the Federation was aiding each state with the forces under the orders of Treviño and Canales, that is, 4792 men of the three branches, to which number soon would be added another 2000.

The country, evidently, was not being consoled by knowing that Treviño had at his disposal such a number of military elements, or that the government was receiving from its frontier commanders reports as usual. It was "perfectly well known" that foreign forces pursuing a band of wild Indians had penetrated Mexican territory. Then, either the government

> . . . has been maintaining a criminal silence opportunely aware of it without the false patriotism of the men who compose it being wounded by the humiliation of seeing the national soil invaded, or it has been ignorant of it all, notwithstanding the [fact that it has at its disposition the telegraph as far as the border, thus bringing upon itself the scandal] that the newspapers should receive first the grave news that affects the country rather than the men who have usurped public power.

If it were the first, no words were sufficiently strong to describe to the defiled nation the official silence; and if it were the second, one should conclude that there existed scarcely a caricature of a government—incoherent, disobeyed by everyone and causing one to "blush with shame." The "international problem," unfortunately, was taking a not at all reassuring direction, among other things because Díaz, hungry to be recognized, was pretending to play two sets of cards. With one he was disposed to make all kinds of concessions to achieve his selfish aims. By playing the other he hoped to win the approval of the country, boasting of energy and even of a furious desire to come to blows with the United States. Nothing so discomforting as the moral that should be drawn from the invasions:

This is an epoch of social degradation. The great virtues have disappeared only to be replaced by the ruinous and avaricious ambition of the selfish man. The humiliating, the dishonourable is completely tolerated, consented to in exchange for the peaceful possession of miserable employment, of the government of a State, of a credential, of an office of cabinet minister, of the presidency of the Republic. The nation is today prey of the loathsome giddiness of aspirants without faith, without conscience and without dignity.

"What a difference from other epochs!" it added. Some United States soldiers invaded Camargo during the Lerdo government; all the inhabitants, without any arousing, obeying only their patriotic ardor, armed themselves to throw out the invader. And with the intention of not losing such a heroic gesture, the federal troops of all the region moved swiftly, until the invader fearfully retired and gave ample excuses. There was not, then, any doubt; but now:

We feel at our back the whip of the invader, and we answer with a smile. . . . The race of Juárez and of Zaragoza has disappeared; we live among vice and degradation. Infamy and ignominy cover us!

The United States was a country that had already used up "the catalogue of indiscretions and infamies in relation to our country," and, apparently, Vallarta believed that he could dispose of the honor of Mexico "as with his own purse."

Time passed without the public being able to see tangible signs that relations between the two countries were improving. The instructions given to Ord, hanging like a sword of Damocles; the rejection of Mata and the apparently contradictory attitude of the United States government of sustaining in Washington the fiction that Lerdo continued being the legitimate President while it maintained in Mexico a minister plenipotentiary and a legation despite the reality that Díaz was the only governing officer of the country; the rumors that Treviño had yielded in his dealings with Ord more than was necessary or decorous; the forced silence of the government and the lack of consideration of the United States press; all this was firing Mexican resentment and turning it more clearly against the government and the people of the United States rather than against the Díaz government.

The news from Washington was of a marked pessimism even in November, five months after the order of June 1. Congress had been called into special session; the message of President Hayes said nothing about Mexico, but it was feared that Texas congressmen would take advantage of the first opportunity to explode the bomb. The conclusion was that

. . . a plan preconceived earlier by the White House cabinet was being unrolled little by little, and that plan involved the ruin of Mexico, by threatening us with an international conflict for which the Mexican government should be prepared and prepare the nation.

It seemed necessary to sound the alarm, for

. . . now it was not to be doubted: the conflict with the North is inevitable. . . . The Yankees want a piece of Mexico.

Brigadier General Ord sent to his superiors his annual report on October 1, all of it dedicated to the frontier situation; and its publication in the Mexican dailies loosed the reins of a resentment that now seemed unlimited:

In the opinion of the people of the United States, the same as of that disloyal and perfidious government, we Mexicans are a stubborn horde of savages that, lacking civilization, have the instinct of evil and carry it wherever we go.

The dislike between the two peoples and their differences in customs; the annexationist instincts of the Americans; their strength and Mexican weakness—all these things made the Mexican unconsciously transform himself into the passive victim of the excesses of his neighbors, "without ever, neither now or before, having the right even to complain." For this reason,

> ... it is now time that Mexico show itself worthy of proclaiming itself free, without limiting itself to the passive attitude in which it is maintained.

The "cunning and malevolence" of the Texans were spoken of as proverbial, and, in consequence, reproach of Treviño for his condescensions to Ord surged forth.

In the first days of November there was a new invasion by United States forces under the command of Lieutenant John L. Bullis, who seems to have specialized in them. A detailed account of how it had occurred, and an explanation of why the Mexican soldiers put up no resistance whatever, was then demanded of the government:

> Duty requires that they present their breasts nobly and loyally to enemy bullets, and not to do so, has shown them unworthy sons of a free people.

And when there arrived in Mexico news of some adverse act or statement by United States authorities, spirits became even more inflamed. When Senator Richard Coke of Texas, for example, declared in a congressional debate that the Mexicans respected only brute force, the time came when the official newspaper of Nuevo León felt itself obliged to join the chorus of the national press:

> The violation of international law is obvious in this case, and that makes it necessary to demand satisfaction and ask for reparation of

that insult from the nation that forgetting its duties, belittling the eternal principles of right, has had the audacity to break the pacts which placed on it the obligation to fulfill. . . . It should be so done in order to make our neighbors understand that we do not fear to cover our dear soil with the blood of the invader, however powerful he is supposed to be, when he dares to insult us and obliges us to wash with that blood the stains that they are trying to stamp on the honor of the country.

A language of rancorous insult each time more painful and arro-- gant was issuing forth—the Texan "rabble" is the true author of the depredations of the frontier; "universal" justice clamors against President Hayes; Díaz and Vallarta are disposed to cede as much as may be compatible with the national interests, but if his (Hayes's) demands go farther, Hayes may be sure that Mexico "will pay dearly for the insults done against it"; the Governor Richard Hubbard of Texas and Brigadier General Ord are "the men most disposed to promote a conflict with Mexico."

VIII
THE EXIT FROM
THE ALLEY

United States Secretary of State William M. Evarts and President Rutherford B. Hayes were impatient and worked in haste. They seemed to think, moreover, that since for Mexico a rude policy was the only fitting one, its efficacy would always more than compensate for the risk that it might involve. The order given Brigadier General Edward O. C. Ord had the purpose without doubt of forcing Mexico to give a collaboration that was considered truly indispensable for terminating the banditry on the frontier; but the order was achieving another goal as well—to oblige Mexico to give in on cases of little or no relation with the banditry on the frontier, such as the suppression of the Free Zone, the exemption of United States citizens from extraordinary taxes, the payment of damages caused by the revolts of La Noria and Tuxtepec and the authorization to acquire real estate on the border.

Besides having the very weak foundation of Lieutenant Colonel W. R. Shafter's report, the order was precipitate; for it was given in an unfavorable moment for the United States, a fact that weakened its strength of negotiation from the beginning. And as with so many decisive turning points of his political career, Porfirio Díaz solved this problem with singularly fortunate results.

John W. Foster suggested to Ignacio L. Vallarta as early as December of 1876 the necessity of the Mexican government's taking the first step toward the extermination of banditry on the border by dispatching to the North a competent federal force and placing it under the command of an experienced leader of high rank, who would be able to cooperate with his American counterpart on the opposite side of the Rio Grande. Foster attributed the greatest importance to that appointment, and for Mexico not to make it immediately visibly irritated him. It was suggested first to Vallarta and afterwards to President Díaz, and when time passed without its being adopted, official relations began to cool. In one of his conversations with Vallarta, Foster cited this delay as proof of the indifference of the Mexican government. Vallarta felt the pressure of the United States minister so strongly on this point that, besides admitting it as a good suggestion, he believed himself obliged to explain that only the most urgent necessities had impeded its adoption. It was thus natural that when Foster, at the end of six months, learned of the appointment of Jerónimo Treviño, he hastened to communicate to his government that Mexico "had awakened" at last to the gravity of the situation on the frontier.

Foster's dispatch was dated May 28, 1877, three days before Brigadier General Ord was granted discretionary power to cross the international boundary to pursue, capture and punish marauders and recover stolen property. The order, once given, could not of course be withdrawn openly and immediately. To do so would have been equal to the United States government's admitting its own haste, and it would have caused it to renounce obtaining the other ends that it was pursuing. The designation of Treviño, being, as it was, an unquestionable demonstration of the good intentions of the Mexican government, did not in itself assure the solution of the frictions. In spite of this uncertainty, the appointment brought forth an immediate and pronounced response from both sides, even though it was made known to the Mexican government late, and even though United States approval did not originate from the Department of State, but from the War Department.

In fact, General Sherman, Commander in Chief of the United

States Army, on June 9 communicated to General Sheridan, chief of the Military District of Missouri, to which belonged the department of Texas, whose chief was Brigadier General Ord, that the President of Mexico "had awakened at last" and had seen the importance of curbing the frontier disorders, and that in order to initiate the task a large force under the command of a prudent leader, instructed to cooperate with Ord, would be sent to the border. In view of this fact, the latter was ordered to receive the offer of cooperation with "cordial reciprocity," begin personal or written relations with him, "and not to be hasty in pursuit across the border, except in a grave case." The rectification did not stop with this general order not to hasten to invade the Mexican territory, but extended to specific resolutions not to invade it in concrete circumstances that well could have been classified as very grave. On June 12 a group of troops loyal to Porfirio Díaz had an encounter, on Mexican territory very near the Rio Grande, with a Lerdista band that penetrated the country from the United States. The Porfiristas won a victory and, to complete it, they pursued the opponents to Texas territory, where yet another skirmish occurred before the Mexican troops returned to Mexico. As soon as Lieutenant Colonel Shafter was informed of the event, he telegraphed Ord saying that he had his troops entirely ready to look for the invaders in Mexico and if he succeeded in catching up with them, he would attack them there. That dispatch was read to President Hayes, who approved the orders of Sherman and Ord that Shafter should not cross the border.

The Mexican public and government, ignorant for some time of those changes in Ord's powers, attributed a decisive importance to the first contacts of the latter with Treviño. A Porfirista newspaper reported that Ord had solicited an interview with Treviño, that this had occurred in Piedras Negras on June 17 and that the conversations were loyal, frank and friendly; an armed conflict was not, then, "imminent"; on the contrary,

. . . by pacific and accepted methods, our government was able to obtain just satisfaction in every way that the unfortunate order of Hayes may have been able to wound the national honor.

The first news from the lesser officers on the frontier revealed equal optimism, and the official organ of the State of Nuevo León scattered through the Republic the description of the setting in which the conversations occurred. Ord made the first visit, and when Treviño reached the United States camp in order to return it, he was saluted by a salvo of cannon, besides having troops in parade dress ready for review. These honors— happily commented a Porfirista daily—were not vain ostentation; they revealed the good will of the government of the United States that peace with Mexico should not be interrupted,

. . . for it is impossible that the neighbor Republic, that marches in the vanguard of civilization, and respects foreign liberty and rights, can ever think of accepting and putting into practice the right of conquest, which is the most enormous absurdity and much more so when sanctioned by a free and independent people.

Ord, it was reported, told Treviño that his government had sent him to put an end to vandalism on the frontier and that he hoped to count on the aid of the Mexican army to do it, particularly by punishing malefactors who operated in its own territory. Mexico learned through a telegram made public that Ord, on informing his superiors of the interview with Treviño, asserted having achieved a good understanding, but "on the basis of my instructions," and that his Mexican colleague seemed now to be convinced "that nothing but good results would be obtained" from the passing of his troops further than the international boundary.

For his part, the commander of Fort Brown, respecting Ord's instructions, sought out General Servando Canales, military commander of Tamaulipas, in Matamoros. After communicating to him "the tenor and substance" of his instructions, he told Canales that the Mexican troops, in complete reciprocity, would be able to pass into United States territory if they wanted to pursue marauders. The United States commander commented:

It is evident to me that although studiously polite, and profuse in his expression of a desire to maintain friendly relations, the tenor of my instructions was not palatable to him.

Canales told him that he ought to ask for instructions about the crossing of the frontier, and asked what would be the decision of the United States commander prior to receiving them, if an occasion for crossing it should arise, to which he was told that it would be done "without hesitation." Canales replied that, in that case, he "simply would ignore the crossing." To Canales' inquiry, the Secretary of War replied that Canales should submit to the arrangements made between Ord and Treviño, which he would communicate to him immediately.

The results of the first interview between Ord and Treviño were not quite brilliant; a possible cause for failure was the claim of the latter that his next campaign against the malefactors of the frontier was matched, through "reciprocity," with one by the United States military forces in order to prevent the Lerdistas from organizing their revolutionary expeditions in Texas. The official newspaper of Nuevo León asserted that Treviño had offered to cooperate in pursuing the Indians and rustlers,

. . . demanding reciprocity, and his words were attentively heard, that General Ord immediately ordered the apprehension of Winkar.

Ord informed his superiors, on July 6, that on July 3 he received a letter from Treviño expressing Treviño's desire to converse with him personally but the impossibility of doing so because of illness, and that meanwhile he would send his representative with instructions. Treviño wanted to inform Ord that, in compliance with his desires, he had already forbidden his subordinates to penetrate into United States territory, besides having moved his troops to give more security to frontier cities and to apprehend the Indian tribes camped in the woody areas. And he added:

I trust that you have given orders not to permit armed groups to organize in Texas in order to invade Mexico under any pretext.

Ord answered him immediately, in a courteous letter, but told him that after his visit a large group of Lipan Indians had invaded Texas in order to steal a hundred horses and had seriously wounded a peaceful citizen. His troops followed the trail that seemed to indicate that they were fleeing toward the inaccessible and uninhabited mountains of Coahuila and Chihuahua, where the Mexican troops were not penetrating; and as Treviño had said that his soldiers would protect the frontier "cities," Ord believed that, given his instructions and even if he were personally inclined to suspend them, he could not avoid the pursuit proceeding into Mexican territory while there was a possibility that they might be caught. On the other hand, Ord assured Treviño that "strict orders" had already been given to prevent the organization in Texas of armed bands that might invade Mexican soil on a revolutionary pretext. Ord sent him a copy of his instructions, informing him that he would execute them; and Treviño, in the face of that situation, asked that "only regular forces be allowed to cross under the orders of discreet officials."

In any event, when Bibiano Villarreal interviewed Ord in the name of Jerónimo Treviño, he left Ord a copy of his own orders to repel force with force and asked him to suspend his incursions into Mexican territory until the two countries concluded a treaty. In spite of telling Villarreal that he would continue in all cases as he judged necessary, however, Ord took the precaution of asking Washington by telegraph if his instructions remained in force. This did not prevent Ord, on the whole a good military man, for whom surprise by the enemy is the worst nightmare, from announcing that he was bringing together enough troops to cross the frontier regardless of what Treviño was able to oppose him with. The United States War Department ordered him to find out what the Mexican forces were and if he thought them capable of lending effective cooperation. It confirmed its orders but clearly forbade him to cross the river if on the other side there were Mexican forces ready to continue the pursuit.

The War Department twice limited the first and generic order to Ord, first by circumscribing the crossing to grave cases, and afterwards to those where Mexican forces ready to continue the pursuit were lacking. Ord did not give very encouraging news. Treviño's forces were estimated between 400 and 3000. They would not be able to prevent the incursions unless they received the aid of the ranchers of the region, and, to crown the jest, his dragoons rode horses stolen from Texas by the wild Indians. But when the commander of Fort Duncan had his first interview, on July 20, with General Francisco Naranjo, Treviño's second in command, both examined at length the problem of how to prevent the incursions of wild Indians into Texas, since recently one had occurred, and Naranjo

. . . pledged himself to put a stop to the raids by Indians from Mexico as soon as Escobedo and Valdés and other Lerdista revolutionaries could be disposed of.

And they were stopped, in fact. Lieutenant R. A. Williams, of the Ringgold Barracks, found out that the steamboat *Ackley* would arrive on July 21 with arms and munitions on board to be disembarked at Camargo; also he was informed of the concentration of a hundred horses on a river ranch. He knew that General Mariano Escobedo, who had been pursued the previous week, was mixed up with all this. He supposed that the movement would occur as soon as the steamboat arrived, and considering it his duty "to take measures for maintaining the laws of neutrality," he took measures to legalize the apprehension of five colonels and of General Escobedo.

When the *Ackley* arrived, on it were discovered several boxes of Remington rifles with their accompanying complement of supplies, none of it declared in the manifests, nor was the consignee identified by name. The prisoners were sent to a criminal court. They remained free under bond but were obliged to present themselves periodically to the court until the case was decided. Brigadier General Ord communicated such good news to General Naranjo and the latter expressed his satisfaction for what had been achieved and for the promise of Lieutenant Colonel Shafter to dictate the necessary orders for pursuing "Winkar"

Valdés. Ord, in fact, telegraphed Naranjo asking him for information on the revolutionary activities of Escobedo and of "Winkar" in order to send troops to disarm and disperse them.

The Díaz newspapers did not delay in drawing logical conclusions from these events:

. . . the imprisonment of Escobedo under these circumstances is highly significant, for it clearly demonstrates that the American authorities do not support the pretensions of Lerdo and his followers. It means furthermore that the United States government, if it has not definitely recognized ours, considers it as an established government against which it is not lawful to conspire.

And the reaction of the Lerdista press was even more significant. On the one hand, it labeled with the worst epithets of despicable and vile the Porfiristas who applauded the imprisonment of Escobedo, bad in itself but made worse because brought about by a government that had not yet had enough of humiliating and threatening Mexico. Then it protested angrily against the idea that the government of Mexico, through reciprocity, should respond to the imprisonment of Escobedo by actively pursuing the bandits on the frontier, for how could the notion of reciprocity equate the hero of Querétaro with assassins and rustlers? But more significant still was the reaction of "Winkar's" men. Convinced that the United States authorities would prevent the purchase of arms and ammunition and the organization of rebel groups, they asked amnesty of Naranjo in exchange for the assurance of being allowed to live peacefully in Mexico. The imprisonment of Escobedo and his followers, like Pedro W. Valdés, alias "Winkar," improved the frontier situation, because Treviño, Naranjo, and Canales, without the immediate fear of a counter-revolution, disposed their troops more freely to guard it.

Notwithstanding, Ord's instructions were to suffer another trial in less than a month. On August 11, 1877, Captain William R. Price, commander of the Ringgold Barracks, wrote to the political chief of Camargo telling him that on the previous night a group of armed Mexicans, captained by Segundo Garza and

Rodolfo Espronceda, had crossed the Rio Grande from Mexico, had proceeded to the jail in Rio Grande City and, firing in all directions at all those who were nearby, had entered it and had freed two prisoners, wounding several people in the process: the county attorney, three jailers and a woman. He begged him "in the name of good harmony and the conservation of order" to procure the apprehension of the assailants and to turn them over at the earliest moment. He added that if he could not count on the aid of the Camargo authorities, he would find himself obliged to use his forces to enter Mexico and to apprehend the culprits. Price, not content with the written communication, went to Camargo accompanied by two soldiers, and there received the assurance that the investigation had been begun with the arrest of the owners of the boats used to cross the river.

The news spread in the United States like a powder blast and soon the Washington reaction was known: "The United States is tired of promises and now shall demand action." The act, besides, interrupted the diplomatic negotiation on recognition and would delay it indefinitely. Undersecretary Seward asserted it and Mata declared having much regretted "the aspect that things had taken with this *casus belli.*" In fact, it was believed that the eve of war had arrived. Governor Hubbard of Texas, neither slow nor lazy, addressed Servando Canales, "demanding" the extradition of the culprits, and Brigadier General Ord wrote to Treviño lamenting that an act of such magnitude should ruin the cordiality that both were creating on the frontier. He hoped that the authorities of Tamaulipas would reprimand the culprits and return the freed prisoners, for, if not,

. . . it would be very difficult to convince the President of the United States that those authorities did not sympathize with the bandits or that they were not impotent to restrain their incursions.

The Department of State, for its part, transmitted to Foster a copy of the telegram sent by the governor of Texas to President Hayes, commenting indignantly that "To the long catalogue of raids into Texas for the purpose of theft and plunder have now

been added two deliberate hostile invasions of American territory by armed bands from Mexico." He was instructed to communicate these acts to the Mexican government immediately and
to ask for the arrest and punishment of the culprits and the
consequent reparations. Foster, of course, did so; but Vallarta
this time was able to tell him that, besides the activities of the
local authorities of Camargo and the state of Tamaulipas,
Treviño already had orders and resources to help in the search
and apprehension. He added that, according to their information, the culprits were of Mexican origin, but of United States
citizenship, that the attack was planned in Texas and that the
attackers fled to Mexico after executing it.

The energetic and even haughty reaction of the United States
authorities and the weak defense that Mexico was able to make
in this case did not escape public comment, generally disfavor-
able to the Mexican government. The national dignity ought to
be considered "profoundly wounded" and all responsibility fell
on the Mexican authorities who, "blinded by their ambition, are
sacrificing the country in order to satisfy their party rancors and
their insatiable thirst for power." And when Vallarta, acting on
very controversial juridical powers, agreed to the extradition of
the culprits, imprisoned and indicted by the civil authorities of
Camargo, his conduct was approved only because it put an end
to the "harmless" but vexatious question. And as those extradited seemed to be Mexicans, a case in which Mexico, according
to the treaty of extradition, was not obliged to turn them over,
it was called an offense, and it was said that the lives of three
Mexicans meant nothing to Vallarta "if in exchange he obtained
the recognition of that nefarious government of which he formed
a part." It was proposed, therefore, that Porfirio Díaz and his
secretary, Ignacio L. Vallarta, be "dragged" before the Grand
Jury of the Congress to answer "for the despicable delivery of
the Mexicans."

Ord's report of October 1, made public in the United States
without any apparent reason, did not help to dissipate the misunderstanding. It lacked tact and was ruder than necessary, be-

sides reiterating that little or nothing could be expected from the Mexican authorities and that therefore the military forces of the United States should take the problem exclusively into their own hands. Ord recognized that the situation on the Tamaulipecan frontier had improved with the retirement of General Juan N. Cortina and with the energetic action of Governor Servando Canales, and that the good will of the Mexican federal government was not lacking; but he repeated the old accusation that the local authorities sympathized with the criminals to the degree of protecting them. Besides, the report was contradictory. On the one hand, it affirmed surprise (and satisfaction) that for "many years" he had received reports, such as the present one, that there was nothing to report, although he attributed this situation to "my instructions having been complied with"; and, on the other hand, he reasoned that as the local authorities were in connivance with the rustlers and the federal authorities could not dominate these, "it is for us to apply the remedy."

The Mexican government, needing to reinforce Treviño in order to succeed in a better vigilance of the frontier, and at the same time desirous of not increasing the irritation of public opinion or the fear or the simple suspicion that the movement of troops ordered for him were, in reality, preparation for an international war, moved them quietly; and when Treviño could not hide them, he explained them carefully. A short time afterwards Ord recognized these facts and in somewhat more significant circumstances. The United States Congress had named several committees and had charged them with investigating the true situation on the frontier and with deciding if the Mexican political policy of President Hayes was correct.

The Texas sounding box which accepted with credulity and loud applause all of Ord's acts and words was missing in the federal Congress. There Ord suffered long interrogations to ascertain if his opinion corresponded with the facts; in them, besides, were sought the contradictions between Ord's conduct and that of the Secretary of War; between the latter and the

Department of State; and between both and President Hayes himself. In such an atmosphere, Ord's declarations were much more measured. He recognized that the Mexican government was working in good faith and with efficacy, for it already had on Mexico's northern frontier 4000 men of the federal army, to which would be added very soon 2000 more; and he did not doubt that "the Mexican officers who are commanding those troops will comply with their duty." He added that that force would be enough to efficiently guard the Mexican side of the Rio Grande, and that not doubting, "as he did not," the sincerity of the Mexican authorities, there was now no need or reason for United States troops to cross the river, inflicting "an affront to the sovereignty of a sister Republic."

Mexican public opinion had reached such heights with the year of rising tension, that far from relaxing it quickly, in reality these declarations only provoked cautious reflection. It was thought, for example, that the desire of the United States Secretary of War to reinforce Ord contradicted them. Then, the great danger of having two great armies face to face, although engaged apparently in a common task, was pointed out: "That is to trust peace too much to an accident." In fact,

. . . the peace of the two neighboring republics should not be made to depend on the discretion of some young and giddy lieutenant ambitious of being a hero of the day in the newspapers of his country.

The tension had been so great that, far from registering protests, a great relief was felt when it was known that Lieutenant L. F. Ward, who arrived on the Rio Grande behind some horse thieves, was invited by the chief of the Mexican forces to accompany him on the Mexican side. "The Mexican troops are in great harmony with those of the North," commented a Roman Catholic newspaper.

IX
ANOTHER BLIND ALLEY

John W. Foster, optimistic and energetic in spite of everything, nonetheless committed the error of his life by negotiating
with Ignacio L. Vallarta in writing, submitting, one after another, proposals for agreements, pacts and treaties. Foster was
an intelligent man and a public official who took his work seriously. He traveled throughout the country, knew its people,
read its papers and even studied its legislation. Last but not
least, he had the support of its government. All those favorable
talents and circumstances made him the best—not to say the
only effective—minister of the United States during all of the
Díaz regime; but in presenting his cases from a purely legal
point of view not only was he dealing with a body of law quite
different from the United States juridical system and tradition,
but he was up against a most distinguished jurist, the best constitutional lawyer in a nation swarming with lawyers. Inevitably,
he turned out to be no match for Vallarta.

On June 23, 1877, Foster left with Vallarta one memorandum
on the border problems; another for the reclamation of damages
and injuries through the detention in Mazatlán of two United
States schooners; a third asking for compensation of $10,000 for
the apprehension of the United States consul in Acapulco; a
fourth on the forced loans, proposing their restitution to those
affected in money or gold value, plus interest from the date of
imposition until that of payment; a fifth on the Free Zone, de-

manding the assurance that the Mexican executive would present to the Congress in its next session of September 1 a bill for abolishing it; and a sixth on the wild Indians living in Mexico— Lipans, Kickapoos, Mezcaleros, Seminoles, Apaches "and others" —asking that the Mexican military authorities deliver them to the border so that the United States authorities could reinterne them in their respective reservations.

A new incident, nonetheless, tore up by the roots this multiple beginning of negotiations on so many different matters. On June 22 an editorial appeared in the *Diario Oficial* that imputed the delay in recognition to the hostility of President Hayes and his cabinet. Foster, of course, thought it necessary to ask that a "concise and exact" declaration of the position of the United States government on the subject be published "without delay." Vallarta assured him that he did not know of the article, and offered to read it and to accommodate him if his government did not find serious objections to the publication of the declaration; but Foster announced that, in view of the instructions sent to General Jerónimo Treviño and of the tone with which the Mexican press treated the whole matter of recognition, he had already sent a copy of the declaration to the members of the diplomatic corps.

Vallarta visited him four days afterwards and showed him the *Diario* of the day before, in which appeared an explanation of the article which Foster had charged as being offensive to his government. He told Foster that the Mexican cabinet had considered Foster's request, even though it hoped that with the second article Foster would be satisfied. It believed that the publication of his memorandum presented very serious difficulties, but if Foster insisted, it would be done, though accompanied by a reply from Vallarta. The satisfaction thus obtained was not complete, above all because the initial article was reproduced by all the newspapers and the second by only a very few; also, because whereas in the first article private reports received by the Mexican government were given as its source, that of the second was given as the United States press, which did not dissipate the doubt in regard to the good faith of the United States government.

Vallarta then offered to make the memorandum and his reply public on the following day. But the Secretary of the Treasury, Matías Romero, visited Foster immediately to tell him that his request worried Porfirio Díaz because a public polemic would alienate public opinion even more and further embitter the relations between the two governments. Therefore Romero offered in the name of President Díaz to publish the memorandum in substance, but without indicating where it came from. Foster accepted this proposal and Romero remained in charge of condensing it; but even so it did not appear in the *Diario*. Romero visited him again to tell him that President Díaz had not been satisfied with the condensation, that he persisted in his fear of the bad effects of the polemic, and that therefore he asked that the request be completely withdrawn. Foster acceded immediately in view of the very friendly terms of the presidential request, even though he declared that he continued to believe that the publication, far from damaging, would be useful in dissipating prejudices.

But it ended by being published, along with Vallarta's reply. Vallarta thought that on withdrawing his petition Foster was removing from consideration the existence of the memorandum itself; but when Romero explained to him that the intention of the United States minister was that it should remain in the archives of the Department of Foreign Relations as a diplomatic document—and Foster in person so confirmed it a few days afterwards—Vallarta consulted with President Díaz on the case, and both resolved to publish Foster's memorandum and Vallarta's counter-reply.

Foster's memorandum was a good document, even though it was not exactly a model of diplomacy. Stubborn, argumentative, well joined, its reading gives an idea that he was right in every way and that therefore he was able to permit himself the luxury of scolding the Mexican Secretary of Foreign Relations and the Mexican government generally; but when one reads Vallarta's reply, one becomes convinced that that is not so. Vallarta's reply is also combative. He countered each and every one of his adversary's arguments, and, except in one case, answered them "victoriously," as he himself said with modest pride.

Foster affirmed without restrictions, conditions or limitations that Mexico had not taken "any adequate or vigorous measure" to prevent the depredations on the frontier and to punish their authors; and that the worn-out explanation of the Mexican government was that the internal political upheavals impeded diverting large military forces to the vigilance of that region. Foster, making it a bird of evil omen, asked:

If one of the rival claimants to the Presidency succeeds in establishing a foothold on Mexican territory and in organizing a counter-revolution, will not necessity again compel the Government to devote all its energy and power to the suppression of this new revolution and abandon the Mexican side of the Río Bravo to the raiders and outlaws?

Also he held that the Mexican government had erroneously interpreted the instructions to Brigadier General Edward O. C. Ord, for "they are not an unconditional order to cross over to Mexican territory freeing the frontier from danger." And in order to demonstrate it, he described with fastidious patience the many and long steps that had to be taken to arrive at the invasion. First, Ord had to give notice of the instructions to his subordinates and second, to the Mexican local authorities; third, he had to invite these latter to cooperate in the suppression of the frontier banditry; fourth, he had to give them notice that the depredations could no longer be tolerated; fifth, he had to declare that if the Mexican government continued to overlook its international obligations, the fulfillment of these would fall to his country; and sixth, and only when all the foregoing had been done, could Ord enter Mexican territory. Consequently, the declaration made by the Mexican Secretary of War in the instructions given to General Treviño to the effect that the orders given to Brigadier General Ord were contrary to the existing treaties between Mexico and the United States, to the norms of international law, and to the custom of civilized people was unjustified. Those accusations, made in an official document, were sufficiently grave to cause fear for the cordiality of the relations between both countries and could be explained only by the rush with which the instructions to Treviño were written; but the deliberate intention of the executive was seen to be confirmed in the article in the *Diario Oficial,* where it was asserted that the order of President Rutherford B. Hayes to Brigadier General Ord was due to the influence exercised over him by Lerdo and by a United States citizen, Foster.

Vallarta's reply exposed the foundation of the whole problem. To what point could and should Mexico be held responsible alone or even in greater part for the border depredations? Vallarta did not wish to answer such a question by himself but to invoke the opinion of Sir Edward Thornton, the English arbiter elected by common accord of the United States and Mexico to judge the claims of the Convention of 1868, and whose wisdom and impartiality were unreservedly applauded by both governments. Sir Edward had said in the judgment of the claim of William C. Dickens:

. . . it is outside of all doubt that during the last years the theft of cattle in the limits of Texas territory with Mexico has been committed and that that stock has been carried to the other side of the río Bravo; but [to the judge] it seems totally insufficient proof that the thieves have always been Mexican citizens and soldiers, that the bands have been organized on Mexican soil with the knowledge and permission of the authorities of the Republic of Mexico and that the victims of these robberies have been denied reparation when in particular cases they have reclaimed a determined lot of cattle after having proven their ownership.

The judge had studied the mechanics of these robberies, for the claimants alleged that on Mexican territory the rustlers were able to re-unite very quickly, to cross the Rio Grande and intern themselves in Texas when the United States soldiers were far away from the river; but, the judge had said,

. . . if this makes it difficult for the United States authorities to prevent such incursions, with more reason this occurs with the Mexican authorities, for if re-uniting and crossing the river is a matter of an hour, the assembling of a considerable herd and driving it to Mexican territory requires much more time and gives greater opportunity to the United States authorities to attack the thieves and to recover the stock.

Sir Edward's conclusion was that, as a general rule, the vigilance of the Mexican authorities did not seem less than that of the Americans; and basing his judgment on this rule, he threw out the claim because of "not finding sufficient foundation to make the Mexican government responsible."

Vallarta then threw himself into arguing on his own account. The persistence of the evils of the frontier did not prove Mexican responsibility for them, but did prove that these evils were profound, had multiple causes, and were favored by the men and the nature of that region. The evil was so strong and had such vigor that it had not only defied the good will and the weak resources of Mexico, but also the powerful desire and the strength and means of the United States. And it is evident—observed Vallarta, not without irony—that the United States government was not said or could be said to lack the integrity and robustness for making felt its "vigorous action" in separated and deserted extremes of its territory, as was so often said of the Mexican. Vallarta then smoothly presented his favorite thesis: the presence of military forces, however numerous they might be, was not enough to consolidate order and security on the frontier; further-reaching measures that would take away the incentive for robbery and rustling were needed; but the Mexican government had been abstaining from proposing them until now, given the "anomalous" state of relations between both countries. Nonetheless, "full powers and ample instructions" to negotiate these problems had been given to its new minister in Washington.

The Mexican government had understood "completely what was the meaning" of the instructions sent to Ord, and had "appreciated its consequences." The conditional character of the authorization that had been given to Ord "did not attenuate its offensive character," for even though the fulfillment itself of the condition was left to the discretion of a military man,

. . . not even under those conditions can the government of the Republic consent to the national territory being invaded, and that a foreign military leader, to whom neither the law of the country nor that of the nations gives any authority, come to perform acts which are jurisdictional according to his discretion.

He maintained that all internationalists agreed that a sovereign state cannot send its troops into a foreign territory without the permission of the government of that territory, since

. . . the independence and sovereignty of the nations would be at the mercy of the most audacious or of the strongest by only trying to argue that principle.

Even more "robust" was the base of that other norm of international law, according to which a military chief, even having the permission of the government to enter its territory, could not perform jurisdictional acts: he would not be able either to apprehend or to punish criminals, or to recover private property, as the order given to Ord required. The Mexican government had been in the right therefore in affirming that Ord's orders were contrary to existing treaties, to international law and to the practice of "enlightened" nations.

Vallarta's argument that the "paragraph of the newspaper squib" appearing in the *Diario,* the source of the whole incident, did not have official character and was therefore weak. The *Diario Oficial* of those days, besides publishing the laws and disposition of the federal government, presented news and editorials that everybody, beginning with the government itself, took as the official expression of the government. Porfirio Díaz and his Tuxtepecan revolutionaries became so angry with the *Diario,* precisely because it represented the opinion of the opposing Lerdo government, that on entering the capital they suppressed it. They had to renew its publication in a short time, not only because without it the laws could not be laws, but because Díaz felt the necessity of making known in it the official policy of his government. This historic argument escaped Foster, in spite of his having witnessed such acts, and Vallarta naturally did not remind him.

Vallarta was very able in the explanation that he gave of the resistance of the government to the publication of the Foster memorandum and of Díaz' last request for Foster to withdraw it. The Mexican government did not fear that the recriminations made against it were well founded or would appear to be so, nor did it fear of not being able to answer them "victoriously." It wished to help Foster, who believed in good faith that in that form he was going to stimulate Mexican public opinion to a response favorable to his government. On the contrary, he was going to excite even more feelings already heated enough with the knowledge of Ord's instructions. Public discussions were going to be more embittered, and all of it in detriment to Foster's negotiation, whose objective was to reach once and for all "a peaceful and friendly settlement" of the differences between both countries.

FOSTER WAS GREATLY surprised when, two days after having delivered his written proposals for negotiation, Vallarta communicated to him that after a prolonged examination made in a cabinet meeting, the idea of negotiating in Mexico had been abandoned, since for one thing José María Mata had instructions and full powers to do it in Washington, and for another Foster seemed to lack them. Therefore Foster confessed to his government to being vexed to see his negotiations end so unexpectedly and abruptly, and from it he drew the obvious conclusion:

The motive is apparent to me. It was a desire to get my propositions in the definite shape in which I made them, for Mr. Mata's benefit.

Foster was not a man to give up easily, and without even suspecting the reception that the United States Department of State was preparing for Mata, "he hoped that they would pardon him" for expressing his desire that the negotiations take place in Mexico, by their authorizing him to carry them on. For the present he felt it necessary to anticipate that the acts occurring since his report of June 18 had made impossible, as he had then offered, that in the "next mail" he would announce the progress obtained in his negotiations. And, in fact, when William M. Evarts informed him that the Department of State would not deal with Mata, but that it would be Foster who would do it with the Mexican Secretary of Foreign Relations, Foster reported that he would see Vallarta at once, but again he considered it necessary to anticipate that "the condition of public sentiment and possibly of the Government of Díaz had somewhat changed." Vallarta, who at one time was disposed to agree on the condition *sine qua non* of the border problem—that is, the reciprocal passing of troops from one territory to the other—seemed to have changed in accord with public opinion, now suspicious to the extreme.

Foster then advanced his fear that he would find the Secretary of Foreign Relations "more intractable" than six weeks earlier, when conversations with him were begun. He cherished the purpose of presenting the problems in a friendly and equitable manner, by making a special effort to remove Vallarta's prejudice and convincing him that the United States wanted only justice and peace, and that what he proposed in the name of his government was entirely honorable and reciprocal. If he failed, he would appeal to General Díaz, "less of a politician and less influenced by popular clamour, and whose impulses are in the main honest and fair"; but, uncertain, Foster reversed the order by asking for an interview with the President before initiating his conversations with the Secretary of Foreign Relations.

In that interview Foster explained to Porfirio Díaz that he had the powers and instructions to negotiate all pending problems and of reaching as soon as possible the establishment of official and cordial relations between the two governments. Given the importance of the conversations that he would soon have with Vallarta, he had wanted to explain to Díaz personally the opinion of his government and to assure him that it would be guided by a spirit of justice in everything. The proposed pact presented by Mata in Washington contained excellent ideas for the settlement of the frontier problems, but it was not sufficiently explicit on some points and omitted the essential measure, that of the reciprocal passage of troops over the boundary. Foster realized the disadvantages that the measure offered to the Mexican government, accentuated by the order given to Brigadier General Ord, for Mexico feared that the presence of United States troops on Mexican territory would deepen the actual hostility of the frontier population; but he thought that, by concluding a treaty in that regard, that order could be canceled out in a manner honorable for both countries.

Foster's government also assigned a singular importance to the problem of the forced loans from whose payment it aspired to see its citizens exempted. To Díaz' objection that an international agreement that exempted them from it would place the Mexican in an inferior position, since anything conceded now to the United States would be extended to all foreigners by means of the mechanism of the usual clause of the most favored nation, Foster replied that the Mexican Supreme Court had recently favored a Mexican victim in the matter of a forced loan, so that the United States wanted only that its nationals not be in a situation inferior to the Mexicans. Finally, Foster, rather than argue with President Díaz, wanted to reiterate once more his good intentions of proceeding amicably and honestly, and to assure him that President Hayes was anxious to renew diplomatic relations as soon as possible. Díaz, for his part, agreed with the necessity of good relations between the two countries, offering to work to obtain them, for "Mexico is not thinking of resorting to war except in the case of inexorable duty, and without hope of triumph."

From August 22 to August 30, morning, afternoon and night, Vallarta and Foster were closeted for six interminable conferences, in which all problems past, present and future pending between the two countries were examined. By August 31, Foster informed his government that he knew that his negotiations with Vallarta, far from being satisfactory, had terminated in a suspension whose end remained in the hands of Vallarta; and three days afterwards, exasperated, he said: "As will be seen [from his report], the Mexican government has resisted step by step to concede to the reciprocal crossing of the troops."

Foster began his first conversation by indicating that he was now indeed fully authorized by his government to negotiate, and to negotiate all pending questions; that Mata's proposal had been sent to him from Washington in order for it to be discussed in Mexico; and that the Department of State would suspend all conversations with Mata and would postpone recognition of Díaz until receiving Foster's reports on the course of the talks. He had instructions to deal with all problems, but he wanted to begin with the two most important: the banditry on the frontier and the forced loans. He repeated that Mata's proposal was ineffective because it did not include the question of the reciprocal crossing of troops. Vallarta conceded that at the beginning it would not have been improper to accept the proposal because it was reciprocal, but he saw the serious difficulty of the rancor between the settlers on each side of the river that would explode at the presence of foreign troops. Perhaps the measure might do away with the banditry, but at the cost of aggravating the deeper and more permanent problem of ill will and hate. In any case he did not see why the measures counseled in the Mexican proposal were not tried at once; if a trial proved them to be inefficient, others would be considered.

Foster maintained that the troops of his country had passed into Mexico in pursuit of bandits and rustlers several times, and that never had any conflict resulted; and he invoked the testimony of General Ignacio Pesqueira, who as governor of Sonora had authorized that step without any adverse consequences. The question of the frontier was affecting the peace of nine million Mexicans and forty-five million Americans; consequently, the opinions and prejudices of a few thousand on the frontier should not represent an insolvable obstacle to a solution. In any case, if

Vallarta and he could not agree on any settlement that would authorize the reciprocal passing of troops, it was hardly worth the trouble to waste time considering Mata's proposal or any other. Foster, at any rate, offered to draw up his own proposal and submit it to Vallarta.

As he was not progressing very much on this question, Foster tried that of the forced loans, only to find that Vallarta told him that he had personally studied it and therefore he could announce immediately that the claim of the United States "was entirely inadmissable." Foster cited as a favorable precedent the treaty of Mexico with England in 1826, in which English subjects were exempted from the payment of this type of loan. Vallarta, besides alleging that the interpretation of the Mexican government was that the forced loans were contrary to the treaty only when they fell exclusively on English subjects, and that such a treaty, in any case, was not now in vigor, cited the antecedent of an old one with Peru and another recent one with Saxony, in which it was expressly established that the nationals of each one should be subject to the payment of the same contributions that might fall on the Mexicans.

Foster then cited in support of his thesis a recent judicial decision in which the court declared that no federal or local, civil or military authority was able to impose contributions of any kind, since such power was constitutionally reserved to the legislative power.

Vallarta disagreed with that decision, in spite of its unanimous approval, and said that was due to "one of those utopian" theories of magistrate Ezequiel Montes, entirely contrary to national reality. Foster made note that the Mexicans, at least, could resort to the protection of the justice of their country, and Vallarta replied immediately that so could the foreigners.

The United States minister ended the first conversation by lamenting Vallarta's "un-liberal" opinions and his incapacity to overcome the prejudices and suspicions so common in Mexico about the intentions of foreign governments. Vallarta, for his part, assured that he was immune to those prejudices and had, on the contrary, a determined willingness to settle the pending questions; however, as the differences in the opinions of both were so great, he thought it best to submit these points to President Díaz and his cabinet.

The first conference was barely a skirmish, in spite of having been prolonged for more than two hours, and notwithstanding the frankness and even the fire put into it and the variety of the themes treated. Foster, with more diplomatic experience, and Vallarta, with a notion of his responsibility that sharpened his senses, used hardly a part of their arguments and none of their strategic resources. In the subsequent ones, nevertheless, all came to light, and to read the aide-mémoires that each wrote independently at the end of each conversation is to bring to life the great spectacle of seeing two lively and brilliant intellects in a duel to the finish. Furthermore: those aide-mémoires can be compared without finding a single case of concealment of the other's argument or of abusive presentation of one's own. The only differences are the natural ones of reiteration that belonged to the personal temperaments involved or that were products of opposing interests.

On the theme of the acquisition of real estate on the edge of the border, Foster made a very timely and very much American presentation. President Ignacio Comonfort of Mexico had conditioned it in 1856 on an express authorization of the Mexican Congress. This was equivalent to a prohibition that was the origin of many complaints. And Foster added: "if at some time" relations between the two countries were renewed, a violent growth of commerce and of business in general could be expected, which would be dashed to pieces against that "Wall of China" raised by Mexico. Vallarta soon cut off those advances by making the dilatory observation that the problem required study of great depth, for it should not be thought that only Americans were going to be authorized to acquire real estate. It was necessary, among other things, to wait until the termination of the problems created by the government of Chiapas in respect to the Guatemalan population residing in that state.

The theme of the suppression of the Free Zone ran into the same fate. Vallarta recognized that he, as the Secretary of Foreign Relations, and Matías Romero, as Secretary of the Treasury, disapproved of it; but it was a fact that the Mexican Congress was refusing to change it, much less to suppress it. Consequently, he could offer nothing, it occurring to him only to initiate immediately a campaign to enlighten public opinion until the change or abolition should become possible.

The border difficulties were from then on one of the most debated questions. Vallarta, after consulting with President Díaz and his cabinet, began the second conference by explaining to Foster one by one the clauses of Mata's proposal, with the hope that careful examination of the range that the Mexican government was giving them would cause Foster's aversion to disappear. But the United States minister did not give in on his initial point of view but rather now explained it with acuteness. The Mexican proposal gave preference to judging more rapidly and punishing more severely the frontier criminals, but before coming to that, it was necessary to find them and apprehend them. For that purpose a military force was necessary to follow the trail of the criminals until completing the pursuit with the capture of the culprit, who usually eluded the Mexican authorities because he disappeared among his friends. Therefore, without the clause for the reciprocal crossing of troops over the border, that proposal was inadequate and inadmissable.

Vallarta, in turn, insisted on his view, using now the authority of President Díaz. The latter continued to think that the presence of United States troops on Mexican territory would create resistance, provocations and perhaps bloodshed, thus creating for both countries troublesome situations and even more serious problems. Foster turned to another reason already pointed out by him: Mexico had lived in the midst of revolutions during half of the last twelve years; if the future was to be predicted by basing it on the past, that would happen again; then the federal government would spend all its resources and its power combatting the new revolt, abandoning the frontier to its fate. This foreseeable situation would not affect the United States if its troops were already authorized to pass into Mexico.

Vallarta did not think that Mexico would again have revolutions: the belief was common among all Mexicans of that time that they only caused great harm and resolved nothing. Also, the government of Porfirio Díaz had popular sympathy; the constitutional reform that prohibited presidential re-election would make the presidential succession a necessarily pacific process. The Mexican people disapproved of the passage of foreign troops, as demonstrated by the fact that all national governments had refused to concede it; nevertheless if Foster and his government insisted on this measure, President Díaz would turn it down if unrestricted authorization was solicited, but he would approve it conditionally. It could be agreed to, for example, when wild Indians were being pursued in deserted areas, and even in dealing with rustlers, although Díaz did not believe it necessary; but it could not be honorably authorized, even so restricted, until the United States government conceded to Mexico the disauthorizing of invasions into Mexican national territory and the payment of reparations for them.

Foster, on reaching this point, asked peremptorily if President Díaz considered those conditions as prior to the discussion of a treaty. Vallarta answered that yes, even while the conditions were being fulfilled they could be continuing to discuss the treaty; they would have ample time to arrive at the final text since in no case could ratification be reached before the establishment of normal diplomatic relations between the two countries. Foster then said that if President Díaz was thus conditioning the negotiations of the treaty, he should put an end to the discussions, for the United States would not withdraw the instructions given to Ord or offer any reparations for invasions that were not made with a hostile spirit, for his government "could not stultify itself by any declaration which would in any way seem to place it in the wrong." If this treaty should be agreed upon and if the other difficulties should disappear through recognition, the order could be revoked simultaneously and immediately after it was authorized.

Vallarta wanted to know from Foster, in any case, what restrictions on the passage of troops Foster would be disposed to admit. The latter thought that if Mexico consented in returning to the United States wild Indians who had escaped from reservations in order to take refuge in Mexico, the problem of their incursions would practically disappear; but of course, the zone on the lower Rio Grande, the most prodigal in crimes and stock stealing, would remain. There the reciprocal passage of troops could be consented to with two exceptions: when military forces were on the Mexican side ready to continue the pursuit, or when United States troops found a Mexican town capable of using its police for this purpose.

Vallarta, after consulting with President Díaz, presented a new proposition to add to Mata's proposal, a clause authorizing the Presidents of the two countries to consent to reciprocal crossing when they thought it necessary. They could agree, for example, on indicating the points through which it should be done and the time of the enforcement of the authorization. Foster flatly rejected the idea, for there was no better way of paralyzing the functioning of the treaty. It would be enough for one of the two Presidents to resist conceding the authorization, or to concede it only for a special point, or in a given time, so that nothing could then be done. Nonetheless, Vallarta said that was all that the Mexican government was able to concede. Besides, he added hurriedly, there were yet other restrictions such, for example, as that of the troops of one country not penetrating into the territory of the other for more than twenty leagues, and not performing in any case jurisdictional acts but policing ones, that was to say, to apprehend and deliver culprits to the nearest national authority.

The examination of the question of forced loans was begun with a resounding negative from Vallarta, for Vallarta anticipated Díaz' instructions to deny the exemption asked for, founding his reply on Article 9 of the treaty of 1831 between Mexico and the United States. There it was very clearly stated that United States citizens in Mexico were subject to the same charges that might fall on the Mexicans. In that sense and with that foundation, the English arbiter, Sir Edward Thornton, had judged a claim of a United States citizen against Mexico in the Convention of 1868. Furthermore, in all international treaties concluded by Mexico that same principle had been established.

Foster began by asserting that the Mexican Constitution disauthorized the forced loans, and as a fundamental law that was superior to treaties; these were the ones which should be changed in order to make them conform to the Constitution. (Vallarta responded with some irony that he would study that point of Mexican constitutional law raised by Foster.) Furthermore, Foster continued, the translation into Spanish of the opinion of the arbiter was incorrect, for the English text said that foreigners were obliged to pay the extraordinary taxes of war that fell on the whole of the inhabitants. To this Vallarta replied that it was evident that not even the ordinary taxes fell on all the population, since it was the custom to exclude from paying them those who had less means. As far as the argument derived from a recent court decision, it should be kept in mind that, granted that it was very respectable, its applicability was limited to the specific case under consideration; it could not be invoked as a precedent nor could it be given another interpretation in the future.

In Foster's opinion, the most reprehensible issue was not the payment of taxes decreed by the executive by virtue of the extraordinary powers which the legislative body gave it but the true forced loans imposed by the military chiefs on a very reduced number of persons; Foster, therefore, would be disposed to favor an agreement to establish a reciprocal exemption for the citizens of both countries. Vallarta rejected this last idea with a good argument, even though he did not make all of it that he could have made. He said that the United States did not make use of forced loans, but rather of printing paper money, and therefore it would be necessary for the Mexicans resident in the United States to be exempted from receiving it, a thing which he was sure would be opposed by the United States government with very good reason.

Furthermore, President Díaz had already anticipated another important adverse argument. Conceding the exemption to United States citizens would bring about the exemption of all foreigners through the operation of the clause of the most favored nation, with the end result being that the Mexicans in their own country would be in a position inferior to that of the foreigners. Foster replied with good sense that the contrary would occur, for the government not being able to tax the foreigners would not be inclined to make the taxes fall exclusively on the Mexicans. To this Vallarta brought out another objection. In the United States as well as in Mexico, under normal conditions ordinary taxes decreed by the legislative power prevailed; but in extreme necessity, the latter could even approve the suspension of guarantees. On the other hand, if the exemption asked by Foster should take form in a treaty, the legislative power, able to do anything nationally, would not be able to annul, modify or suspend the treaty. For all these reasons Vallarta concluded that "after lengthy meditation," the Mexican government declared it impossible to accede to the United States' demand.

Foster, exhausted, affirmed that nothing had been gained by the conversations; his only conclusion was that the Mexican government had not measured up to that which the United States was expecting of it. He therefore did not see anything further to do but to inform the Department of State. His government, of course, was not disposed to single out only one of the pending questions and to give recognition on the basis of the solution of it.

Vallarta, very calmly, said that the Mexican government "would not lend itself to undue concessions even in order to obtain recognition." He had already submitted this question to the cabinet and he would not be able to make any concessions.

Foster, in the face of this, felt it his duty to break off the conferences *ex abrupto,* and not renew them until receiving new instructions from his government, which without doubt would not wish to grant recognition. In any case, if in the future they should again confer, it would be wise to do so by beginning with written proposals from Vallarta. The latter offered to make them when the occasion should arrive.

X

A BAD BALANCE

The result of his one conversation with President Díaz, the six with Vallarta and three confidential ones with Matías Romero, Foster appraised thus on reporting to his government: Vallarta had come to agree on the reciprocal passage of troops that were pursuing the wild Indians in the desert regions of the Upper Rio Grande. He had not agreed to general permission in the case of the populated zones of the Lower Rio Grande, but proposed giving the power to the presidents of the two countries to agree on it if a trial demonstrated that the measures advised in the Mata proposal were ineffective. Also they would have the power to limit the passage to certain places and to a given period. He desired, furthermore, to limit the distance into the territory the troops could go and their powers to merely policing, excluding the jurisdictional ones. Vallarta had resisted completely the negotiating of a treaty that exempted Americans from the forced loans, had declared that his government could not at the moment abolish or change the Free Zone, agreed to considering within two weeks the fate of the American wild Indians resident in Coahuila and Chihuahua, was not able to take care immediately of the claims for damages made during the revolt of La Noria. Finally he had demanded that the settlement of the frontier questions be the only condition necessary to recognition and that the announcement of the latter precede the settlement. In the face of this situation, Foster counselled:

If Mr. Vallarta was satisfied that acquiescence in our views on the frontier question would bring about recognition,

he thought that he would agree to a treaty similar to that suggested.

IGNACIO L. VALLARTA, loyal to his promise, had John W. Foster called on September 10 in order to present to him his proposal for a treaty. It empowered the Presidents of Mexico and of the United States to conclude agreements authorizing the reciprocal passage of troops in pursuit of wild Indians or rustlers, and to determine the period of duration of the authority and the places through which the passing might take place. The passing would be limited in this way to federal troops pursuing closely or having within sight a party of wild Indians or rustlers, to a limit of penetration of twenty leagues from the dividing line; on reaching that—or before, if they lost the trail or made the catch— the troops should return to their country of origin. The foreign force should not enter any populated centers of the other country or pass within the immediate vicinity of those that had municipal authorities and police forces, or cross the border when on the neighboring frontier there were troops or police able to continue the pursuit. The exercise of all acts of jurisdiction was forbidden. The proposal established the commitment of the two governments to punish the abuses of its troops as if they had been performed on their own territories, and of each one respecting the territorial rights of the other by forbidding the passage of troops without the other's consent and by punishing those troops if such passage took place without authorization.

Foster felt the necessity of unburdening himself to Evarts, again using a confidential letter. Vallarta's proposal meant a rejection of all the American propositions, he said with evident exaggeration, since Díaz had gone from absolute rejection to a conditional crossing. He had trusted in the possibility of an agreement because several common friends had assured him that Vallarta would end by giving in: "but, it appears that still stronger pressure must be applied before this government will yield." The German minister had told him that Vallarta expected a prompt agreement with Foster, but that his political enemies would tear him to pieces if they should be able to use against him the argument that he had surrendered on the issue of reciprocal crossing. And searching for some explanation, Foster said philosophically to Evarts: "It is not so much a question of duty and justice as of popular prejudice against the Yankee, which influences the action of the government."

Five days afterwards Foster talked with Vallarta and recovered some hope. The Mexican Secretary knew, of course, that the precedent that Foster had had in mind was the McLane-Ocampo treaty of 1859; but besides having been negotiated under really extraordinary historical circumstances, it had never been ratified by the Mexican Congress in any manner. He had confirmed that fact in his recent conversations with the leaders of the Senate; but he offered by all means to make a more formal exploration there.

The United States government, meanwhile, had given Foster notice of its approval of his conduct by his conforming "not only to the letter but to the spirit" of the instructions which he had been given. Foster entered into contact with Vallarta fortified by the explicit approbation of his government but weakened by the strong reaction that the invasion of Lieutenant Colonel W. R. Shafter into Piedras Negras had produced on the government and public opinion of Mexico. The impact of that invasion on Foster was visible, for he himself asked the Department of State if this reaction was not partially justified, adding that the Mexicans had come to see in Shafter the personification of the transgressor of the national rights. Naturally, Foster exhibited strength and hid his weakness on beginning new conversations by saying that he had the renewed approval of the Department of State of his conduct and performances and that, consequently, he wanted to give Vallarta one more opportunity to modify his position or to adopt a new one.

The Mexican cabinet had again dealt with the frontier question, Vallarta answered; but the existence of the order of June 1 continued to be the great impediment to reconsidering the problem on better terms. In fact the situation had worsened with Shafter's invasion, for Mexico had asked for reparations for it; not only had none been given, but the Department of State had not even answered the Mexican note. In any case if the proposals made by Mata and by him himself did not satisfy him, Foster should make new ones, naturally taking into account that Mexico would not give "on any conditions" an unlimited permit for the crossing of the frontier. After discussing this further and the problems of the forced loans, Foster again suspended the negotiations, and, on doing so, warned:

. . . desiring so much that our diplomatic relations be re-established, I cannot even give hope of considering it while the government of Porfirio Díaz denies justice to the American citizens and does not fulfill his obligations on the frontier.

Foster now began to relate the conduct of Vallarta and, in general, that of the Mexican government, to Mexico's internal situation. But in his first interpretations he reached the realms of exaggeration and of pure unreality. Not without alarm on November 10 he communicated that he had heard it said that no less than 3000 men—infantry, cavalry, and artillery—had recently been dispatched to enlarge Treviño's forces, already 6000 strong. It was said that the objective of that unusual concentration was certainly that of preventing invasions both of criminals and of the United States Army. And since he had been urging Vallarta to re-enforce the Division of the North, and nothing had been said of these last movements of troops, "there must be something unexpected and extraordinary in it." Furthermore, Foster continued, resentment against the United States was increasing, and each day the belief of the Mexicans in the inevitability of a conflict between the two countries became more general. They also believed that its provocation was the real objective of the United States. To this he attributed Vallarta's not giving in on any point, even though he, Foster, told him and repeated very clearly that he should not and could not expect recognition under such conditions.

Manuel María de Zamacona had told Foster that the Mexican Senate asked Vallarta for reports on the state of relations with the United States and had voted a resolution to the effect that Vallarta should not consent to a recognition conditioned on anything. Zamacona had explained to Foster that Porfirio Díaz could not stop being very cautious in his negotiations with the United States, for even when there was no probability that Lerdo would return to power while Díaz held his present popularity, Díaz would lose it very quickly if he showed himself complacent. In fact, that attitude of rejecting a conditioned recognition seemed to be old, Foster said, for now he saw published in the *Diario Oficial* of November 13 the instructions that were given to Mata in June, and in them it was said that Mexico expected recognition as a right and not as a gift.

Recognizing that Vallarta's position was still firm, and cognizant of the fact that the United States Congress was then conducting an investigation of Mexican-American relations, Foster sent Undersecretary Frederick W. Seward a resumé of the state of his negotiations in case he wished to utilize it in the investigation. The Mexican government would not agree to the acquisition of real estate near the frontier, nor to an agreement that exempted United States citizens from the payment of forced loans; it would not commit itself to abolishing or modifying the Free Zone and had refused to agree to the reciprocal passing of troops even within a zone and subject to some restrictions; and nothing had yet been said about its disposition to hand over to United States authorities Indians taking refuge in Coahuila and Chihuahua.

Foster felt uncomfortable cut off from Vallarta, the more so because the latter was taking no steps whatever to renew negotiations; besides, he knew positively that events in Mexico and the United States were going adversely. He resolved therefore to make use first of Zamacona, on the eve of his departure for Washington, and afterwards of Mata, recently returned to

Mexico from his unsuccessful mission. The first suggested that Foster see President Díaz and talk to him frankly; perhaps he might react favorably toward one new point of departure in the negotiations. But Foster resisted, considering that he had turned to him before initiating his first conferences, and that seeing him now might offend Vallarta, who might think that he was going over his head by negotiating directly with the President. Foster would prefer to have Zamacona talk with Vallarta and induce him to overcome the anti-American prejudices so common in Mexico and to look at the principles of justice and the true interests of Mexico as freely as Zamacona. Foster thought that he could not go to the Secretary of Foreign Relations without a previous indication that he would be welcomed. Zamacona, after making the démarche, announced that Vallarta would visit him "very informally" in order to have a confidential talk with him. But Vallarta did not make the visit.

A few days later Mata invited Foster to his home and conversed on his own mission in Washington and Foster's efforts in Mexico. Mata told him that he had declared to Undersecretary Seward the opinion that Mexico ought to accede to the reciprocal passage of troops as well as that Foster's interpretation of Article 29 of the Mexican Constitution, on which he based the unconstitutionality of the forced loans, was correct. Foster touched at once on the point of his reluctance to go to the Secretary of Foreign Relations, and Mata offered to bring him together with Vallarta in his home in order to establish the first contact. There Vallarta spoke to Foster of his intention to go on studying some of the claims of United States citizens for damages suffered in the last revolt, and charged him with estimating the amount so that he might be able to decide if Mexico would be able to incur the obligation of paying them. Foster hastened to propose to him the idea of a convention to recognize and judge these claims, offering to recommend it to the Department of State as a provisional solution to the great question of the forced loans, for that one and the frontier question were viewed as "essential" by his government for the settlement of all differences between the two countries. He insisted that there was no other solution than that of the reciprocal passing of troops, and that "he could not give in" on that point. Vallarta advanced the notion that the silence of the Department of State in giving satisfaction for the two invasions by Shafter made it difficult for the negotiations to begin properly; but, in any case, it was fitting that Foster submit written proposals.

THUS THE CONTACTS were renewed under poor portents. Foster and Vallarta had a new and long conversation, the fruits of which Foster transmitted in a coded telegram on November 28, 1877:

> Two thousand troops going to Matamoros by Veracruz and the Gulf. The Díaz government has notified me it will consider no question or negotiation until after recognition.

Foster, in effect, presented himself on November 23 with a proposal for a treaty on the question of the frontier. But Vallarta cut him short by telling him that he would not even consider it while the Mexican government had not received satisfaction for the repeated crossing of United States forces into Mexican territory. And Foster, resolving not to lose his contact again, for the first time asked what type of satisfaction was desired. Vallarta, also for the first time, indicated the same that Mexico unhesitatingly gave when a group of its soldiers penetrated the territory of the United States, that was, trial and punishment of the culprits, indemnity for the injuries caused and guarantees that similar acts would not be repeated. That must have seemed monstrous to Foster, but he contained himself; and even when he expressed his ignorance of whether his government would give those satisfactions, he asked whether his treaty proposal would be approved should they be granted.

The invasion of Chihuahua by Lieutenant Colonel W. R. Shafter, at the end of September, Vallarta told him, had excited such national indignation that the Mexican government was no longer disposed to offer its propositions of September 10. In order "to bring them into accord with public feeling," it would be necessary to limit them even more. The authorization, limited or not, for the passing of troops, or any other condition that the United States government tried to impose on Mexico for the resumption of relations, would have to be "entirely thrown out." Even though the Mexican government felt that, apart from the matter of recognition, the United States was justified in proceeding thus, Mexico was powerless to propose or accept such a condition to recognition, for recognition was due it under international law.

Foster, as if not realizing that Vallarta's position had changed completely, again asked if his proposal would be approved in case the United States should give the satisfactions asked. He was told that they would be if the satisfaction was made in terms that would succeed in changing Mexican public opinion. Foster, desiring this time not to interrupt the conversations, armed himself with patience and asked that his proposal of a treaty, in which important concessions were now made to Mexico, be studied.

Nevertheless Foster did not fail to tell Vallarta that as early as June he had informed him of the precise instructions of the Department of State, as he had left a copy of them with him, and to assure him that they had not since changed; consequently, President Díaz and he were responsible for refusing to negotiate before recognition. But on appraising the situation resulting from it for the Department of State, he went still further. Even though the Díaz government was now asking for recognition before negotiating, Foster felt that it had decided from now on to turn down the principal demands of the United States in future negotiations; thus he judged that prior recognition would in the end be useless.

Foster was truthful in saying that his proposals contained concessions to public opinion and to the desires of the Mexican government. In that of the frontier questions he had incorporated several of the measures of the Mata proposal and some of Vallarta's memorandum of September 10. The principal change consisted in proposing that, in place of making the Presidents the resolving agency, the two superior military chiefs would be. He cast out, of course, the idea of restricting the crossing to the pursuit of Indians, extending it to any transgressor of the law, but accepted that of the forces going no further than thirty leagues and not exercising other acts of jurisdiction than that of the capture of the robbers. He agreed also to the crossing not being made when on the other side of the river there were troops able to continue the pursuit, or towns with police forces capable of doing it. It is true that Foster added, as a lost clause from his treaty, the authorization of citizens of either country to acquire real estate on the other side of the frontier. He made more concessions in the other project. He abandoned entirely the idea of an international convention to exempt United States citizens from the payment of forced loans, but proposed a commission to recognize and judge the claims for damages and injuries caused the citizens of both countries since 1868.

When Vallarta spoke with Foster on November 27 about these projects, he was both encouraging and discouraging. He told him first that some of his ideas were unacceptable, others coincided in every way with Mexican opinions and a third group, even though differing, was negotiable; and second, that President Díaz found it improper and useless to continue the examination of these questions because the two governments which they affected were not maintaining normal relations. Until now, Mexico had been inclined to examine them in an informal manner to demonstrate its good will in settling them at the proper time. There had been no other purpose for sending Mata to Washington, and for his conversations with officials of the Department of State. That good will had been more than fully demonstrated already; consequently, he thought it useless to proceed with the negotiations beyond the point at which they had arrived. Besides, the United States government had said that these treaties would be a condition to recognition, and Mexico was not disposed to accept a recognition conditioned on anything.

Even with that squall, the worst that had fallen on him, Foster insisted on ascertaining which ideas in his proposal seemed inadmissible to Vallarta and which seemed admissible to negotiation. Vallarta told him that the passage of troops would be authorized only and exclusively for the pursuit of wild Indians in uninhabited regions; the Mexican government would "in no way" increase the possibility of United States citizens acquiring real estate on the frontier; and the idea that forced loans be repaid with an interest of 10 per cent was unacceptable because the public treasury could not afford it. This being the case, Foster predicted the failure of the Zamacona mission and indefinite postponement of recognition; and, in order to protect himself, he declared that with his proposals he had wanted to "calculate the probability" that the government of Mexico, once recognized, would accept incorporating those stipulations into a treaty.

XI
FRONTIER STREET

Ignacio L. Vallarta's diplomatic struggle had already lasted a year, for it had begun in November, 1876, soon after the revolutionary group led by Porfirio Díaz entered Mexico City. Nevertheless, it was not to be prolonged much longer, for on the one hand the revolutionary faction had been transformed, first to a *de facto* authority and afterwards into a constitutional government, gaining equally in strength, stability, and respect; on the other hand the political situation and public opinion of the United States were changing adversely for President Rutherford B. Hayes and his Secretary of State, William M. Evarts.

The United States House of Representatives and Senate resolved to initiate a public investigation into the military as well as the diplomatic and commercial aspects of "the Mexican question." The inquiry was multiple in origin and yielded to diverse and even opposed purposes. Texas Representative Gustav Schleicher, an old and well-known lawyer of quarrelsome disposition, proposed it in the House of Representatives, while Henry B. Banning, chairman of the Committee on Military Affairs, wanted to give it an impartial tone in the Senate. The investigation, in any case, gave splendid opportunity for the press to be occupied with it and to give birth thus to a considerable current of public opinion, which in the end prevailed. The testimony given and the documents exhibited, plus the questions put by the members of the committees, contradicted in great measure the selfish incentives of the investigation and of those who openly or quietly were pushing it.

Behind the parliamentary claimants existed equally diverse and opposed economic interests or philosophies on the "Mexican question." One of these was the American railroads, which had now reached the Texas-Mexico frontier. Since the southwestern region of the United States was still unpopulated and the West even more so, the financial success of the railroads did not seem immediate. In order to obtain it, it seemed natural and desirable to extend the lines to the capital of Mexico and capture the trade with the populated area of the highland and even to a Mexican port on the Pacific, in order to serve the commerce of the Far East, in which the railroads were placing much hope of quick enrichment.

Representative Schleicher, for example, maintaining that the United States would have to guard its southern frontiers permanently, pleaded for federal subsidies for constructing a railroad parallel to the Rio Grande and the border as far as California. Edward Lee Plumb believed in the necessity of extending the line of the Texas Pacific to Mexico, and, because of his bitter experience as a negotiator for those concessions during Lerdo's government, he seemed to think that only by snatching away Mexican territory could there be any certainty of carrying out an operation of that scope, so necessary to modern civilization. Others believed in all this but judged resorting to force to obtain it unnecessary and disadvantageous, for as neighbors and with complementary economic features, the United States and Mexico were naturally destined to become more and more friendly.

One of the first results of the congressional investigation was to show the disparity of opinions between the Secretary of War and the Department of State. More notable still was the fact that those of the former had a peaceful tone, while those of the latter by inference were bellicose. Secretary of War George W. McCrary expressed himself to be on friendly terms with President Díaz and considering Díaz a liberal ruler deserving of success in the conduct of his administration. The commander in chief of the United States Army, General W. T. Sherman, was convinced that creating a band of territory on each side of the dividing line, in which Mexican and United States troops could enter freely, would provoke a war in less than two weeks. Brigadier General Edward O. C. Ord held that a war with Mexico was "entirely unnecessary" and was opposed to the local troops of Texas participating in the pursuit of frontier bandits, sure that a fight between them and the Mexican army would be fatal to good relations between the two countries.

Foster felt his position weakened from then on. He had made the reciprocal crossing of troops a cardinal point of his negotiations because the Department of State had instructed him to proceed thus and because he always had thought that the order of June 1 enjoyed the approval of the military authorities. Anyone could see in his dispatches the true origin of that order, and it would consequently be believed—as it was already being said in Mexico—that he had demanded much more than his government had authorized him to ask, thus exceeding his instructions. He himself, on the other hand, had considered that the main obstacle to his success as a negotiator was, precisely, the order given to Brigadier General Ord, and that without it an agreement with Mexico would have been easily obtained.

Another of the immediate results of the investigation was that the United States press began to express unfavorable criticism of the aggressive elements and came to suspect the attitude and proceedings of the executive branch of the United States government. One newspaper affirmed, for example, that the Department of State was withholding from Congress documents demonstrating the progress reached in the pacification of the frontier during the last year and a half; another, that none favored war with Mexico except the speculators, the adventurers, and some few Texans, and to prove this it brought to light the opinions of Generals Sherman and Sheridan and Brigadier General Ord. Private individuals began also to express their adverse opinions to a provocative policy by writing letters to the newspapers in which they showed the contradiction between the declarations and the conduct of the Department of State, or argued the economic advantages of peaceful relations with Mexico. And then the time came when this movement of public opinion reached more formal and expeditious expression such as the resolution of the California legislature instructing the representatives and senators of that state to promote in Congress the recognition of Díaz.

THE GOVERNMENT OF MEXICO had lacked for some time a representative of its own in the United States capable of informing it with sagacity on the changes in internal policy and public opinion, as well as of drawing a lucid picture of the forces and interests that were agitating the "Mexican question." In reality, it was relying upon the slow and tardy arrival of news from the United States press. For that reason and because it had become certain that limiting itself to negotiating with Foster might lead up a blind alley, the Mexican government resolved to send Manuel María de Zamacona to the United States, in spite of the bitter experience it had encountered with José María Mata.

Credit for that nomination must be attributed to President Díaz himself. Vallarta had no personal relationship with Zamacona, and it was easy to forecast that serious differences between them would soon arise. Díaz deserves even greater credit for this nomination, for in so doing he sacrificed the natural resentment that any political leader feels when one of his oldest and closest followers abandons him. Zamacona had been in fact the most tenacious and intelligent Porfirista during the hard struggle against Benito Juárez; but when the latter died and Sebastián Lerdo de Tejada ascended to the Presidency, in spite of a real and great disparity between them, he agreed to serve on the Joint Claims Commission of that government. So Zamacona did not participate then in the Porfirista opposition to Lerdo and thus tarnished his title of an unalterable supporter.

Zamacona's three years of residence in Washington, on the

other hand, had prepared him admirably for the great task that was now entrusted to him. His figure and manner singled him out as a distinguished and cultured person. His English was not so perfect that it was comparable to that of a native speaker, but rather it continued to single him out as a foreigner; but not being capable of giving expression to his rhetorical temperament, it prevented him from reaching the excesses to which his own language would inevitably lead him.

Zamacona, very sure and satisfied with himself, trusted without any hesitation whatever in his talents and above all in his capacity for persuasion, to which he attributed powers of irresistible fascination. His temperament and his life, spent in the parliamentary and journalistic opposition, had made him grow before the magnitude and complexity of an adverse situation. His bitter experience as Secretary of Foreign Relations in 1861, under President Juárez, which was translated not only into public repudiation of his treaty with the English minister Sir Charles Wyke, but in the disgrace of having been helpless to prevent the Intervention, made him particularly alert and obstinate in his own diplomatic negotiations and pitilessly critical of those of others. And above everything else, his experience on the Joint Claims Commission had taught him the bottomless depths of the dishonesty with which the reverses of Mexico were taken advantage of; more valuable still, it persuaded him of the possibility of overcoming Mexico's worst enemies if one appealed to the good sense of United States public opinion and gained for the cause of Mexico those who could be interested in its economic fortune.

All this created in him a true mystique of how the relations of the two countries should be conducted, a philosophy which in addition fitted in perfectly with his ability and his oratorical propensity. According to him, Mexican diplomacy in the United States had been until then passive, intermittent and directed to combatting the symptoms of evil, but not evil itself; or, literally, "to settle amicably today a question of claims and tomorrow another of extradition." The only efficient method was to combat the "annexationist principle on its own ground, chaining it and rendering it impotent" within the United States itself.

In order to secure this, American public opinion must be "tempered" and the interest in Mexico among the wealthy classes awakened. Zamacona believed that in the United States there existed an enormous mass of sensible and conservative laboring classes and "a certain number" of honest souls to whom war was repugnant. Therefore he held that Mexican diplomacy should work its influence into laboring and religious circles and into commercial and financial media in order that, with such support won to its cause, the Mexican government could resist the United States government and the annexationist groups that were inspiring it. It was necessary, then, to abandon the "slow action" and resort to "simultaneous and extraordinary methods, capable of producing a strong impression"; capable, in fact, of "electrifying" United States public opinion. The task consisted in presenting Mexico's case in working men's clubs, in religious assemblies, in chambers of commerce or in industrial associations; in winning over the newspapers and even to publishing one of its own, however modest it might be; in refurbishing the Mexican legation in Washington to the extent of making it the most sumptuous, even endowing it with the powers of giving some "native curios" as gifts to persons to whom it owed favors.

Vallarta asked the Mexican Senate on October 17 the necessary authorization to use the services of Zamacona, then a member of that chamber, and ten days later he named him confidential agent to the United States, giving him the salary of a minister and 10,000 pesos for traveling expenses and moving expenses. On November 13, on leaving for the United States, Vallarta gave Zamacona precise instructions. Because of Mata's experience, Zamacona was not formally appointed minister, even though the Mexican government considered him as such and would not recognize any one else in that capacity. His principal mission was to search for the most satisfactory solution of the difficulties between the two countries and to enlighten United

States public opinion in respect to Mexico "and especially about the frontier." He should make it understood that the advantage of settling the differences as soon as possible was mutual, but without the United States trying to obtain unjust concessions, "that Mexico would not concede."

To Secretary of State William M. Evarts, Zamacona would say that he was informed of the negotiations begun by the Secretary of Foreign Relations with Foster, and "that he was authorized to discuss all of them," but without accepting unjust conditions, as were some of the proposals of the United States minister. He would have to report all of his conversations with Evarts, and the "possibilities of a settlement, the probabilities of reaching it and of the dangers that the American policy contained and the manner of avoiding them." Furthermore, he should explain to the United States people that the Mexican government would not accept "any humiliating condition" in order to be recognized, and that

. . . it has been appraising the intervention that the United States has tried to exercise in Mexican affairs, by constituting itself the judge of the legitimacy of the present government, as an act offensive to its sovereignty and independence, and even more hostile to Mexico in that that kind of intervention is not in conformity with the traditional policy of the United States.

He would have to insist on the protests made over the invasion of Mexican territory, and postpone the discussion of pending questions until recognition was secured. As for the extremely important point of the passage of troops, he would make known that Mexico had withdrawn its concessions of September 10, limiting them now to the pursuit of wild Indians in uninhabited regions of the country.

The Mexican press hailed with pleasure the designation of Zamacona, and Foster at once considered him as the most capable man of the Porfirista group, after his failure to be able to negotiate with Vallarta. The press was delighted when it was informed of his oblique acts, like the declaration in Washington that the question of recognition completely lacked importance, as was proved by the fact that neither of the two governments gave it very much attention. On the other hand, much effort was given to securing "some kind" of commercial relations, more necessary than "the mere formal negotiations for diplomatic relations." It was said that Zamacona made a much better diplomat by not acting like one, and that "his" system would produce better effects than if he were to beg recognition "for the love of God." And Zamacona's work was, in fact, quite effective, even though it unfortunately does not seem possible to follow it step by step.*

In spite of his diplomatic philosophy, adverse to merely official conduct, Zamacona made his first contacts with Secretary of State Evarts. And it appears that he judged that the impression he made on Evarts was responsible for Brigadier General Ord's change of conduct, which went from lukewarm reserve to outright cordiality; for Ord now showed him documents from his subordinates demonstrating the friendliness that they found among the officers of the Mexican army, and invited him to the Capitol to present him to the members of the committees that were investigating Mexican affairs. Zamacona reported also that only Ord dared in his conversation with him to suggest a basic reform in the treaty of extradition in order to make the trial and punishment of criminals efficient.

Zamacona also had conversations with Senator Stanley Mathews and Representative Henry B. Banning, who assured him that recognition ought not to be delayed. Ord's testimony had been very favorable, for it had characterized the Díaz government as the strongest that Mexico had had in many years. Even the reservations of Secretary Evarts should be attributed not so much to the basic problems as to his personal character, which

---

*Vallarta, in the instructions, asked Zamacona to write and send memoranda of each and every one of his conversations with Evarts. Zamacona may have obeyed these instructions partially, but the truth is that in the archives of the Secretary of Foreign Relations the memoranda do not seem to exist.

inclined him to give a special value and reiteration to his acts. Furthermore, Banning had invited Zamacona to appear before the United States Senate in order to report also on the problems of Mexico. He accepted with delight, and even though outwardly on the condition that he limit himself to reporting on economic and commercial affairs, he actually had in mind to end his testimony with the problem of "judging the efficacy or inefficacy of the policy of the American Executive in its relations with Mexico."

But Zamacona displayed his greatest activity and collected his best laurels in the public sphere by appearing at meetings of teachers or clergymen, or at dinners given by merchants, bankers and artists. A United States newspaper caught the impact of those appearances:

> If the position of Díaz in Mexico is as strong as Zamacona paints it, there is no doubt that Congress will soon recognize his government and take measures for an agreement, whether or not the Executive likes it.

Porfirio Díaz, nonetheless, did not entrust to Zamacona the entire task of winning United States public opinion, but made use "of everything that was suggested to him" in order to achieve it. General John B. Frisbie, looking in Mexico for mining and railroad concessions who was on very good terms with Díaz himself and also with Matías Romero, was converted into a propagandist for the Mexican government and a harsh critic of the United States Department of State. William Pritchard, perhaps the first explorer of oil deposits in Mexico, met Felix and Porfirio Díaz in Oaxaca, where he resided. Pritchard was a salaried employee of Díaz, under the direct orders of Vallarta. He would give public lectures in which he painted intelligently and pleasingly the great possibilities that Mexico offered to business, industrial, mining and railroad enterprises of the United States.

Pritchard was also a contact with writers of "some literary reputation," like Edward Lester, whom José María Mata had retained during his days in Washington. Lester, a fiery person with an unlimited imagination, was at least as confident as Zamacona in his persuasive capabilities. He wrote feverishly from his retreat in Spencertown, near New York City, a pamphlet that little by little was transforming itself into a colossal book, "written with a strength and vigor of mind that I did not suspect" having. The five thousand copies that were to be printed would reach all United States representatives, senators, merchants, bankers and industrialists. While he was finishing it, he managed to publish a very laudatory article on Porfirio Díaz in *The International Review*. He finally finished the book, and it was published and distributed without its impact being as effective as he had expected.* For his part, Pritchard obtained from United States representatives and senators reserved documents for his political campaign.

FOSTER was called upon by the United States Congress to report on his activities and the questions that were dividing the two nations. And in spite of the fact that it was obvious to all that his testimony was decisive, Vallarta maintained toward him an attitude of incredible frigidity. When Foster visited Vallarta on January 12, 1878, to announce to him his approaching trip to Washington and to ask if the Mexican government had anything new to propose to him, Vallarta told him that he had nothing to communicate to him. Foster made another trip three days later, repeated the question and received an identical answer. A third visit occurred, two days later; in it he announced that that night he would leave for Washington, so that that was the last opportunity to communicate something to him. Vallarta had nothing to tell him.

Foster's testimony was very elaborate and exceptionally intelligent. He began with the liberal revolution of Ayutla in 1854, the liberal victory and the progressive break-up of the triumphant party. Confining himself to the problem of recognition,

*Edward Lester, *The Mexican Republic, an Historical Study* (New York: The American News Co., 1878).

he admitted that Secretary of State Hamilton Fish had given him discretionary powers, but that he, Foster, had thought it unwise to be hasty. Nevertheless, in May, 1877, after the Mexican Chamber of Deputies had been installed, the electoral computation made, and Díaz declared constitutional President, Foster had suggested the necessity of reconsidering the question. After he received the dispatch of Undersecretary Frederick W. Seward which conditioned recognition on the settlement of pending questions, he dedicated his efforts in that direction, but with very little success. The Mexican government and people had rejected as dishonorable the purchase of recognition with prior agreements.

Foster thought that the official inefficiency in resolving the frontier problems was due not so much to ill will as to inherent defects in the system and political customs, as well as the physical characteristics of the terrain. The principal cause of it was that the revolutionary condition of the country made it dangerous for the central government to send too many military units too great a distance from the capital. On the other hand, the Mexican forces tended to desert in great numbers because of the difficulty that the government had in paying them promptly, and because of the area's proximity to the United States. The northern frontier, besides, had always been the favorite birthplace of rebel movements against the central government; because of that, all presidents took care not to give cause or pretext for the Northern states to rebel.

On the other hand, jealousy and distrust between the frontier populations of the United States and Mexico had existed for a long time. This prevented the Mexican federal government from making itself respected when dealing with crimes committed by Mexicans, as the local authorities usually sympathized with the criminals. Díaz had proof of this when he sent General Miguel Blanco to Matamoros as his representative; but when Servando Canales did not recognize Blanco's powers, Blanco could do nothing but abandon the place and return to Mexico City to report his mission as unsuccessful.

Díaz, furthermore, had to be extremely cautious in his relations with the United States, since his Lerdista enemies were taking advantage of the occasion to revive anti-American feelings in order to snatch away his popularity. Therefore whatever concession Díaz made was presented by the Lerdista press as a humiliation to the country. The order given Brigadier General Ord singularly excited those feelings and consequently made a settlement more difficult.

Foster, of course, passed through the galling pillory of questioning by the committee members. One asked him his opinion of Zamacona's thesis, and, forgetting that it had been Vallarta's, he answered that the principle was to maintain that recognition would remove all the obstacles to undertaking a fruitful settlement of the difficulties. Another asked him his personal opinion of recognition, and he responded that only the Secretary of State should be asked to answer that.

Both Foster and Evarts were called to report on February 16. The first question to Foster was if he thought the President of the United States was "now more sincere and vigilant" in preventing the organization in his territory of rebel groups enemies to Díaz. The reply was that "in general terms," it was so. And did Foster not fear that the irregularity of relations would prejudice trade between the two nations? This was undeniable, although the greatest obstacle was in the insecurity of capital and property in Mexico. Another thorny question was asked: Had President Hayes been impartial or had he favored one of the factions that were in the dispute for power in Mexico? The reply was that he had been so impartial, that through express instructions of the Department of State, Foster had informed the Mexican authorities that the United States did not want to intervene in the internal affairs of the country or even to judge if a government were revolutionary or constitutional.

But the committee returned to the principal point of whether Foster believed or not that the moment for recognizing Díaz had arrived. Foster answered that he supposed he had been brought to Washington to make reports, not give advice, whether to the legislative power or to the executive. He was serving the latter following a policy dictated by the Department of State. Nonetheless he ventured to say that lack of recognition was irritating the Mexican people without distinction of creed or faction; in Mexico it was thought also that to deny it was the first step of a whole preconceived plan to conquer the country. As for the rest, the decision of the Congress to make an inquiry into the common problems of the two countries created in Mexico the hope that at last justice would be done it; therefore if the Congressional Committee approved a recommendation to the executive branch of the government to give recognition, the hostility of the people and government of Mexico would grow to dangerous extremes if the executive should ignore it.

Evarts declared that there would be no antagonism between the two powers if the Congress succeeded in understanding the problem of Mexico as the executive understood it. The general principle was that of recognizing the government that firmly maintained itself in power; but in Mexico the rule was revolutionary action that overthrew the constituted government. He did not think, therefore, that a republic like the United States should encourage with a premature recognition the rapidity of those changes. In fact, through having delayed it, the United States had fortified the Díaz government and had created the hope that it would be longer lived. The delay had also made that government feel the magnitude of its obligations on the frontier. Precisely for that reason, Foster did not hesitate to say that the Díaz government had already manifested a clear disposition to fulfill them; and when the investigations of the Congress ended, the executive should decide "very promptly" if he was to concede recognition immediately with the hope that thus the pending questions would be settled, or if, on the contrary, he should demand their settlement before granting recognition.

The real problem that Mexico presented consisted in that

. . . with all the pride and self opinion that belongs to a strong civilized nation it has not the power to carry out towards us the obligations which such a condition imparts.

That difficulty could not be solved with the formalities of diplomatic negotiations. Therefore his conclusion:

There must somehow be brought about an impression in Mexico that we cannot receive as an excuse for bad neighborhood in fact, good intentions or the dignity and importance of the Mexican Republic.

The question was whether the Díaz government could master public opinion and temper the pride of the Mexican people. Since Evarts had returned to the Department of State, he had never contemplated the necessity or the possibility of war, unless the people of the United States should want it. But the people did not appear to want it, nor did he think that Mexico desired it.

Foster intervened then, and following the vein of collective psychology explored by his chief, affirmed that because the Mexican people had believed that the President of the United States was hostile to its government and to the country, Porfirio Díaz had been able to appease partisanship by appealing to the patriotic sentiment of remaining united in face of foreign danger; but

... when we once recognize them that basis is taken away and then, in my opinion, commences the disintegration of this administration and Díaz may find himself in a worse condition after recognition than he does now.

One member of the committee asked Evarts what conditions he would propose for conceding recognition if the Congress approved a resolution recommending it, meanwhile proposing a compromise to avoid a misunderstanding between the two powers. The legislature would admit that the executive had responded to its duty and to the difficulties of the problem. The committee would declare that, in its opinion, the Díaz government had sufficient stability to be recognized and that it was leaving the executive free to decide whether negotiations should precede or follow recognition.

The Mexican press became optimistic at the beginning of the investigation by the United States Congress. One capital daily observed "with great pleasure" that the United States press was speaking more considerately of Mexico and its government. Another, thinking early recognition to be assured, reasoned moderately that "better late than never." In this, of course, the Mexican dailies were only following those of the United States, which were nearer to the source of the stories and better informed. The New York *Herald* anticipated that Foster would on his return carry instructions from the Department of State in keeping with the results of the congressional investigation; and the Washington *Republican* gave details of meetings in the department, which not only Evarts and Foster attended but also Texas Representative Schleicher, chairman of the Committee on Mexican Affairs in the House of Representatives, a sign that even the most rabid opponents of Mexico were now searching for a compromise.

Nothing, however, awoke so much expectation as the import of Foster's testimony. It was said that, more than anything, he was recommending postponing recognition until the Mexican government should demonstrate its capacity to control the banditry on the frontier. At that point, some gave in to doubt; others, to indignation. A Catholic newspaper recently converted to Tuxtepecanism said

We have thought that minister to be a just man. Has he deceived us? Could it be that he belongs to the rabble of American public figures, who, casting all reason and right aside, wish to launch their country into the most censurable acts without heeding any law other than that of the power of the strongest?

The conclusion was, of course, that Mexico should not beg for recognition; it could very well get along without it. *La Libertad* had accused the Lerdista press of favoring the solution of war because once Mexico was conquered, the United States would deal with the Lerdo government, the only one that was considered legitimate. Now it suggested that Díaz, making use of "the right conceded him by international precedents," ought to refuse to receive Foster as minister of the United States; and if anyone was fearful of the consequences of such a measure, he should take the trouble to "leaf through any treatise on international law" to realize that "the results would not be as serious as might be imagined." On the other hand, other newspapers became partisans of the Indianapolis *Journal* of Foster's home state. That newspaper had asserted that the testimony of the latter had decided the question favorably, on his sustaining that the United States was not benefitting by postponing recognition. But someone said that the "loyalty of Foster is a little doubtful," and that the favorable complexion of his testimony was hardly "a strategem to keep him from finding spirits badly prepared on his return."

In the face of such opposing reactions, D. S. Richardson, chargé d'affaires for the United States during Foster's absence, communicated to his chiefs that the "nervousness" was visible on learning of the testimony. Furthermore, he transmitted a statement of Vallarta that his government did not share the opinion of some newspapers of the country that Foster was the only obstacle to the renewal of relations.

WHEN THE United States minister left Washington on his return trip to Mexico, he actually carried instructions from the Department of State to recognize the Díaz government. They were written in a considerate tone and admitted that the change of face was made by the government of the United States and not that of Mexico. They recalled that the Department of State had wanted to make certain that Díaz' government had popular support, had sufficient stability and was disposed to comply with the rules of international amity and with its contractual obligations.

Foster's reports revealed that the Díaz government was maintaining peace in the Republic of Mexico and that his authority was respected in it. The United States government recognized with satisfaction that the Mexican authorities had shown a greater desire to pacify the frontier and had exerted a more effective effort to achieve it. Furthermore, it had now made two prompt claims payments, thus giving another important proof of its wish to comply with its contractual obligations. Foster had reported, nevertheless, that the Díaz government did not feel free or comfortable enough to arrive at a satisfactory settlement of the pending difficulties, because of not being recognized:

> If this view of the situation be honestly entertained by General Díaz it is better for this Government to waive its own preference as to the fittest manner and the time of adjusting the difficulties.

By virtue of all these considerations, Foster was instructed to notify Vallarta that relations between the two countries would be entirely official, and to invite him to negotiate immediately permanent measures to preserve peace and order on the frontier and to better protect the lives and interests of United States citizens.

Foster returned to head the United States legation on April 8, and on the next day he visited Vallarta in order to inform him of the decision of the United States government and to leave with him a copy of Evarts' instructions on recognition and the note in which he communicated it.

The impatience, that "nervousness" as Richardson called it, had reached such a point in Porfirista circles that on April 10, twenty-four hours after having been officially notified of recognition, a newspaper spoke of Foster as "that dissembling enemy of the Republic," and said that the United States government was usually involved "in the blackest hypocrisy and duplicity and most aggressive intentions"; but the notes exchanged between Foster and Vallarta were published on April 11, and after that there was no room for doubt.

That of the former was excessively formal, lacking any note of cordiality and not even avoiding the declaration that the United States government was recognizing Mexico after "taking into consideration" the conduct of the latter, Vallarta must have noticed the difference in tone between it and Evarts' instructions, for in his reply he did not fail to emphasize that with recognition, justice had simply been done his government; nevertheless, he decided not to maintain in writing his original thesis that Mexico had the right to obtain it and that it could not be given as a premium for good conduct.

The Lerdista press, giving free rein to its dismay on seeing all hope for a quick return of its leader disappear, did not fail to say that recognition had been obtained

. . . after eighteen months of humiliation; after the shameful surrender of Mexicans; after the invitation made to prudent and discreet American officers to violate the territory of our country; after the offer to hold General Cortina in prison; after the secret promises relative to the Free Zone; after so many and so great debasements, that the Tuxtepecan usurpation has accumulated at the feet of the cabinet in the White House.

And *El Federalista* was also—as an enemy of the regime, and especially of Vallarta—the only one that said that "in all the diplomatic annals" not one single document similar to Foster's note could be found,

. . . because the sovereign rights of a country are derived from within and its recognition is not subject to the prior examination of the conduct of its government.

According to that newspaper, the Díaz government was possessed with an insane fever to obtain recognition of other countries, like France and Belgium, and, of course, "we are sure that it has made use of measures that will be made known later."

The Roman Catholic newspapers were those which expressed the most indignant dissidence, although crude in idea and expression. It seemed to them that Foster's language was so haughty and so condescending that Vallarta should have rejected a recognition that carried "the most audacious insult . . . of that nation of shopkeepers." The Mexican government did not need to demonstrate its good conduct in order to be recognized:

Is the government of that prostitute and degrading nation . . . permitted the bold insult of judging the conduct of the government of General Díaz?

That was the opinion of *Voz de México* insofar as the Foster note; while in regard to Evarts' instructions, it reported that they made "our blood boil in our veins." Those instructions seemed, in fact, so monstrous that their acceptance could only be explained by the fact that Vallarta was not a Mexican, for Mexican blood did not flow through his veins.

But the general reaction was one of approbation, even though disparate. At last, said one newspaper, Mexico and the United States can present themselves again before the Old Continent as two great republics that "united by bonds of friendship, go forward carrying the American continent along the path to a great future." Even for those who pretended to be cautious by sustaining that Mexico could get along without it, the recognition of the United States "forms an augury of a prosperous future for the nation of which we are sons."

XII
AND WHO WILL CARRY
THE CORPSE?

Formal recognition of the Mexican government by the United States was accorded after a year and a half of tension in the relations between the United States and Mexico that at times was as extreme as the danger of an armed conflict was real. That danger alone sufficed to explain why the feeling in Mexico was now generally one of relief; but it was still felt that only one step, though an important one, had been taken. The real problems—the causes of the delay in granting it and of the harshness of the dealings between the two countries—still remained.

La Libertad giddily minimized the magnitude of those problems and exaggerated the magic power of the Mexican government to resolve them:

... the eloquent facts have come to prove . . . [that] the recognition is without conditions: no passage of troops, no free zone, nor anything that would offend or wound the national honor. . . . Difficulties and claims will come. . . . And, well, let them come, for there is no nation that does not have them. But all humiliating, onerous, unpatriotic and exaggerated pretensions in the face of the inflexibility of the present government, its integrity, loyalty and patriotism, will be dashed to bits.

More representative was a Roman Catholic daily which sensibly declared that "a natural sadness comes over our heart," for, "what will come after the published notes?" Washington had clearly instructed Foster that once recognition had been made known, he should invite Vallarta to negotiate permanent measures to bring order to the frontier and to protect American lives and interests. To authorize the passage of foreign troops, beyond being a violation of the Mexican Constitution, would cost the country "much blood and long years of mourning," and to permit Americans to acquire real estate on the frontier would lead to colonization in the Mexican northern states that would end with a drama like that of Texas. *La Libertad* accentuated then its strong feelings against Lerdo, by saying that recognition meant that the United States would not now permit Lerdo partisans to arm themselves in its territory in order to revolt against Díaz, and to post a large army on the frontier would permit Díaz to have the laws of neutrality rigorously respected.

The credulity of *La Libertad* was revealed by the facts that John W. Foster did not allow even a week to pass before renewing his conversations with Ignacio L. Vallarta, and that the tone of the first of them was so demanding. Furthermore, Foster had such complete faith in the strength of his position that he had offered to communicate telegraphically the success of his efforts, besides predicting that Vallarta "would cede in everything," upon which United States Secretary of State William M. Evarts' frontier policy would have been fully triumphant.

Part of Foster's assurance, nevertheless, proceeded from a disposition to make adjustments, a disposition which Vallarta seemed to lack. The latter, in fact, again defended an old thesis of his, the one which had inspired the treaty presented by José María Mata in Washington: to reform the internal laws of the two countries and the treaty of extradition in order to facilitate the prosecution and the punishment of criminals; for example, penal legislation to bring the crime of rustling under federal jurisdiction, and an extradition treaty to make obligatory the extradition of co-nationals accused of that crime.

Foster, of course, besides considering impossible the solving of the constitutional problems that would be created in the United States by the modifications of internal legislation proposed by Vallarta, also obstinately persisted in his old thesis that nothing would work but the passing of troops over the border, a measure which he still considered capital and urgent. Nevertheless, he was now ready to come to an agreement which was not exactly an international treaty but a military-technical accord between the two supreme commanders of the frontier forces. Moreover he was ready to accept what Vallarta had offered him some time before, namely, to limit the passage of troops to the pursuit of wild Indians in unpopulated areas.

Vallarta, disarmed by this change of face, asked for time to consult with Díaz; and when he had done so, he subordinated the consideration of the new offer to receiving first satisfaction for the invasions of Mexican territory. Foster, for his part, defended himself by replying that since that subject was being dealt with directly by the Department of State and the Mexican legation in Washington, they should let them take care of it there; but agreement on reciprocal passage was a serious and urgent matter, and Vallarta ought to worry himself more with preventing future evils than finding consolation in past ones.

Vallarta then announced the possibility of yielding: President Díaz would ask the Mexican Senate for authorization for reciprocal passage across the border if the United States would give beforehand reparations for past invasions and revoke the unfortunate order of June 1. He was so confident of his new proposition that he pressed Foster to telegraph it to his government. The latter began by making a rotund declaration that

. . . we have no apologies to make, and that the instructions to Ord will stand until the Mexican government by its own action makes them unnecessary,

but he ended by asking what satisfaction Mexico desired, and by arguing that the invasions had occurred under such diverse conditions that "the same principle cannot be applied to all of them." Vallarta, in turn, replied by declaring that Mexico desired exactly the same satisfaction as the United States had asked and that Mexico had given when its own troops had invaded United States territory in pursuit of some revolutionary Lerdistas; but it was agreeable to him to treat this problem of the past without great urgency, though he was not inclined to yield on the forthcoming one, that of the withdrawal of the instructions to Brigadier General Edward O. C. Ord. Porfirio Díaz, nevertheless, insisted on both conditions. Foster then offered in one of his notes to try to fulfill them, although he asked that the note be returned to him if it did not win the approval of both Vallarta and Díaz.

Foster presented first a draft of a note, which was returned to him as insufficient, and then a second one that Vallarta returned to him because he was leaving the post of Secretary of Foreign Relations in order to return to the presidency of the Supreme Court. In them Foster expressed doubt that Lieutenant Colonel W. R. Shafter and Lieutenant John L. Bullis had entered Mexican territory in disobedience of higher orders; they had done it in pursuit of some bandits, and without causing any damage. In any case, the conditions peculiar to the frontier caused the invasions and they in no way had the purpose of offending Mexico. The United States government had always wanted to conclude a treaty for the reciprocal crossing of troops, which would make measures such as the instructions that it gave Ord unnecessary.

VALLARTA as well as Díaz must have admitted at that stage the impossibility of resisting indefinitely an agreement on the famous reciprocal passage of troops. In the first place was the perseverance with which the United States had sustained and continued to sustain its thesis that without this point all other measures for pacifying the frontier were useless. A position so irrevocable had only the exception of the adverse opinion of General W. T. Sherman, which was not important, for if Foster, with very recent instructions and after the conclusion of the congressional investigation in which that opinion was expressed, insisted on it, it was clear that his government was continuing to hold to the old demand.

Then one by one Mexico's dilatory resources to agree to passage were being exhausted. First it had said that the old rancorous feelings among the frontiersmen made passage dangerous. From there it had agreed to allowing reciprocal passage at times and places to be fixed by the Presidents of the two countries. Then followed the invasions into Mexican territory, and at that time it was argued that the popular indignation produced by them had renewed the danger of its execution, and it was proposed to limit crossings only to uninhabited regions and in the pursuit of wild Indians. Afterwards, Mexico argued that all negotiations be postponed until recognition had been granted, in order to avoid the appearance of this having been unworthily purchased. And now Vallarta, in the face of the renewed insistence of the United States minister, announced that the Senate would be asked for approval of reciprocal passage, but conditioning it on satisfaction for the invasions and the withdrawal of the order of June 1. The fact that Foster, far from rejecting the idea of giving satisfaction, set out to search for a means of giving it, demonstrated that the United States would be able to grant one of the two conditions asked, and that perhaps it would grant the other. In that case, it would be absolutely unavoidable to arrive at an agreement on the passage of troops.

On the other hand, the realistic consideration that United States troops were crossing the frontier anyway and that the Department of State was not even answering Mexican protests against those acts could not fail to enter into the appraisal of the position of the Mexican government. A formal agreement between the two countries might control the invasions and, when they went contrary to the agreement, make protests from either country viable. Nor could it overlook the consideration that the banditry on the frontier was as damaging to Mexico as to the United States, and that consequently, its extinction was a work of mutual benefit.

But all this did not touch, nor could it touch, the great political problem and responsibility of who was to take on the obvious unpopularity of the measure. Sharply and brutally Evarts had said in his declaration before the United States Congress that the great problem of the renewal of relations resided in whether Porfirio Díaz was capable of mastering the public opinion of Mexico and moderating the passions of his countrymen. And Porfirio Díaz, still uneasy in power, facing the possibility that Lerdo would gain as much popularity as he would lose, felt the slow, dangerous and inevitable process of losing supporters and having substituted for them indifferent ones and even adversaries. In the face of the facts that he could not be re-elected and that there was in sight an early electoral battle whose result would inevitably be a serious loss of his political support—under those conditions of insecurity and confusion—Díaz did everything in his power to disentangle his name from the unpopular measure of authorizing the passage of United States troops into Mexico.

On May 15, 1878, the President himself and his secretaries, Trinidad García, of Government; Protasio Tagle, of Justice; Vicente Riva Palacio, of Public Works; Matías Romero, of the Treasury; and Manuel González, of War, met in the National Palace. There was no Secretary of Foreign Relations, but Ignacio L. Vallarta, at that time president of the Supreme Court, attended, because of having conducted the negotiations. Vallarta pointed out the need of asking the Senate immediately for the authorization, in conformity with paragraph III, letter B, part 3a of Article 72 of the Mexican Constitution as amended in 1874, according to which it was exclusive power of that chamber to authorize the Executive to permit Mexican troops to leave the country, the passage of foreign troops over Mexican territory and the stationing of squadrons from other countries in the waters of the Republic. The urgency of submitting the proposal to Congress for action stemmed from the state of the negotiations with Foster and from the fact that the Senate would close its session on the last day of May and would not meet again until September. During that recess, Vallarta feared, "incidents might occur" that would make the settlement of pending questions still more difficult.

The executive's proposal of the law, in essence, explained that the problem of the depredations of the wild Indians was a very

old one; the unquestionable fact that they committed their misdeeds on the territory of one country and fled to the other to
gain impunity made it necessary to fight them on both sides of
the Rio Grande. Then, the frontier states suffered many damages
from these depredations, and in fact the local governments as
well as the federal one had been trying for a long time diverse
measures for combating them. Finally, the reciprocal character
of the passage and the "solemn protestations" of willingness to
adjust its differences with Mexico now made a decorous settlement with the United States admissible. In addition, the authorization asked for was to be limited to the pursuit of wild Indians
in uninhabited regions, and the agreement would contain protective dispositions, such as the punishment of the abuses of
troops on foreign soil as if they were committed on their own.

Matías Romero made some observations of form that were
promptly accepted; Protasio Tagle and Trinidad García gave
explicit support; and the proposal was unanimously approved.
Porfirio Díaz then expressed the opinion that the subject was
very serious; therefore he thought that the proposal would be
better received in the Senate if it were signed by Vallarta, "placing on it a date at which he was still the Secretary of Foreign
Relations." Vallarta feared exposing himself to a "serious
charge," since he had been out of the department since May 2.
Besides, the aide-mémoire of his conversations with Foster were
already closed and in the archives of the department; so

it was not possible to antedate the proposal without committing a
notorious falsehood, a falsehood even less excusable insofar as Foster
knew very well that the communication could not be referred either
to the last days of April or the first of May.

On this, of course, Vallarta was right, for Foster could not have
failed to report to his government such an important act as his
departure from the Department of Foreign Relations and the
consequent suspension of his activities in that area.

Matías Romero, in support of the presidential idea, sustained
that not only in Europe but in Mexico as well it was usual for

the Secretaries of State to sign documents relative to their activities even after resigning from their positions. Trinidad García, Protasio Tagle, and Manuel González supported Díaz and Romero, but Vallarta insisted on his refusal, explaining that it was not dictated by his desire to shun a responsibility, for he was offering to persuade verbally some senators in order to achieve the approval of the proposal. Porfirio Díaz then ordered the writing of a detailed report of the meeting of the group and that all present sign it in testimony of what each one had said.

The Senate approved the law. It authorized the executive to allow Mexican federal troops to leave the national soil, and the federal troops of the United States to enter when pursuing wild Indians in uninhabited regions. The Presidents of the two countries should determine by common consent which those regions were. It was established that the pursuing forces should retire immediately to their country of origin when they had subdued the pursued, when they had lost the trail or when they met with forces of the country on whose soil they were making the pursuit which were ready to carry it on. It was determined that the abuses committed by the forces of a country in the territory of the other would be punished by the former and according to its own laws. The authorization was valid during the full term of Díaz' Presidency, and the only thing asked of him was that, the arrangements once made, he should send the official documentation to the Senate.

There is no room for doubt that Porfirio Díaz felt strongly that his personal sentiments and his political well-being had to lead him spontaneously and logically to a bellicose attitude toward the United States. At the same time he must have been very conscious of the personal and national risks that such an attitude represented. A draft of a declaration that Matías Romero prepared for him on his learning of the order to Brigadier General Ord which was not published, gives a very clear idea of his personal feelings. With moving desperation he asserted that his had done more to satisfy the demands of the United States than any other Mexican government. He was disposed to permit the crossing of the international boundary for the pursuit and punishment of wild Indians. He was maintaining on the border, at countless sacrifices, five thousand men under the command of Jerónimo Treviño; and the success achieved by them directly and indirectly by cooperating with United States forces was very well known. He agreed to turn over Mexican criminals although the extradition treaty excused him from doing that. The country was living in peace and the property and the work of nationals and foreigners were protected. He had paid the first claims installment promptly.

In spite of all this, the United States, in addition to denying him recognition, ordered its army to invade Mexican soil. What could he do under those circumstances? The bitter tone of the relations were displeasing and preoccupying him. He rejected a break and, even more, war. And, for the reasons expressed, things seemed to impose this path:

... I feel obliged to demonstrate that I have the firm decision, difficult as it may be to me, of not consenting to wound the honor of the nation . . . by armed forces of any foreign nation, high as the stakes may be that I have in them, personally and officially, and however great may be my desire not to alter in any way the good relations. . . . The head of a nation that has shed so much blood to defend its honor and its independence, cannot do otherwise in complying with his highest duties.

Even in September, 1878, five months after being recognized, Díaz felt that conflict between his personal feeling and his public prestige and the hard necessity of finding a solution to the American problems. In his presidential message of September 16 he insisted that Mexico should not be held responsible alone for the frontier banditry and in its good disposition reach an agreement with the neighboring nation. Desperate, nevertheless, he languished at last, when he expressed the weak hope that "the feeling of equity of the American people" and the "justification" of its authorities would end by finding him to be right.

In a private document of the same period he expressed his

perplexity at the behavior of the United States, which had come to make itself incomprehensible to him. General John B. Frisbie had come to Mexico in search of rich concessions, and on the eve of returning he had asked Díaz four questions in writing in order that he might use the answers in a great campaigr in favor of Mexico and its government which he proposed to make in the United States. Porfirio Díaz recited again all that he had done to come to an understanding with the United States government, dramatically stating in his exposition that in spite of great delay in the payment of civil employees, he had not failed to give to Treviño resources to maintain his forces active.

Also he declared his disposition to intern in the southeast of the country all wild Indians apprehended in the campaign of the North and to propose the reform of the treaty of extradition and to agree to marking off a strip of land on each side of the Rio Grande so that all crimes committed within it could be judged in the federal courts of the offended country "without regard to the nationality of the accused." Likewise, he expressed his intention to encourage United States immigration and investment. Frisbie's absurd idea of creating a "mixed committee of distinguished citizens of both countries to meet in Mexico to consider, advise or determine a line of action regarding the political, industrial or commercial problems that might affect both countries" came to seem acceptable to him. All of this was one more reason for revoking the order of June 1 before agreeing on the reciprocal passage of troops.

PORFIRIO DÍAZ was not the only character of this drama who felt his political and historic responsibility in the presence of the problem of consenting to the passage of foreign troops over the international boundary. Upon the granting of recognition, Manuel María de Zamacona accepted promotion from the position of confidential agent to that of Mexican minister plenipotentiary in Washington. Thus on April 9, 1878, his nomination was extended to him, and on May 13 he presented his credentials to President Rutherford B. Hayes; but on June 14, by telegraph, he asked the Secretary of Foreign Relations to present his resignation to General Díaz, alleging the ravages that the climate of Washington was making on his health. That must not have seemed a very compelling reason; the almost natural reply was that the state of relations with the United States made his immediate resignation hardly advisable. Zamacona acceded for a moment, for learning that another invasion had taken place and that the interventionist clamor was being newly agitated, he wrote that he would look out for the interests of Mexico as long as "a breath of life remained to him" and even if he had to have himself carried "on stretchers" to the Department of State.

But soon he repeated his resignation in a long and expressive communication. He had given in support of it the impairment of his health; for, in fact, the "gigantic" activity that a good minister of Mexico ought to display in the United States frightened him; but now he openly adduced the true motive: his disagreement with the central idea of the negotiations between the Mexican Department of Foreign Relations and Foster; or rather that of authorizing the passage of United States troops into Mexican territory. Zamacona opined that that passage would create "a new order of delicate questions more easily converted into a *casus belli* than resistence to such a pretension," and that those invasions of the United States army made without authorization indicated what they would be in any case, so that

. . . on the least expected day the imprudent declaration of 1846 that war existed because of acts of Mexico would be heard here.

It was true that now the authorization was being conditioned on receiving excuses and reparations for the invasions made up until then, and on the revocation of the order of June 1; but it was also true that authorization of the Mexican Senate had already been asked, and that the text itself of the proposal of the executive was objectionable. For Zamacona, experience demonstrated that condescension brought bad results. Having done so delayed recognition, when in fact the latter was obtained "in some few months" when Mexico altered its course by resisting the "irregular" demands of Foster. He noted, finally, the coherence of his attitude, for when Vallarta proposed to name him as confidential agent, he had refused, saying that he would not be able to follow—much less oppose—in Washington a policy with which he was in disagreement; and he accepted the appointment only when he was told that President Díaz required his services even with that reservation.

The political problem that Zamacona posed was not insignificant, either for José María Mata, then Secretary of Foreign Relations, or for Díaz, finally responsible for the conduct of all the agents of the executive power. Therefore Mata, without finding precedents for it in the department, began by communicating Zamacona's version to Vallarta and asking Vallarta his. Vallarta recognized as true Zamacona's nonconformity with the propositions made by Foster in the memorandum of September 10 and his consequent declining of the nomination. However, while Zamacona and Vallarta had been discussing Mata's appointment, the invasions of Mexican territory had occurred, and also the reconsideration by President Díaz and his cabinet of the propositions of September; and the accord limiting invasions to the pursuit of wild Indians in uninhabited zones was reached. Then Zamacona, satisfied, had stated that now he would not be embarrassed to accept the position offered. The instructions that he had been given and the correspondence exchanged with him was proof of all this.

Mata answered Zamacona's new resignation on August 25. President Díaz reported himself surprised at the reason given for it, for that was the first notice of Zamacona's discontent with his own policies. In fact, not only was Díaz unaware of it, but he believed in a complete identity of opinions between him and Zamacona and in the resolute disposition of his minister in Washington to accept the policy of his government as a guide for his actions. Zamacona knew of Díaz' willingness to agree on the reciprocal passage of troops in uninhabited regions in the pursuit of wild Indians, for in his instructions an express reference was made to it in addition to telling Zamacona that he could declare to the United States authorities that he was acquainted with the negotiations with Foster and that he, Zamacona, could continue them in Washington if it was thus agreeable to the United States government.

It was true, as Zamacona alleged, that those instructions had been given to him on the day of his departure, but it was clear that when the nomination of minister was offered to him he had had "an ample opportunity" to manifest his opinions fully. In several of his dispatches, which Mata cited literally, Zamacona had spoken of the passage of troops, expressing his conformity with it and with the specific measures for executing it. Mata was building up all this evidence not to reproach Zamacona but in order to prove that President Díaz was not trying to keep him in a strained position and against his will. In short, Zamacona's resignation was accepted and his letters of retirement were sent to him on August 25.

Five days after having written this note, however, José María Mata seems to have resigned from the Department of Foreign Relations, for the newspapers reported the news of such a fact, although it was not known officially until September 19, at which time the text of the resignation and its acceptance were made public. No one explained Mata's departure satisfactorily, for even though the official reason given was that of bad health, it was supposed that, as the head of the cabinet, he had not succeeded in bringing it to a minimum of uniformity or cohesion. Everybody agreed, nonetheless, in the necessity of replacing him immediately with someone of the importance of Joaquín Ruíz or of Francisco Gómez del Palacio, and in not leaving the office of Secretary of Foreign Relations in the hands of a chief clerk lacking the prestige necessary to continue, much less conclude successfully, negotiations with the United States. That was, nevertheless, what happened. On September 15, before giving formal notice of his taking possession, Eleuterio Ávila, named to the office of chief clerk of the Department of Foreign Relations, telegraphed Zamacona telling him of having proved to

President Díaz the great importance of Zamacona's remaining in Washington, and, as Díaz thought the same, "he charged me to beg you not to leave your position now." Besides, Ávila asked Zamacona to answer by telegraph "if he would make this sacrifice for the country and friendship," and Zamacona agreed to it.

But Zamacona had previously received Mata's note accepting his resignation, and he had already answered it, lamenting above all that his correspondence with the department should end with considerations of a personal nature, to which he felt obliged to respond. Vallarta had given the department a report that did not correspond with the facts, whose true nature and sequence were otherwise. It "was nearly a year" since Vallarta had offered him the post of confidential agent, and at the moment, his only argument for turning it down was that he had also declined that of minister in South America. But, in the face of Vallarta's insistence, he ended up by explaining to him the real reason for his negative reply: he disapproved of the authorization of the reciprocal passage of troops and did not want to take part in negotiations that would lead to giving it. All this was going on long before the cabinet had agreed to withdraw the propositions of September 10.

Zamacona did not say in this note anything different from his first one; but he recounted something new afterwards. When the Mexican Senate asked Vallarta for reports about Mata's nomination and mission, he showed to the committee named for that purpose by the Senate the instructions given to Mata. The Senate committee rendered an opinion saying that, after having seen that and other documents, it was satisfied that neither the Department nor Mata had any desire to make undue concessions to the United States; but Zamacona, then a senator, was, as confidential agent, up to date with the negotiations with Foster and consequently knew of the consent of the government to authorize the passage of United States troops. He found himself in a dreadful conflict which he resolved by getting the Senate bill to confine itself only to the documents really seen by the committee. Furthermore, his disagreement on this point had been continuous and manifest, for always he counseled the department to proceed thus:

My humble suggestions, more or less direct, had always been in the sense that once the opinion of this country was suitably tempered, demands on our honor and our security could be resisted without danger.

Seeing now the robust fruits of his labor of ten months, the bitterness provoked by the acceptance of his resignation was abating:

. . . they prove that the Mexican legation has succeeded in forging the only rein that is able to keep at bay greediness and conspiring ambitions in this country against our nationality. . . . I believe I have gone even a little beyond what my position strictly requires and, above all, much more so than that done here by any of my predecessors.

Ávila answered Zamacona's note by first telling him that he had read all of it to President Díaz and had received instructions to answer him "in the following terms." His having said that the Department of Foreign Relations was ignorant of the repugnance of the Mexican government to authorize the passage of the United States troops and of the reasons for that repugnance should not be considered as a reproach. On the one hand were the "positive" interests of the Mexican frontier states of the "West"; on the other, an inevitable necessity: to agree on it was preferable to the "entirely arbitrary" passage of those troops, and much more preferable than war. The government was as far from reproaching Zamacona for his lack of understanding as without doubt Zamacona was in blaming the government for its disposition to agree to that step. The end of Ávila's note revealed the true motives of the apparently contradictory attitudes of first accepting the resignation and afterwards "begging" the withdrawal of it:

The President of the Republic is sure that you never have placed in doubt his patriotic feelings, and understands that you have and

always will do him the justice of not believing him capable of compromising the independence of the nation nor the integrity of its
territory in any way.

Zamacona was forced to admit then that his disagreement was
only in the means, not in the end:

. . . whatever were the differences between the views of that Department and my personal opinion over the passage of troops, I was sure
that it did not refer to the final objective, which for the government as
for me and all Mexicans, could not be other than to guard our Republic from the dangers that the actual state of relations with the
United States presents.

Porfirio Díaz must have been profoundly uneasy on seeing that
Zamacona, a famous, battling, indiscreet man and, especially,
very possibly a presidential candidate, should hold his head high
as a champion of resistance to the United States and flaming
critic of the passage of United States troops over the boundary.
His attitude, besides being threatening for purely personal reasons, was the more so because it represented an unquestionable
national reaction. When the public learned of the authorization
by the Senate, the heated comments were a clear index to the
currents and the climate of public opinion. The authorization
was called "criminal," contrary to the Constitution, because it
contemplated only passage *through* the national territory, indicating clearly that it was dealing with transit of foreign forces
to a destination different from their starting point. Also it was
said that to give it was equivalent to raising the famous order of
June 1 "to an international treaty," and that it was impossible
to imagine that a single Mexican would approve handing the
country over "to the mercy of our enemies of the North." The
authorization was the height of "scandal, of effrontery and of
shamelessness." For all of it

. . . the people should rise up in mass to stone the traffickers in the
national honor.

Whatever arrangement that might be injurious to the national dignity "shall be unanimously rejected by all the country" was said repeatedly.

THE SIX MONTHS following recognition, besides, were a real trial for the prestige and even the stability of the Díaz regime. In June and July elections were held to renew the Chamber of Deputies and to elect four magistrates of the Supreme Court. The group supporting Justo Benítez, the most organized and ambitious, considered the elections a firm step toward the presidential campaign of 1880, so that they displayed an activity which was exaggerated by their enemies. There was talk that thanks to the pressure on the Supreme Court constantly maintained by Protasio Tagle, Secretary of Justice, and to the election of the new magistrates, Justo Benítez would have a majority on it, and that he had "made a clean sweep" in the election of the Chamber of Deputies. If that was so, it was concluded, Porfirio Díaz would be a king of fools, but not the President of the Republic. On the eve of the installation of the Ninth Congress a small group of conspirators determined to counteract the political hegemony of Benítez was organized; but, in reality Benítez' candidacy to the Presidency was about to be proclaimed at a great public banquet.

To such an uncertain political situation were added rebel outbreaks in different regions of the country, symptoms of an unrest that seemed to give foundation to the prediction of the most discontented: "One rebellion scarcely put down, another will come and afterwards another, until Díaz falls to earth." The most significant of all was that of General Mariano Escobedo, who entered Mexican territory from the United States at the beginning of June. It was because of the great renown of this leader, for his known ties with Sebastián Lerdo de Tejada, and because accompanying him were men of military prestige; but it must have seemed more significant to Porfirio Díaz because the military authorities of the United States, who made another revolutionary attempt of Escobedo fail when his regime was not yet recognized, proved incapable now when relations were normal of preventing Escobedo from leaving United States territory with his revolutionary forces.

The United States press itself drew that conclusion. It reported that the movement had been organized "within sight" of Brigadier General Edward O. C. Ord's general headquarters, and that the arms and ammunitions passed through San Antonio en route to their destination on the Mexican border without any obstacle whatever. And Díaz knew, of course, that Vallarta had been asking Foster since April to transmit to his government the information that Mexico had of the revolutionary preparations that the Lerdistas were making in Texas. Nor could the fact escape him that the United States Secretary of War declared that he was aware of those preparations only after they had already evolved into Escobedo's revolution.

At times it was not rebel movements but spectacular disagreements that created the impression of poor cohesion in the Porfirista group. When Miguel Negrete, military commander of Mexico City, learned that General Ignacio Mejía, former Secretary of War under Juárez and Lerdo, had returned from his exile with the authorization of President Díaz, he had his resignation of the command and his request for retirement from the army published in all the newspapers.

The new invasions by United States troops, and even the circumstances under which they occurred, must have seemed more impressive to the Díaz government; and more yet the disconcerting reaction of the United States authorities toward them. On June 17 a more than respectable force of 1500 men of the three armed forces under the command of Colonel Richard S. McKenzie invaded the state of Coahuila to recover cattle stolen in Texas and which was supposedly hidden on El Remolino ranch. It was said that another 2000 men were concentrated near the place where McKenzie crossed in order to give aid in case he was attacked by Mexican forces. On July 24, Captain J. M. Kelley, at the head of 100 men, besieged Villa Jiménez for seven hours, also in order to recover stolen stock. The mayor of the Villa, requested to return the stock, accompanied the United

States troops to identify it, a fact that called forth a very attentive note from Foster to Mata thanking him for that cooperation and commenting that "it is only to be regretted" that a spirit of helpfulness "in favor of law and order on the frontier" did not exist among all the Mexican authorities. In spite of the fact that Mata immediately instructed Zamacona to protest the McKenzie invasion, the Department of State scarcely acknowledged receipt of his note "respecting certain acts that the government of Mexico supposes having been committed" by that military chief. And Eleuterio Ávila, on answering Foster's note of thanks, said, with less firmness than he thought, that the conduct of the mayor "shall receive the most severe and explicit reproof" from the Mexican government.

The Mexican as well as the United States press presented those acts thus. The Mexican press wrote that the McKenzie invasion "indicates a considered plan, a scheme whose purpose we do not even wish to calculate, but that undoubtedly has by design the most pronounced hostility"; and the United States press said that no precedent existed in the history of the United States of a formal authorization to invade the territory of a country with which official friendly relations were being maintained.

A situation of this nature lent itself marvelously to exaggeration, fear and threat. Representative Gustav Schleicher of Texas announced that the government of his country had resolved to occupy militarily the Mexican border states, or to buy them, as the only means of protecting United States interests. Also it was said that the United States Secretary of War, far from thinking of revoking the instructions to Ord, had elaborated them, ordering still more active pursuit of malefactors when they flee to Mexican territory. They were not to seek conflicts with the Mexican forces, neither should they flee from them if the pursuit should be opposed, and they were not to consider as an act of war anything that might occur on the frontier as a consequence of these new instructions, unless the Mexican troops crossed the river in reprisal. The only thing that was lacking was what one person asserted having heard from the lips of Secretary of State

William M. Evarts, that is, the necessity of taking advantage of the recess of the United States Congress to "precipitate events" by carrying them to such a point that on reconvening it could do nothing but approve of them.

XIII
FOR MY RACE MARS
WILL SPEAK

Not receiving a reply to his formal proposition of signing an agreement for the reciprocal passage of troops over the boundary as soon as the instructions to Brigadier General Edward O. C. Ord of June 1 were withdrawn—a circumstance that preoccupied José María Mata to the point of impatience—had an explanation of which Mata, of course, was unaware. It was a fact that the depredations of wild Indians and cattle thieves were continuing in the territory of the United States as well as in that of Mexico, in spite of the fact that the United States troops were more numerous, and the officers who commanded them should have been more experienced; in addition they had discretional powers to pursue malefactors into Mexican territory which they had been using often enough to expect some tangible results. Another factor should have contributed to improving the situation; but, apparently, it exercised insufficient influence also. It was the increased number and activity of the Mexican forces.

In effect, this fact perhaps more than any other came to concern the United States Secretary of War and the officers who were directly commanding the United States forces, for they all thought that, although little could be expected from cooperation with the Mexican forces, the danger of coming to blows with them was perceptibly increased. Ignacio Mariscal, from his voluntary exile in New York, came to credit the final change in the attitude of the United States government to that fear. In any case, Ord admitted that the 12,000 troops whose concentration on the frontier he estimated for September, 1878 formed a considerable force. Furthermore, he was impressed by the fact that Treviño was now being given a quarter of a million pesos to move them, by the announcement that a general of greater reputation, perhaps Ignacio R. Alatorre, was on the way at the head of new reinforcements assembled in the interior, and by the fact that to crown these preparations, Porfirio Díaz was going to ask the Mexican Congress permission to take command of all of them himself.

Colonel Richard S. McKenzie, who, together with Lieutenant Colonel W. R. Shafter, had the greatest experience in the invasions into Mexican territory, now believed the instructions that he had to be insufficient. Neither he nor his men had confidence in them "when the risk of collision with the regular troops of Mexico is so imminent." That lack of confidence must have been great, for in order to put an end to it, McKenzie made the unusual request that President Rutherford B. Hayes himself give the new instructions. And General Philip H. Sheridan, on transmitting the request to his superior, approved it also as a necessity to give "confidence in the face of the danger of conflict with Mexican troops." Furthermore, he added that because of the lack of new instructions "no permanent good has so far attended the pursuit of Indians and thieves into Mexico."

Secretary of War George W. McCrary then thought it necessary to consult with Secretary of State William M. Evarts and to ask the three principal actors of the drama, Generals W. T. Sherman and Philip H. Sheridan and Brigadier General Ord, for a "careful and formal" report on the border frictions. General Sherman, more of an executive, asked that the examination of possible solutions be limited to four questions which he presented: Would the proclamation of martial law in the Texas counties bordering Mexico help to discover and to punish the accomplices of the bandits, or to make their confederates fearful enough so that they would not aid outlaws or would aid them less? What effect would the violent and sudden military occupation produce on the Mexican border towns to the south and west of the Rio Grande? If in reprisal Mexican stock should be taken, by force and at random, in equal number of heads of cattle to that stolen in the United States, would it be possible to awaken in the honest people of Mexico the desire to cooperate in the extermination of the cattle thieves? What would be the effect of recalling the United States minister if the government of Mexico did not pay immediately a compensation for prior damages?

It seemed difficult for the answers to result satisfactorily sure and pertinent. They could not be based on facts; for, in effect, they signified an appreciation of possible consequences of problems whose solution, moreover, could not be conditioned on a single factor. And if this was not enough, the evaluation was going to be made outside the technical-military field, the only one in which it was supposed that the ones being questioned had any personal background and experience.

Brigadier General Ord, in fact, paid no attention to the questions and went directly to proposing some measures in whose efficacy he trusted. First, a conciliatory policy toward the "renegade" Indians should be attempted, by inviting them to return to the United States and offering them amnesty for their past crimes and lands to work and to live on peacefully at the side of their brothers and under official protection. Also the Mexican government should be persuaded that it was so costly to maintain forces for a prolonged, difficult and uncertain campaign that it would be wise to allow the free passage of the United States army. If it failed, the United States government should announce that its troops were crossing the international boundary without any reflection whatever and "armed groups of Mexicans" that in any form molested their operations would be attacked as accomplices. As for the problem of rustling, Ord favored limiting the reprisals in kind to whoever bought stolen cattle.

General Sheridan answered the questions one by one; but first he thought it necessary to paint what he considered the social background indispensable to an understanding of the frontier problems. The Mexican population on the frontier was a mixture of Indian and Spanish, and even though it had the manners of the latter, by nature it was Indian. The rural population that represented nine-tenths of the total was even more so. This explained their ignorance of government and of law, and even the lack of consideration toward and the rebellion against them. The same condition also explained why the three hundred families of Lipan, Kickapoo and Comanche Indians living in Mexican territory should be so well understood by that population and also why they should receive protection from it. To that it should be added that the great majority of the inhabitants of the Texas counties bordering the Rio Grande were of Mexican blood and were United States citizens only in the legal fiction of nationality. Therefore the bandits from Mexico found friendship and aid among them, to the degree that United States forces never received reports on their movements. That feeling of solidarity among the Mexican populations on both sides of the frontier made of Texas a propitious place to organize rebellions against the local and federal authorities in Mexico, the consequence being repeated that the United States authorities failed to prevent them.

General Sheridan, therefore, judged that martial law would help to dissolve the revolutionary groups adverse to Díaz and to make aiding the Indians and cattle thieves riskier, and some would hesitate to continue doing it. The effect of the measure, however, would be limited to those two rather modest advantages. The violent and sudden occupation of Mexican cities on the south of the Rio Grande certainly would end the depredations, but it would oblige the Mexican government to oppose it and to formally declare war on the United States, "for otherwise it would be overthrown by its own Mexican people." The reprisals would provoke a situation of anarchy and confusion, for, on such a long and unpopulated frontier, groups without any authority whatever would end by carrying them out. And this was without taking into account that such a measure was unworthy of a great country and that its final influence would be limited, because in Mexico few honest people existed. More doubtful still would be the result of recalling the United States minister from Mexico. The cause of the evils along the frontier was the impotence of the central government to make itself respected there, so that the measure would leave the people of the frontier undaunted.

Sheridan, such an accurate judge of the measures proposed by his superiors, did not have anything especially attractive to propose. He suggested, however, that the United States Congress approve a law whereby the President of the United States could authorize the occupation of Mexican territory from the Rio Grande to the Sierra Madre if the incursions of the Indians and cattle thieves continued after a set date, and to retain it until the assurance that the lives and interests of United States citizens were safe. The fear of the occupation would be so great, he thought, that the Mexicans would give up their robberies, "and if it is not, we would already be in a position to stop it effectually ourselves."

General W. T. Sherman, Commanding General of the United States Army, felt more keenly his role of greater authority. He laid aside the questions that he himself had posed, and his opinions were extreme and haughty. Due to the hybrid character of the Mexican population, the length of the frontier and the facility of robbing and escaping to Mexico, he deduced that the question did not lend itself to a quick or full solution. Also, he concluded, and with much greater firmness, that nothing would be gained, as Sheridan and others believed, by moving the dividing line to the south, because apart from not counteracting the stimulus to rob, the United States would only have more Indians to contend with, and if this trick was repeated again and again, instead of anglicizing the Mexicans, "they could make Mexicans out of us."

On the other hand, Mexico was patently incapable of preventing its people from entering Texas in order to rob; but that fact should not relieve Mexico of the responsibility for all the stolen property that could be located on its territory. This payment should be demanded of it, and if not paid promptly, ships of war should be sent to Veracruz to destroy Fort San Juan de Ulúa and to bombard the port, since the latter, Mazatlán and Acapulco "are commercially vital to Mexico's existence as a nation." One should be forewarned that all of this would not be enough; land forces of the United States would occupy, retain, and fortify Matamoros, Nuevo Laredo and Piedras Negras, giving powers to the military to levy taxes whose application would be "to pay our just demands and the cost of its execution." Finally, the forces on the frontier should be augmented immediately, giving the officers that commanded them not only absolute control of the telegraph lines, but also funds to construct blockhouses every fifty miles with communications between them so as to transmit from one to the other news about the bands of invaders.

General Sherman counseled other more intelligent measures, such as the extension to the Rio Grande, with official funds, the railroad that had already reached San Antonio, and to do the same with all others near the frontier. Thus would be stimulated immigration of Anglo-Saxons who would defend themselves from small groups, so leaving to the army the task of dealing with the larger bands. And as in that program the Free Zone might be an obstacle, he suggested suppressing it by force. The United States government should prevent foreign merchandise from entering Matamoros by way of the Rio Grande unless Mexico charged the same duty as levied on it in Veracruz, Tampico and other ports. "This will enable our merchants to compete with them, will revive trade in American goods and increase the American population in the towns on our side of the river." Thus, in a "very few years" the latter would be strong and prosperous, and its population capable of protecting its lives and interests, although "with such aid as military force can always render."

The warlike opinions of their subordinates posed new problems to Secretaries McCrary and Evarts, and to President Rutherford B. Hayes, who knew the gravest phases of this great problem without having solved a single one of the old ones. Until then, for example, at no time had the United States executive even suggested making Mexico financially responsible for the damages of the depredations. The destruction of San Juan de Ulúa, the bombarding of the port of Veracruz, the military occupation of Matamoros, Nuevo Laredo and Piedras Negras, the charging of import duties and its application to pay for the indemnizations, all required the United States to sustain that thesis, or, rather, required that it should have sustained it from the beginning, since, apart from other weaknesses, sustaining it now would have the fault of seeming to be a justification at the last hour of aggressive acts that could lead only to war. This was the opinion of General Sheridan, and he gave it thinking that the aggression would be limited to occupying a part of Mexican territory.

Then, the declaration of war as well as the approval of a law to empower President Hayes to proceed so militarily, required sending "the Mexican question" to the United States Congress again, and immediate past experience had clearly demonstrated that it was Congress that overrode the President, and not the reverse. In fact, the disparity and incongruity of the measures suggested, and above all those proposed by General Sherman, must have weighed heavily on the spirits of President Hayes and of his secretaries of State and War. If Sherman, for example, proposed to obtain a monetary indemnity from Mexico, and he himself declared that Veracruz was a port vital to the economic life of Mexico, then bombarding it signified destroying the small possibility of receiving it. Ord's advice of pacifying the wild Indians by inviting them to return to the United States, assuring them of amnesty for their crimes and lands for their future life, was contrary to the policy and the interests of those who in some form were managing Indian affairs, aside from the fact that similar projects had been tried more than once with very uncertain results.

In fact, these warlike ideas were old ones, and from that point of view the secretaries of War and of State did not gain much by again listening to them. Representative Schleicher of Texas had set the tone of the investigation made at the end of 1877 by the Committee on Foreign Relations of the House of Representatives. He posed the problem of the relations with Mexico as a dilemma between the necessity of the United States of counting it among the foreign markets for the new American manufacturers or the breaking of relations which the depredations on the frontier would logically lead to. He judged that the temporizing policy of the executive of his country was erroneous, for

. . . temporizing is the most dangerous method of dealing with evils of the character we have thus described. A slight demonstration of power would have stopped them in their incipiency, and they would never have assumed the proportions to which they have grown.

The committee, as was natural, concluded its findings with a joint resolution advocating that the United States maintain on the frontier a military force of over 5000 men, and that the instructions of June 1 be continued until an international agreement that would resolve all the pending problems had been signed.

Brigadier General Ord testified before that committee; and although on some points of interest he did not hesitate to decline to venture an opinion, or to manifest one in spite of its not being expected by Schleicher, the general tone of his testimony was mistrust of all that smelled of Mexico or of things Mexican, thinking of the military solution as the only one. He thought that the initial incursions of wild Indians certainly were from the United States into Mexico; but that for a long time now raids only in the reverse direction had occurred. Diplomacy had failed to solve the frontier problems, and the military solutions had made scarcely any progress, among other things because it was relying on some 2700 men to guard something more than 1250 miles of frontier. He asked for at least 5000, since it should be understood that the Mexican forces had never been any good and he doubted that at any time they would lend effective service.

He favored the recognition of the government of General Díaz because the more the peace and stability of Mexico were encouraged the more the frontier would benefit; but, at the same time, he did not advise any other measures than the ratification on the part of the Congress of the orders that the Secretary of War had given for the invasion of Mexican territory in pursuit of malefactors. "If you yield to the demands of those people," he said on concluding his testimony, "they will attribute it to fear, not to reason or justice." And he confirmed the old Texan belief that "the Mexicans only respected force."

Lieutenant Colonel W. R. Shafter, whose ten years of continuous service on the frontier gave great weight to his opinions, supposed that if the Mexican army cooperated, not more than 1500 men would be needed on the United States side; but as it was useless to expect such aid, it was necessary to have 5000 or 6000, in spite of believing that there were scarcely 200 wild Indians causing the depredations.

Even an officer of lower grade and of limited experience, like Lieutenant John L. Bullis, who commanded a group of Seminole scouts, roundly affirmed that the civil authorities of Mexico never had tried to prevent the incursions of the malefactors into Texas. He did not advise, however, by his detailed description of how the Indians made them that one could infer less passivity on the part of the United States authorities. According to him, the Indians passed into Texas territory in groups of two to thirty-five, on foot and shod, if anything, with moccasins. They hid during the day in advantageous positions and at midnight began to gather the stock that they proposed to steal from a nearby ranch. They would round up herds of a hundred or more, and the operation completed, they would head for Mexico, traveling now by day and night to reach the river, crossing it up to two hundred or two hundred and fifty miles from the nearest post of United States soldiers. The Indians penetrated up to one hundred miles into Texas territory, for at one time they almost reached San Antonio.

WHILE IN HIGH CIRCLES such advice was being pondered, Brigadier General Ord felt it necessary to give new instructions that Colonel McKenzie and his other subordinates had asked of him. If United States troops were met in Mexican territory by "hostile" Mexican forces, they should notify the latter of their intentions and give them the opportunity to choose between aiding or opposing; they would be attacked if they should elect the second. If it should be discovered that some of the marauders were taking refuge in some village and that the Mexican forces were occupying it in order to protect them or resist attack on it, "the commanding officer of our troops will consider said protecting or opposing force, in every respect, as a party to the raid and attack accordingly." Before so doing, however, but only when the safety of the troops of the United States or the possibility of catching the malefactors would not be jeopardized, the officer in charge should ask the Mexican commanding officer to punish them or to return the stolen property, and if it seemed possible that that procedure would bring good results, he could defer action. In any case, the troops that penetrated into Mexican territory should carry ammunition and food enough to go as far as the lairs of the malefactors, and to have the rear guard supported by other forces that would cross the frontier at any point.

These instructions incorporated the ideas that Ord submitted to the consideration of his superiors, and he put them into practice at once in order to quiet the uncertainty of his officers in the presence of "hostile" Mexican forces. Some one of them must have transpired, for not only the alarmed Mexican press commented on them but a short time afterwards the senators from Texas, John S. Ford and P. R. Storms, telegraphed Ord asking him to authorize the commander of Brownsville to arm the civilian population, because a break with Mexico seemed inevitable. The Mexicans of Matamoros were already organized; "and if they assume the offensive, we are not prepared to defend ourselves." Ord refused to supply arms of the federal army because the law forbade it, but he suggested applying to the governor of Texas, who did have the authority to do it. He added that there was no cause for relations with Mexico to be broken, and that the invasions of United States forces in the past three years had increased the respect toward the United States among honorable and sensible Mexicans.

ONE VOICE of sanity was heard opportunely. Secretary of War McCrary ordered General Sherman to transmit confidentially to Sheridan and Ord the opinion that President Rutherford B. Hayes did not see in the crossing of the frontier the aim of provoking Mexico into a war, and that United States forces ought not to attack the Mexicans except to defend themselves. Consequently, care should be taken not to commit any hostile acts against them. Only Congress could declare war, and President Hayes was proposing to go to it in order to ask for new powers leading to the settlement of the frontier problems. Meanwhile, McCrary instructed his subordinates "to avoid all conflict with the Mexican troops."

XIV
THE LAST CHAT

Ignacio L. Vallarta found himself obliged to leave the Department of Foreign Relations and return to the presidency of the Supreme Court; nonetheless, under instructions from President Porfirio Díaz he continued for some time in charge of negotiating with John W. Foster. Thus, on May 10, 1878, he communicated to Foster that his first proposal did not express in a sufficiently explicit manner the request to cancel the order of June 1, and that only by giving a clear surety that it would be so done could the risk of a negative action by the Mexican Senate be avoided. Foster refused definitely to go further and after a new consultation with Díaz, Vallarta accepted his proposal and informed him of the resolution of the President to ask the Senate for the authorization. The *modus operandi* would be the one outlined in Vallarta's memorandum of September 10, even though the crossing would be authorized only when dealing with wild Indians and only in uninhabited regions of the frontier. Díaz thought that once the first authorization was obtained from the Senate, he would later be able to extend it to the cattle thieves and other criminals of the lower Rio Grande.

An entire month was spent by President Díaz contending with the Supreme Court in order to retain Vallarta in the Department of Foreign Relations and, failing in this effort, to find a substitute. Thus, Foster heard nothing more of pending matters until June 17, when José María Mata told him that he had been invited to take charge of the Department of Foreign Relations, but that he would not accept the post if the possibility of settling the differences with the United States was discouraging, since that was now the subject of greatest importance. Foster must have described the state of the negotiations to him, but, in any case, he assured him that he did not see any insuperable obstacle to their being terminated happily.

Mata, whom the United States Department of State now considered "eminently just, sensible, and courteous," entered the department well armed for negotiation: he had the authorization of the Mexican Senate. With it he could formally ask Foster for the revocation of the order of June 1 as a condition to President Díaz' making use of the authorization given him by the Senate, anticipating that his own government would no longer have any reason not to sign a treaty on the reciprocal passage of troops over the international boundary in pursuit of wild Indians in uninhabited regions.

Foster not only opposed such conditions but again insisted that the crossing of the troops be in order to pursue any criminal and not simply wild Indians. He gave necessity as one reason, as well as a more convincing one: that United States troops were already authorized by the President of the United States to enter Mexican territory. Notwithstanding, Foster agreed to transmit this proposal to his government, even after having failed to get Mata to put in writing the promise to sign an agreement. On transmitting it, he could no longer conceal his vexation: the order given to Brigadier General Edward O. C. Ord continued to damage the relations of the two countries. It was not possible to place the blame on him by saying that his dispatches had inspired it, and neither did it come from the Secretary of War of the United States, but from President Rutherford B. Hayes. Thus it was up to Hayes to decide whether to reconsider the order.

Negotiations were progressing somewhat, but much more slowly than the facts to which they corresponded. Mexico was complaining of the invasions into its territory by United States troops and of the incursions of wild Indians, one of which had culminated in the killing of seventy persons and the robbery of more than five hundred head of cattle. The United States, for its part, clamored against wild Indians taking refuge in Mexican territory who periodically entered Texas to steal cattle and murder the owners or to take vengeance against them by kidnaping their children, whom they carried into the mountains of Coahuila as hostages. Therefore, while Foster was pressing for the order of June 1 to be reconsidered, he continued to advise that if the difficulties with Mexico were going to end in war, the American people should be informed, for

. . . I fear a larger portion of our own countrymen think Mexico is right and we are wrong. If we are to have trouble, we must and can have the support of our own people.

Foster made no mistake in pointing out this other solution, for the Department of State in no way was inclined toward the revocation of the order. It professed the opinion that, in spite of recognition, the situation on the frontier was "practically" the same. It did not doubt the good faith of the Díaz government and even recognized that some effort had been made to improve the situation; but all these factors weighed little in the face of the indifference and the hostility or the complicity of the local authorities. Neither did the Department of State doubt the good faith of the Mexican government when it asserted that part of its repugnance to consenting to the passing of the troops proceeded from the certainty that to do so would excite still more the anti-American sentiments of the people of Mexico. But, at the same time, it was difficult for it to consider such a fear as reason enough for the United States government to cease protecting the lives and interests of its citizens. Since that was its only reason for being, any government that ignored it would be useless.

The idea of the United States' pretending to conquer Mexico or to reduce its territory was "fallacious and absurd," and the Díaz government knew it. The only motive for complaint and the only real and true problem was that Mexico did not give sufficient cooperation in bringing law and order to the border once and for all; and that, before this real and unquestionable situation, the government of the United States did not conform with the vague hope that "at some future day or at some future session of the Mexican Congress laws may be enacted or treaties ratified which might offer the solution of the difficulties."

In the overall estimation of the frontier problems as well as in the examination of concrete cases that were arising, the language of the United States Department of State was becoming each time more acrimonious and more biting. One time Eleuterio Ávila, chief clerk of the Department of Foreign Relations, defended Mexico by arguing that a good number of the frontier depredations were organized on Mexican territory, but under the direction and with the resources of United States citizens. The Department of State replied that Ávila, besides having the candor of assuming at that time that nothing would be so efficacious as a good intelligence between the military chiefs of both countries, did not perceive that the jurisdiction and the responsibility of the Mexican authorities was determined not by the nationality of the leaders but by the place where they operated. And if Ávila considered that the invasions of United States forces offended the government and public opinion of Mexico, "it is hoped that he will make a due allowance for a similar sentiment here and especially in Texas at the murders and robberies and burnings by Mexican outlaws."

Although the depredations on the frontier made it react more quickly, the Department of State also showed increasing irritation in regard to the other problems, whose solution did not advance either. It continued considering unnecessary, contrary to international treaties, and "entirely incompatible with friendly relations" the prohibition forbidding United States citizens to acquire real estate on the frontier. The origin of this prohibition was the fear that the imaginary offenses of the old Texas colonists would be repeated. This time, nevertheless, the case was radically different, for great concessions of agricultural

land had been given the earlier colonists, while now it was a
question of being prohibited to buy any kind of real estate. Such
an exclusion was impolitic and unjust and was causing an irritation that "sooner or later might lead to other than peaceable
courses to make such acquisitions." The United States could not
allow Mexico, "nor any other foreign power," to place its citizens
in a situation of such inferiority. It was true, according to the
treaty of 1831, that the equality of United States citizens with the
Mexican seemed to be limited to commercial affairs and to navi-
gation, but "it can also be interpreted to include the right of
acquiring real estate."

The United States seemed to have resigned itself as far as the
subject of the Free Zone was concerned, and this in spite of the
fact that on referring to its failure, Foster commented that no
other question illustrated "more clearly the incapacity of the
present government of Mexico to discharge its plain duty toward
the United States." The department then limited itself to
"lamenting" that the government of Mexico was refusing to
repeal or even to modify the laws relative to the zone. But when
it was known that Baghdad might be declared the one port of
entrance for foreign merchandise for the Free Zone of Tamaulipas, Foster was asked to attend quickly and energetically to the
correction of a measure that the Department of State thought
wrong, "for it would injure greatly the commercial relations
between the United States and Mexico in favor of European
trade."

This was, however, a false alarm, although expressive of the
ease with which the United States Department of State made
private interests the condition for complaint and even of national policy. The truth was that the Mexican Free Zone had
hurt Texas merchants because during the Civil War the United
States had been converted to protectionism; it then raised the
duties on imports to such an extent that they worked as an
irresistible incentive to the smuggling of European merchandise
from the Free Zone. In the twenty years since, progress in industry and, above all, in communications permitted the Texas

merchant to offer merchandise whose price could compete with European contraband; but it was necessary for Foster to have an opportunity to visit the frontier and to talk with the interested parties in order to arrive at the conclusion that the Free Zone, "which was originally intended to be a protection to Mexican interests and an obstruction to American commerce, in its practical working is just now proving the contrary."

IT WAS INEVITABLE for Foster, considering the meaning and the tone of the instructions which he received, to resume a demanding and exacting attitude. He carried to Mata a pamphlet in which a group of Texans called on the United States Congress to put an end to the depredations, a pamphlet which Brigadier General Ord had sent him with a covering letter. In it he urged Foster to convince the Mexican government of the necessity of delivering any wild Indians taking refuge in its territory to the military authorities of the United States or to remove them from the frontier. Also he asked him to get the Mexican Secretary of War to instruct Jerónimo Treviño to join with Ord in a united campaign against the wild Indians camping in the mountains of Santa Rosa in Coahuila. Foster presented Ord's ideas as a concrete military campaign that should be undertaken and executed by both leaders. Porfirio Díaz, he argued, now had the Mexican Senate's authorization to agree to it, and it would not be considered as a precedent for the future.

Foster felt very sure of the urgency and simplicity of the measure that he was advising; so much so that he declared that Porfirio Díaz would approve if he were well informed of the situation. Mata then secured an interview for him in which the President told him that he was now inclined to agree to the removal of wild Indians to a distance from the frontier. Foster could count on the military commander of Coahuila to cooperate with Ord in the campaign; Díaz, however, would not consent to the passage of United States troops until the order of June 1 was revoked. As soon as that was done, he would sign an agreement authorizing it.

In order to give Foster an idea of the reaction of Mexican opinion, Díaz told him that Manuel María de Zamacona had resigned his position as minister in Washington on learning of his disposition to allow the passage of troops across the frontier, and that the Senate had made him promise not to use the authorization until the "national honor and dignity" were saved from the humiliation caused by the order. His appeal to the Senate and the latter's having given the authorization demonstrated in an "unquestionable" manner the good will of his government, and gave the United States the best opportunity and the most convincing argument for revoking the order. Foster, with a discouragement which he did not even attempt to hide, reported his complete failure to convince Díaz, ending that now indeed he was persuaded that the Mexican government would not consent to any agreement while the order was in force.

In the face of this situation, Foster advised his government to partially rectify its policy; but he also recommended that it apply greater pressure. He hoped, for example, that President Hayes in his annual message to Congress would use vigorous language that would bring "an instant solution" to all the pending problems.

Foster's superiors were not even surprised at his discouragement. They told him, in fact, that the success of his "just and honest" complaints was "evidently nil"; that the condition of the problems, pending for such a long time, was "the least satisfactory," and that the repeated appeals "to international good will in order to obtain principles of right and justice" seemed sterile. The Department of State, in spite of everything, hoped that Foster would not relax from inculcating a sense of responsibility into the Mexican government, and trusted that his steadfast efforts in favor of good international relations would some day yield positive fruit.

In Mexico, on the other hand, Foster felt happy, for he ably took advantage of his failure in the principal affairs to realize favorable and quick solutions in the minor ones. Besides being allowed the luxury of announcing his visits to Eleuterio Ávila scarcely half an hour in advance, he recommended repeatedly and clearly the requests of American companies like Western Union, which wanted to connect with an undersea cable the Atlantic Coast of the United States with the ports of Tampico and Veracruz, or he echoed the complaints of small merchants, who were not even his own nationals, as occurred in the case of the withdrawal of the copper coins called "Zacatecas' quarters."

Mata had waited impatiently for the United States minister to communicate something to him about Mexico's formal request to the repeal of Ord's instructions. It was natural that he was disagreeably surprised to receive from the former a complete copy of Evarts' instructions of August 13, and a note in which Foster justified it on the necessity of the Mexican government's knowing directly the United States' opinion in regard to the situation on the frontier. Mata replied to Evarts' proposals, and Foster offered to send them to the Secretary of State. Even so, Foster thought that some progress was being made, for Mata in his reply had put in writing, for the first time, that Mexico was disposed to signing an agreement for the reciprocal passage of troops across the frontier as soon as the order of June 1 was revoked.

And even a personal incident that occurred then helped him to confirm to his government the order's unpopularity. During the *soirée* in which he took part on September 16 of that year of 1878 in the Arbeu Theater, one of the participants read a poem "a large portion of which was devoted to a bitter and insulting tirade" aimed at the government of the United States; the public applauded the speaker noisily and, rising to its feet, broke into cries of war and death to the Americans, "the most frightful confusion" reigning in the theater. Foster retired, but decided not to take the incident as an official insult.

In spite of this and of everything else, Foster continued to send good news. Díaz was complying with his promise to make a formal campaign against the wild Indians in Coahuila, notwithstanding the great poverty of the government. In fact, Foster ventured the opinion that in that form the order to Brigadier General Ord would soon be unnecessary. Besides, Díaz was consolidating himself in power, for one after another of his enemies' rebellious movements had failed. And Foster also reported, as a partial explanation of his failure, that the Porfirista faction was very much divided, and that only the fear of a war with the United States gave it an appearance of unity, this being a situation from which Díaz was drawing every advantage imaginable.

The Department of State and its secretary, nonetheless, agreed entirely to disregard Mexico's complaints over the damages the wild Indians caused in Mexican territory. The lack of reports from the Secretaries of War and of the Interior induced the United States to suppose automatically that the Mexican charge of damages must be imaginary, and even more so when it was presented without copious proof on which to support it. Without further examination it was held that the culprits were not Indians coming from the United States but the "renegades," those who were now living in Mexico. Or the United States took very seriously the argument that the wild Indians were "nations" that were in a state of war against a nation friendly to Mexico, namely, the United States.

Its own military authorities occasionally admitted that in fact some incursions into Mexico had left from the United States; but did not the latter suffer from Indians coming from Mexico? And when in the Mexican complaint a reproach directed at certain Texas authorities slipped out, Mexico was indignantly asked to withhold all judgment until it had irrefutable proof in its hands. In short, all the situations and arguments that Mexico had been making use of to defend herself, and that the United States had rejected as fallacious or untruthful, were now being used in order to disallow damages from the other side. And certainly the skeptical attitude of the military authorities did not help much. When Brigadier General Ord received in June, 1878, news of the campaign being carried out against the

wild Indians by Colonel José María Garza Galán, his only reaction was to order that the "veracity" of the news that he received be proved.

The position of the United States Department of State was
vulnerable on another point also: that of the satisfaction and
reparation for military forces invading one country from the
other. Those terms had been thunderously demanded when
Colonel Fructuoso García pursued a group of Lerdista rebels
into United States territory in June, 1877. Mexico gave them
quickly and without vacillating. But two years later Foster was
still expressing his disagreement concerning purely procedural
questions. On the other hand, the Department of State did not
even answer Mexico's protests against invasions by United States
military forces, and Foster maintained that it was not his business to examine them because they had been presented in Washington.

All of these past occurrences explained the determination
with which the Mexican government emphasized those cases in
which its cooperation was effective. Early in September, 1878, a
band of rustlers lead by one Arriola appeared in Texas between
Fort Duncan and El Jardin. Even though it made its first raids
near Piedras Negras and only "threatened" to make them in
Texas proper, the Department of State instructed Foster to ask
the Mexican government if it knew of Arriola's deeds and what
measures had been taken to prevent those that might be committed "on the soil of a friendly State." Very soon the military
commander of Piedras Negras was accused of providing Arriola
with arms and "taking care" of the stock stolen. The government of President Díaz was asked to give immediate attention to
this subject and was warned that the United States in no case
would agree to a monetary compensation which would not be
enough to satisfy

. . . the continued harrassment and apparently ceaseless turmoil
which is kept up on our otherwise peaceful borders by these marauding
parties of Mexicans which crossing secretly and in the darkness of

the night, from their own territory, emerge upon the farms and fields of American citizens, carrying perpetual alarm and dread, and rendering life in that region of our country insupportable.

Foster, of course, incorporated those instructions almost in their entirety in a note and dispatched it immediately to the Department of Foreign Relations. Soon the chief clerk, Eleuterio Ávila, reported that President Díaz had ordered that the Arriola band and the military commander of Piedras Negras be watched. He reiterated the willingness of his government to combat cattle rustling on the frontier but suggested that if it failed in its efforts the reason would be the same as that for which the United States was impotent to suppress it on its own territory. The Department of State found such a reply not very satisfactory, being shocked that the Mexican government should flee from its responsibility in the case of crimes committed by persons within its jurisdiction; but it would find it impossible to shirk this responsibility in this instance, because a high official of the Mexican army was involved.

In reality, Ávila, perhaps due to his experience as Mexican agent on the Joint Claims Commission, was preparing a very elaborate note, with the purpose of presenting the Mexican government's final position on all pending problems. He must have been greatly surprised when Foster declared that he did not propose to give an extensive reply to it, for the time for giving these topics high priority for general discussion had already passed; he could only examine them concretely and according to the promises of the Mexican government

. . . to adopt vigorous and adequate measures to prevent its territory from being made the secure base of operations for raiding parties into the United States, and the safe and profitable place of deposit of the plunder of these bandits.

Fortunately, on December 18, Foster was told that Arriola had been arrested by the Mexicans and was asked for information about his crimes in order to proceed against him. Shortly thereafter Foster was entirely calm. The United States consul in Monterrey had confirmed the apprehension. But Foster, in the face of such good news, could not repress his skepticism and commented that "the Mexican government wants to make of this deed a proof of its disposition to resolve the frontier problems."

In some matters Foster could have been plainly satisfied because the outcome of such and such a case coincided with his desires and those of his government. Unfortunately for him, they were not always those in which he had intervened. Thus it happened in the case of Ceferino Ávalos, a Mexican soldier who killed one of his countrymen in Texas and returned to Mexico after having committed the crime. The Díaz government agreed to his extradition, in spite of the fact that it was not obliged to do so under the treaty with the United States, and Ávalos was tried in Texas and sentenced to death. The Secretary of Foreign Relations communicated all those facts to Foster, commenting that this was how the Mexican government acted when it was convinced of the justice of a cause. Foster thanked him, but asked for a duplicate copy of the record of the case, because "it could serve as a precedent." The Mexican government, in fact, using that and another case, eventually asked reciprocal conduct of the United States authorities in matters of extradition, a request whose approval Foster immediately recommended.

But Foster still retained a skeptical attitude about the real cooperation of the Mexican government to pacify the frontier, to the extent of not realizing that he was thus contradicting his argument that the order of June 1 be reconsidered. In December, 1879, he ended an inspection trip with an extensive visit to the Mexican frontier states and did not hesitate to admit that "much greater" peace and order existed in them "than usual along the Río Bravo." He became acquainted with Jerónimo Treviño and Servando Canales, the two military commanders on the frontier, as well as with the governors of Coahuila, Nuevo León and Tamaulipas. He received attentions from all of them and the expression of a uniform desire to maintain the peace. He discovered, as well, that the feeling of the frontier Mexican population had changed very favorably. From all of it he concluded, however, that although he "never" doubted his good intention, General Díaz could not maintain large military forces far from the capital for his resources were very limited; besides, Díaz personally was living in a constant turmoil. This combination of events caused the abandonment of frontier affairs to the hands of local authorities.

The improvement now shown was consequently due to the fact that the United States government was combating banditry in its own territory and in that of Mexico besides having succeeded in forcing Díaz' participation in a task beneficial to both. Even so, part of Treviño's forces had been dispatched to Chihuahua to put down a revolutionary uprising, and the next fight for the Presidency of the Republic presaged traditional disorders and pronunciamentos. Furthermore numerous groups of Indians were continually escaping from reservations in the United States to take refuge in the inaccessible mountains of Coahuila and Chihuahua, to which it was very improbable that the Mexican government would send its own troops. Under these conditions it would be unwise to reduce the military forces of the United States along the frontier, or to limit the discretionary authority of their officers, that is, to revoke Ord's order, as Foster unwillingly concluded.

FOSTER RETURNED to Mexico City after his long and arduous tour of inspection through the west and north of Mexico at the end of December, 1879. One month later he was offered the legation of the United States in Russia, and he telegraphed gratefully accepting it. On March 2, at a formal ceremony in the National Palace, attended by President Díaz and his full cabinet, the diplomatic corps and "society," he presented his letter of recall and bade Mexico farewell. Only the day before, the Department of State, still addressing itself to him, informed him that Secretary of War Alexander Ramsey, successor to George W. McCrary, had resolved on February 25, 1880, to revoke the famous order of June 1, 1877. It sent him besides a copy of the note in which

Secretary of State William M. Evarts gave the news to Manuel María de Zamacona, a note which said:

This signal proof of the President's conviction that the Mexican government is in a position to ensure the full protection of life and property on the borders lately the scene of marauding incursions, is but another of the many recent evidences of the good will existing between the two Republics.

Thus Foster did not even reap the laurels of the revocation of the order. The resolution was not taken as a direct answer to his recommendations, and the Department of State had previously communicated it to Zamacona. Nonetheless, John W. Foster did recommend prudence when others wished to add new difficulties to his own. He feared, for example, that President Hayes and Secretary of State Evarts would sympathize with a recent resolution of the House of Representatives recommending the naming of a committee to go to Mexico to negotiate treaties of commerce with and for the protection of United States interests. The preamble of the resolution, Foster said, might offend Mexico, because the treaties of Guadalupe Hidalgo of 1848 and of Gadsden in 1853 were basely given as friendly demonstrations, when they could only evoke Mexico's two most lamentable setbacks. Besides, it was being said that the negotiations would include not only matters of a purely commercial character but also the suppression of the Free Zone, the exemption from forced loans and modifications of the treaty of extradition, all subjects of his fruitless negotiations. Finally the resolution recommended putting in the hands of a court of arbitration all pending problems as the only form for avoiding delay in their settlement.

JOHN W. FOSTER was replaced by P. H. Morgan, who arrived in Mexico City on April 15, 1880, and who presented his credentials six days later. His instructions asked that he attend "intelligently and jealously" to the interests of the United States and to the promotion of good relations between the two countries. With the revocation of the order of June 1 and the change of minister it seemed that all was going to slip into place as in a mild, tepid sea. The Department of State, filled with satisfaction, informed its minister that, as new proof of the good will that existed now between the military forces of the two countries, Brigadier General Ord had ordered that military honors should be rendered Servando Canales on the occasion of his visit to the general headquarters of the Military District of Texas at San Antonio. A little later, the commander of Fort Brown ordered the flag to be flown at half mast on learning of the death of the wife of General Díaz.

A slight, first cloud appeared on the horizon when the Mexican forces of one frontier post acquired the habit of shooting at deserters inside United States territory. Morgan was asked to transmit this information, but without presenting a formal claim. A large group of wild Indians crossed the dividing line during the middle of June, and the commanding officer of Fort Craig judged it necessary to drive them into the mountains of Chihuahua in order to prevent the incursions that they might make later into New Mexico. This commanding officer reported that the Mexican state authorities were agreeing to permit the passage of his troops, but that the authorization of the federal government should be asked. President Hayes personally made this request his own, and Morgan was instructed to present it. Two days afterwards, in a coded telegram, the latter gave an account of the results: the Secretary of Foreign Relations, after consulting with President Díaz, refused to consent to the crossing of the United States troops over the boundary.

Miguel Ruelas, then Secretary of Foreign Relations, argued that there were enough Mexican troops in Chihuahua to take charge of the situation; besides, the citizens of that state could be counted on, for a bitter experience disposed them to lend aid. At any rate he would inform President Díaz, and he was sure that Díaz would immediately order the cooperation of the Mexican army with that of the United States, but with each one within its respective territory. Ruelas afterwards told Morgan that he met President Díaz with Mexican Secretary of War, whom he ordered there on the spot to send the instructions necessary to combine operations with the United States forces. In regard to the crossing of the troops Ruelas told him, "and repeated to him several times," that President Díaz would consent under two conditions: first, that the authorization given in this case would not serve as a precedent for asking for it on another occasion; second, that the United States should authorize by reciprocity the passage of Mexican troops into its own territory.

Morgan tried to sidestep the second condition, but as Ruelas insisted on it, he began to compose in Ruelas' office a telegram with the purpose of showing it to him and thus obtaining his approval. While he was writing it, Ruelas was called by President Díaz, with whom he remained for some time. When Ruelas returned and Morgan gave him the telegram to read, he maintained that he had been misunderstood, for he had said only that the Mexican government was disposed to sign an agreement for which it already had the authorization of the Senate; in any other case, it would have to ask for it again. Morgan, feeling deceived, thereupon expressed surprise and said he regretted that "the Mexican authorities had changed their thinking so suddenly."

But Ruelas left a written statement of the position of his government on answering the note in which Morgan asked for authorization for this crossing into Mexican territory. Since May of 1878, he said, the Mexican Senate had authorized the executive to negotiate an agreement subject to the five standards approved by the Senate itself. The Mexican government had quickly communicated these standards to John W. Foster, and consequently, it was not responsible for the fact that an agreement had not been concluded since then. The authorization was still in effect, and the executive still had the powers and the disposition to conclude an agreement; but to permit the entrance of United States troops without a prior agreement which would grant the privilege reciprocally would go beyond the authorization of the Senate and would thus be to operate outside of the constitutional powers of the executive.

The United States Department of State then instructed Morgan to express the hope that the Mexican government would disarm the wild Indians to whom "it was giving asylum" and that it would make itself responsible for the damages that they might cause. Ruelas, of course, rejected not only the idea that Mexico was giving asylum to the Indian "enemies" of the United States, but also that of making itself responsible for the damages that they might cause. To refuse permission to United States troops for crossing the international boundary could not be interpreted as a concession of asylum; in fact, the Indians were escaping from reservations in the United States, where they armed themselves and committed their first depredations, and then were taking refuge in Mexico only in order to continue them. He repeated the reasons for denying passage and reiterated the disposition to enter into a formal agreement for making it reciprocal, adding that it was not Mexico's fault "if the government of the United States had not resolved to accept it."

The Department of State, therefore, looked for a new way of stating the problem. It then asked that the Indians be disarmed, and it threatened to claim compensation for damages. A short time afterwards the band of the Indian leader Victorio attacked a United States military post, caused some casualties and fled to Mexico. Immediately Morgan was instructed to present the problem in that form. Morgan now displayed great activity. He looked for Secretary Ruelas, who was ill. He found the chief clerk, but Ávila lacked authority. He asked to speak with President Díaz but was told that Díaz could not receive him because he was too busy. When he finally did talk with him, Díaz, to Morgan's great surprise, told Morgan that he would ask the Senate immediately for the authorization, because the Constitution so required. He did so, but he met violent opposition, which ceased when he proposed to conclude a treaty for only three months. The crossing of troops might be made in places six miles or more from the nearest populated area. It should be announced as soon as possible to the nearest civil and military authorities of the other country, and pursuit should be suspended when the trail of the pursued was lost or upon meeting troops of the other country ready to continue it. Abuses committed by the forces of one country in the territory of the other should be punished according to the laws of the first.

Ignacio Mariscal informed Morgan of an adverse reaction in the Senate and in public opinion because it was rumored that Morgan had threatened an invasion if official permission for the crossing was not given. Soon, also, doubt arose as to whether President Díaz had really been authorized to permit the crossing since May 28, 1878; besides, the comment was made that it seemed that the Mexican army needed foreign help to perform its functions, and that it would be impossible to put out the United States army once it was installed in Mexico. Morgan ended by telegraphing his government that those were the best conditions that could be obtained.

But just as the famous agreement for the reciprocal passing of troops was being initiated, the Indian Victorio and his band were caught by the forces of Colonels Luis Terrazas and Adolfo T. Valle, and in the encounter the chief and his principal followers died.

There were only forty-five days remaining from that October 15, to November 30, 1880. They passed with an exasperating slowness, but they passed, finally, without any new incident occurring to impose the necessity of negotiating and signing the agreement for the reciprocal passing of troops over the international boundary. At the striking of twelve o'clock of the night of November 30, 1880, the satisfaction and the relief of Porfirio Díaz must have been immense, for with the last chime of that singular hour, he successfully ended his first Presidency; and he concluded it without having signed that or any other agreement that the United States demanded for the recognition of his government.

It seemed that the prediction of Ignacio L. Vallarta had then been fulfilled. Recognition would create an atmosphere favorable to the peaceful negotiation of any differences between the United States and Mexico. It was negotiated for four years, and the differences resolved themselves, to whatever extent that they were resolved. The prediction of Manuel María de Zamacona seemed to have been fulfilled, that once public opinion in the United States was "conveniently tempered," Mexico could resist the "irregular" demands of Foster and his government; and to temper it meant basically to win the rich people of the United States to the cause of peaceful penetration of Mexico. And above everything else, the "axiom" of Professor Walter Prescott Webb: "When a Texan fights a Mexican, he can win; but when he parleys he is doomed," was proven retrospectively.

Manuel González, the next President, was the one who consented to signing on July 29, 1882, the agreement for the reciprocal passing of troops over the border; and he did it with a freedom from bias that Porfirio Díaz was never able to have, although three circumstances helped to give this freedom to González. The internal political situation had become much brighter: Manuel González felt more secure in power, and his personal and political ties with the leaders to the north made his influence on the frontier great. His government, one with an impeccable constitutional origin, did not have the embarrassment of a pending diplomatic recognition. Finally, it fell to his good fortune to deal with a new United States administration, for President Rutherford B. Hayes and Secretary of State William M. Evarts had left their offices on March 4, 1881.

Things, in fact, were to change greatly. One day Zamacona interviewed the new United States Secretary of State to ask for authorization for General Francisco Naranjo to enter United States territory to pursue a party of wild Indians, and James G. Blaine talked to him in a confidential and affectionate tone. He assured Zamacona that, in general, these goings and comings of troops from one country into the territory of the other were repugnant to him, adding that he did not fear so much the Mexicans entering the United States as the Americans entering Mexico. And he told of an act occurring in his native state of Maine in order to better explain his thinking: bears and wolves, very abundant in those days, were causing great damage to the stock, and the local government had assigned a sum of money to remunerate the services of some soulless men to pursue them. The latter once asked for a higher salary, and the governor answered that, at the moment, the state was busy protecting the stock from them and that, once that was achieved, it would take care of defending the cattle from the wolves and bears.

Blaine, in fact, not only confided his opinions to Zamacona privately, but also made public declarations that expressed a new policy toward Mexico, that of peaceful penetration, whose principal champion, in fact, turned out to be Blaine. Blaine came to classify the eagerness of securing the reciprocal passage of troops as "openly aggressive" and destined to provoke an international war, and his condemnation of the idea of annexing Mexican territory or making Mexico a protectorate came to have a certain monotonous tone of religious conviction:

. . . it is in conflict with the higher interest of all American citizens of the present generation and of the countless generations that through the providence of God will inherit our proud name and our responsibilities that continually increase.

These circumstances and the fact, fortuitous but fortunate for the government of General González, that its publication coincided with the election of deputies and senators and with the serious diplomatic incidents with Guatemala,* explain the official manner of making the agreement known, the extremely few comments that it provoked and the purely formal and empty quality of those that were made.

The Mexican government limited itself to announcing signing of the agreement and to justifying its action by saying that the frequent and bloody incursions of wild Indians "had demanded it for some time," and that the best results for "the cause of civilization and progress" were expected from it. The Roman Catholic press, which from then on would comment bitterly on the expansion of the United States interests in

*See Daniel Cosío Villegas, *Historia Moderna de México*, vol. V (Mexico: Editorial Hermes, 1960).

Mexico, limited itself to saying at this time: "May God deliver us from an international conflict," while the liberal-conservative daily *La Libertad* reproduced the government's extremely poor justifying preamble and added for its part that "those reasons" were the ones that had led the two governments to sign it. Much later, this same paper essayed a justification by insisting on its reciprocal character and by explaining its principal clauses. Furthermore, the agreement was renewed every two years some five or six times, without incident or any special negotiation, Porfirio Díaz authorizing it on returning to the Presidency in 1884. It did not provoke at any time the black tragedies foreseen and those that had been so talked about, particularly in Mexico.

United States Representative Gustav Schleicher of Texas, the champion of an aggressive policy toward Mexico, died before Porfirio Díaz completed his first Presidency; and Zamacona, on informing the Department of Foreign Relations of so fortunate an event, had the nobility and the professional sense to comment that, after all, he had been a good representative, for he represented and defended the interests, sentiments, and the ideas of his constituents.

Jerónimo Treviño, whose military prestige suffered so much because of Brigadier General Edward O. C. Ord, in the end became good friends with him—such good friends, in fact, that he eventually married Ord's young, blonde and dazzingly beautiful daughter. An unusual importance and an unparalleled international meaning were given to this apparently merely personal and private act. A newspaper in San Antonio, Texas, described it as if it had been the result of a deliberate decision of Generals Treviño and Ord:

To banish all kind of grudges in both countries; to cause the citizens of each nation to maintain strong and intimate relations; to unite with fraternal bonds these two peoples that are so congenial because of their ideas and even because of the similarity of the institutions that rule them; there you have the great purpose which is being proposed by the two distinguished persons that have just united with intimate family bonds as a consequence of one having united with the daughter of the other.

It was reported that "never" had there been seen in Texas a marriage of such great significance, for besides awakening local and nationwide curiosity and interest, it provoked "thousands of comments" abroad. The international meaning of the event was underlined, even to the bride's wedding cake:

. . . It was a beautiful construction of ices, in gothic style and crowned by a parapet above whose walls appeared a bronze cannon and the American and Mexican flags, with the whole being mounted on a statue representing a bride.

Brigadier General Ord, in whose residence the guests were entertained, seemed to have proposed, in effect, to display the signs and the feeling of international friendship. In the garden he had arranged extremely lofty arches of immortelle, whose pinnacles, repeated several times, were enormous flags of one or the other country, achieving, apparently, really fascinating effects:

. . . all that was illuminated on all sides with brilliant lights made of that beautiful and magnificent mansion such a pleasing sight that it almost dazzled those that proposed to contemplate it.

The chronicler came to perceive that a totally new atmosphere was born, and one certainly the opposite to the old, distrustful, fearful, if not odious one:

During the meal one heard the most animated and happy conversations, and as if nature itself wanted to take part in embellishing that enchanting scene, night had hardly fallen, when the moon began to send its rays over that enchanted paradise, at the same time that a soft breeze began to blow, bringing the perfume of the flowers to refresh the brows of the guests, on whose faces one saw signs of the most lively satisfaction and of the most innocent and enthusiastic happiness.

Roberta Augusta Ord de Treviño traveled in triumph through the states of Coahuila, Nuevo León and Tamaulipas, and wherever she went she witnessed the importance of her husband and the respect rendered him. A short time afterwards, Treviño reached the height of his career with the nomination as Secretary of War, and then his American bride shared the adulation that the rising Mexican middle class lavished on the agents of public power. All that did not last very long, however. His wife's health declined rapidly, and in order to recover it Treviño was obliged to leave his post to return to Monterrey. She died some time afterwards, but not before giving birth to an idiotic son, who has dragged out his misfortune for seventy-four interminable years, and who is still alive today.

BRIGADIER GENERAL EDWARD O. C. ORD, who during the four years of the first Presidency was the blackest nightmare for Porfirio Díaz and of his government, obtained a "most honorable" retirement after having seen his daughter married. He was invited to come to Mexico as an official guest, and then *La Libertad* sang of his moderation and prudence, "well-known everywhere" and the "many and sincere demonstrations of sympathy he has given." Furthermore, it demanded of the Mexican government a reception as "attentive and courteous," at least, as that which was given to former United States President Ulysses S. Grant, also visiting then; and as it logically fell to Secretary of War Treviño to do it, and the latter might feel the embarrassment of his relationship to give it all the desired display, *La Libertad* asked that the President take charge of it in person.

Ord arrived in Veracruz, where the wife of the Secretary of War awaited him. He was lodged in the home of Landero y Coss, the Secretary of the Treasury, and was carried to Mexico City in a special train placed at his disposal. On his arrival on March 5, 1881, several newspapers adorned their first pages with extensive laudatory biographies of the illustrious guest. Porfirio Díaz organized an excursion to show him Mexico's eighth wonder of the world, the caves of Cacahuamilpa, where they went "to amuse themselves for a short time" together with a caravan of more than a hundred persons. And when General Díaz took possession of the government of the state of Oaxaca, Ord attended the ceremonies but now not as a guest of state but as agent of the Mexican Central Railroad, which was trying to construct a rail line to that state.

He was treated, in short, as a friend, and as a friend he responded. Without any apparent great effort, he recognized that after all Mexico City was much more attractive than San Antonio, where the poor man had had his general headquarters for long years. And in the face of this situation, *La Libertad,* wishing "to help the press to greet him with enthusiasm and affection," made an unfaithful and short story of all that has been related in this book:

Our readers know that the valiant and wise General Ord, at the present moment our illustrious guest, was the head of the United States forces in an epoch of difficult complications. With flagrant violations of the existing treaties between both countries, and with manifest infraction of the principles of International Law, the government in the White House authorized General Ord to cross the boundary line and to pursue with his forces the wild Indians in Mexican territory. . . . The farseeing and tolerant conduct of General Ord had to make a contrast and to struggle with the lamentable policy of Mr. J. W. Foster, that man determined to cause all the damage possible for Mexico by converting the immunity and respectability that his character of Minister gave him into an instrument of petty passions.

But a rectification about Foster was also forthcoming. The latter, who in time would crown his career by ascending to the height of United States Secretary of State, resigned as Minister to Russia, returned to Washington, and at the end of October, 1881, was included on the regular roster of the Mexican Legation as its legal adviser; in fact, the legation did consult him, among other things, on how to make less demanding and compromising the agreement for the reciprocal passage of troops across the international boundary. Some opposition newspaper protested against such a nomination and such utilization of Foster's services, whereupon, the Mexican government justified it by publishing a letter Foster had written to Ignacio Mariscal, Secretary of the Department of Foreign Relations from Saint Petersburg, shortly after the initiation of the government of Manuel González. In it he had said:

> . . . no Mexican understood so exactly as you what was my position and what were my sentiments while I was in charge of the Legation; and it is a special pleasure for me, today when I cannot be suspected of having any private interest in it, to be able to write to praise the proper policy that your country has lately adopted. . . .

And Foster, in fact, became not only a private lawyer for the Mexican Legation in Washington, but also a public advocate for the entire country and its people. The New York *Evening Post,* for example, published toward the middle of 1882 an article by one of its correspondents who had traveled through Mexico, and who expressed opinions, not exceptionally new, about the imperfect political systems of the country and the limitations of its governing officials. Foster felt it proper that "those slanders should not go without a reply," especially because the proprietor of the *Evening Post* was a member of the cabinet of former President Hayes. Not satisfied with coming to Mexico's defense, he sent his article to all the major newspapers of the country, which reproduced it with embellishments.

Many years afterward, in 1909, Foster published in two thick volumes his *Diplomatic Memoirs,* no small part of which refers to Mexico. He gives in these volumes a picture of his conduct that varies greatly from that which his dispatches and his private correspondence reveal, which it was already possible to read in the National Archives and in the Library of Congress in Washington at the time that the *Memoirs* appeared. He said in them, for example, that Secretary of State Hamilton Fish authorized him to bestow recognition "if it became necessary in order to enable Mexico" to comply with the Joint Claims Convention and to make the first payment; and he added:

> . . . but the Díaz government, realizing this situation, agreed to make the payment through Señor Mariscal, the Mexican Minister in Washington accredited by the Lerdo Administration, and through the accom-

odating spirit of the Díaz Government that question was for the moment avoided.

The most serious discrepancy, however, is that Foster appears in his *Memoirs* to accept in every way, and without tinge of any doubt, the existence of a United States plot to provoke a war against Mexico as a means of making the government of President Rutherford B. Hayes secure and to cause its fraudulent origin to be forgotten.

Foster attributed to himself, of course, the whole credit for recognition of Mexico's new government having been granted by the United States, and could not describe more remorselessly his situation during the eighteen months in which it was postponed:

> This period had been one of intense anxiety to the Díaz Administration and of great embarrassment to me personally, as it was my duty to support my Government loyally, and I could not intimate to the Mexicans that the policy as to recognition was contrary to my recommendation and advice.

It was natural, thus, that Foster's dedication as a friend of Mexico should reach Genaro Estrada, a most keen reader and an astute and circumspect Secretary of Foreign Relations, who, not knowing the history of Foster's conduct except through what Foster says in his *Memoirs,* describes him as

> . . . one of the diplomatic agents that, with a certain breadth of vision of the realities of that epoch, knew how to use a rare gift of a winning way among the Mexicans, of simplicity and moderation, and of prudent behavior to manage the task that was entrusted to him by his government, as is easily seen in his *Memoirs,* and in the revelations *a posteriori* that, [as such is the searching caution used in matters of this nature, that are found in some of the chapters].

AND THINGS ALSO CHANGED because Brigadier General Ord was not the only one who traveled, now as a friend, to the country to which he had once been an enemy. Porfirio Díaz, in turn, made a long trip to the United States. Recently married to Carmen Romero Rubio, he went to Oaxaca to take possession of the governorship of the state. Bored with the social poverty of the place, the preparations for his next re-election advanced, and in the face of the danger of his election as president of the Supreme Court of Justice being consummated, he accepted the invitation of Jerónimo Treviño to be the godfather at the baptism of José Jerónimo Treviño y Ord, and so he embarked at Veracruz for Galveston. The authorities of Galveston expressed their desire that his transitory passage be converted into a formal visit and immediately began to make "preparations on a grand scale." Then the Texas legislature, on February 28, 1883, approved a resolution unanimously—that *La Libertad* classified as of "an admirable simplicity"—formally inviting Díaz to visit the state and to be received in Austin, its capital, in an official manner. *El Siglo XIX* then congratulated the Texas legislature because "it knew how to honor so worthily distinguished Mexicans."

Díaz received invitations to visit Saint Louis, Missouri; Chicago; Washington; and New York. From Washington Matías Romero and his adviser, John W. Foster, went to Saint Louis to meet him, and joined with the local authorities to board the special train on which he traveled some twenty-five miles into Saint Louis. From the railway station to the hotel he was escorted by militia forces with bands playing all the way, and a banquet given by the Knights of Saint Patrick stood out in a program of gracious receptions that lasted for three days. He went to Chicago and could not resist escaping from there with Carmelita to Niagara Falls. In Washington he could not be received officially, for his visit coincided with the death of a member of the President's cabinet; but President Chester A. Arthur and all his secretaries received him, and he made the pilgrimage to Mount Vernon. And in New York former President Ulysses S. Grant entertained him as his guest.

A southern United States newspaper declared that "no statesman, no prince or potentate had ever had such a brotherly reception"; and one New York newspaper estimated that the reception that was given him greatly exceeded those that had been accorded the Emperor of Brazil and the Prince of Wales.

XV
RELEVANCE AND MORAL

It has been said that Porfirio Díaz ended his first Presidency without signing any agreement that the United States demanded in exchange for recognition of his government; likewise, that conditions began to change shortly thereafter; and that still later some issues came to be diametrically opposed to what they were initially. Nevertheless, they did not change to such a marked degree only because others occupied the places of President Rutherford B. Hayes and Secretary of State William M. Evarts, or simply because the internal political situation of the United States was more propitious to a better understanding with Mexico. The transformation was due more than anything else to the change in the conditions underlying the problems that separated the two countries to the extent of carrying them to the brink of armed conflict.

Consider, for example, the forced loans. One of John W. Foster's "irregular demands," as José María de Zamacona angrily called them, was that Mexico should be conventionally obliged to exempt United States citizens from them. However, the forced loan, child of the urgency and the arbitrariness of the rebel uprising or of the authority that fought him, completely disappeared when the Porfirista peace became general and permanent. The problems born of the Free Zone also were decreasing to the degree that United States industry was providing products of the quality and at prices similar to European goods introduced into Texas as contraband, as soon as the rail lines of the United States could carry them to the frontier cheaply and regularly. Its isolation, which was one of the most convincing reasons for creating and maintaining the Free Zone, disappeared also when the Mexican frontier became linked by railroad to the central region of the country. Things there changed so much that smuggling from Mexico into Texas ceased completely—to be replaced by smuggling from Texas into Mexico. Thus the problem was no longer one for the United States but one for Mexico.

Even the conditions at the bottom of the most dramatic problem, that of cattle rustling and the wild Indians, changed noticeably and in a rather short time. To the stability that he inherited from Díaz, Manuel González added his own; the influence of the central government on the northern frontier grew for that reason alone. But it was greater yet because of the particular circumstance that Manuel González had better personal and political relations with the leaders of the North. Jerónimo Treviño was his first Secretary of War, and Francisco Naranjo took command of the Division of the North; they changed positions when Treviño resigned from the Department of War.

At the same time, these leaders were being replaced by professional military men. On the death of Servando Canales, General Rómulo Cuéllar took command of the federal forces in Tamaulipas, until then called the Canales Division, so strong had been the personal stamp of its leader. General Carlos Fuero commanded directly part of the federal forces of Coahuila and Chihuahua, and General José Guillermo Carbó and Colonel Bernardo Reyes those of Sonora. Those chiefs, strangers to the economic and political interests of the regions where they operated, saw the control of the cattle thieves and of the wild Indians as a purely professional problem. And the central government did not hesitate to give them all resources possible, sure that they would not be employed against it. Besides, the local cacique, whose indifference or complicity was always an impediment to an intelligent and sustained pursuit, now fell under the vigilance of an authority of a different origin, and it did not take him long to estimate its greater strength when in conflict with it. Furthermore, among those local caciques some began to stand out, like Terrazas in Chihuahua and Garza Galán in Coahuila, whose interests coincided with the extermination of the cattle thieves and the wild Indians.

The North, in addition, was slowly being populated with people from the central states, accustomed to a stable occupation and with decidedly more sedentary and less adventurous inclinations. Finally, a most important factor began to take effect. The Mexican government, a little freer from demands and pressure from the United States, gave more efficient attention to this problem when it could be presented not as an imposed preoccupation, but as a genuine and spontaneous one. Progress in communications contributed to this same result, for they could, at last, carry directly to Mexico City the cry of pain and wrath that was drawn forth by the criminal deeds of the barbarians in the territory of the Mexican North.

The transformations were greater and more rapid on the United States side. The migratory wave advanced impetuously and unrestrainedly toward the West and left behind it a stable agricultural population, devoted to cultivating small properties. That meant that the wild Indian was disappearing and that the white settler was acquiring means of livelihood which made violence and crime unnecessary. It meant also that the immense vacuum that made possible the birth, development and culmination of the cattle kingdom was being narrowed until it disappeared when the farm fenced with barbed wire began to appear and to flourish in it. The great opportunity and the easy pretext of stealing cattle disappeared when cattle raising was practiced in a civilized manner and on a small scale. The change was so great in this sense that when the immense empty spaces in Texas disappeared, the cattle industry redeveloped in Chihuahua, the nearest similar empty space.

A presidential election like that of Rutherford B. Hayes did not repeat itself, and the relations of the United States federal government with the former Confederate States improved. The latter came to participate fully in the political life of their country, and for Texas, its immediate relation with Mexico was no longer so important.

One change affected both Mexico and the United States. The thesis of Zamacona of opposing the "irregular demands" with the opinion and influence of Americans interested in the economic fortune of Mexico soon became a reality. And soon mistrust of the Colossus of the North ceded to the urgency of economic progress and the inevitable conviction that only with foreign capital could that progress be achieved. Thus, Porfirio Díaz, who in his period as a rebel was a determined anti-imperialist, now fought tenaciously against the nationalistic zeal of the Mexican Congress until he secured, scarcely three months before leaving the Presidency, its authorization to contract with two United States enterprises for the construction of the Central Railroad to Ciudad Juárez and of the National Railroad to Nuevo Laredo.

ALL THESE CHANGES, in effect, were definitely those which brought on a stable and basic solution to the problems that had divided the United States and Mexico. But while they occurred, diplomatic negotiations between the two countries had the tremendous feeling and anguished urgency of avoiding war. From this point of view Zamacona's diplomatic mistique was mistaken because it was exaggerated. It was all right to oppose official pressure and the annexationist current with sane public opinion and the interests of capitalists who invested money in Mexico; but while those forces were gaining impetus, growing, balancing, and finally overthrowing the others, was it possible for Vallarta and Porfirio Díaz to refuse or to cease to negotiate with Foster and with Evarts? It happened as it had to happen. Recognition was not obtained, as Zamacona said, "some few months" after the government of Mexico decided to resist; it was obtained when United States public opinion made itself felt and when the political elements adverse to President Hayes put him on the spot. This occurred seventeen months after the problem had been presented; but these favorable forces did not prevail for another year, and during that year the negotiation and concession, apparent or real, that all negotiation involves were not only necessary but not postponable. It was natural and inevitable that one should resist less and concede more at the beginning than at the end.

Ignacio L. Vallarta began his negotiations directed to the recognition of the Díaz government under very adverse conditions. On arriving in Mexico City, Porfirio Díaz was no more than a military chief, victorious for the moment. He was disputing for power with Sebastián Lerdo de Tejada, a popularly elected constitutional President, a civilian of great prestige, above all in the foreign world, since as Secretary of Foreign Relations for Juárez or as President he had managed the foreign relations of Mexico for more than ten successive years. Díaz also had as a rival José María Iglesias, a civilian of great renown, with claims to the Presidency inferior to those of Lerdo but very superior to those of Díaz, since as president of the Supreme Court of Justice he was the Vice President of the Republic. And on top of all that, Porfirio Díaz seemed to be planning a complete upheaval in Mexican society.

Vallarta, thus, was the Secretary of Foreign Relations of the least viable faction, constitutionally speaking, and the least desirable politically. And in spite of the fact that for that reason the heads of accredited missions in Mexico declared to him immediately that they would only maintain personal relations with him, he persevered in maintaining them even in that character. He informed them that Porfirio Díaz had taken charge of the executive power and he himself, the Department of Foreign Relations; that Díaz, on leaving for a campaign, would be replaced by General Juan N. Méndez, and when he returned he would again take charge of that power. And more rightly, he later informed them that Díaz had been elected constitutional President and that he had taken the oath of office. That is to say, Vallarta, in spite of his weak and undesirable position, observed the first rule of diplomacy, to maintain communication with the outside world; and unquestionably aided by Díaz' military security and by the transformation of the latter into a legitimate authority, he obtained the recognition of all countries which had recognized Mexico after the restoration of republican government after defeat of Maximilian and the imperialists and which had missions in Mexico during the administration of Sebastián Lerdo de Tejada; and by so doing he isolated the United States, the only one to resist granting this recognition.

Vallarta could then maintain that the government of Porfirio Díaz filled all the requirements for recognition, as the unquestionable fact that it had been recognized by all other countries represented in Mexico demonstrated, and that consequently the United States owed it to him by law and not as a gift. The United States reply that its location and the extensive common frontier made it look more closely at the problem of its relations with Mexico did not operate dialectically and juridically, as demonstrated by the fact that President Hayes found himself obliged to recognize in an official document that he had in this case varied the traditional policy of the United States in the matter of recognition.

Vallarta had great difficulties in negotiating the only problem that escaped him. He had to face an exceptionally intelligent United States minister, a man familiar with Mexico, supported by his government, and very much aware of the power of his country. Also, Vallarta mistrusted the adherence to the Díaz government of the Mexican diplomatic representatives in Washington and the consular officers all over the United States, especially those in New York and in the posts on Mexico's northern frontier. And to crown his misfortunes, it seemed impossible to use the first arm of negotiation, the payment of the claims, for he was ignorant of the final results of the Joint Claims Commission, he lacked money, and he did not know where to turn to obtain it.

Vallarta tried persistently to solve each and every one of those difficulties. His negotiations with Antonio Escalante finally provided the money. He made an approach to Ignacio Mariscal in case it was necessary to use him. He asked Foster to transmit to his government the decision to comply and the fear of not being able to avoid some little delay. Finally, he decided to send José María Mata and Ciro Tagle with ready cash to make the payment.

A man moving among so many adverse circumstances was exposed to failure, and Vallarta erred by hastening to declare that he would not understand as an act of recognition the fact that the United States would receive from the Díaz government the first payment of the claims. Of course he did not know, as we now know, that Hamilton Fish doubted that his government could receive it without maintaining official relations with Díaz, and that precisely for this reason Foster was authorized to recognize Díaz. But Vallarta, a lawyer to the last, yielded too easily to the thesis, juridically correct, that the debtor was the nation and not one particular government, and that thus the payment could not be made in the name of the latter but must be made in that of the former.

In Vallarta's favor it must be said that when he made such a declaration he did not yet know positively the resistance with which the United States would oppose recognition. On the other hand, he knew that by making the payment at all costs he was fulfilling the most difficult of the three requirements that the traditional policy of the United States demanded for recognition of a government of revolutionary origin: that is, the capacity and the desire to fulfill its international obligations. The other two requirements, those of stability and of popular approval, would be satisfied in a short time. But, nevertheless, as Foster—in the same interview in which Vallarta made his declaration—was already talking to him of the problems that the United States Department of State would consider *before* granting recognition, Vallarta should then have suspected that the United States was going to vary its traditional policy, and that, in consequence, recognition would not come easily.

Vallarta wished to use the claims payment as a way to approach directly the United States government, to probe the possibility of recognition and to count on an officially recognized Porfirista representative in Washington. For that reason he did not even try to make the payment through Foster, with whom he already was, and could continue, in good relations, in spite of the fact that thus the handling of the funds would have been simplified and cheaper. Also he rejected Mariscal (in spite of what Foster says in his *Memoirs*), for to trust him with the payment would have confirmed the fiction that Mariscal was the only diplomatic representative accredited and recognized by the United States, and that, for that same reason, the government of Lerdo was the legitimate one.

Vallarta foresaw this conflict, as his instructions to Mata demonstrated. In them he told Mata that if the United States government refused to receive the payment, he should consign it judicially, which was equivalent to resolving not to make the payment in any manner through Mariscal. Mata could, of course, have thought until the last moment that he would do it, since he accompanied Mariscal to the appointment with Secretary of State Hamilton Fish and even entered Fish's antechamber. But such a belief should have vanished when Mariscal, heeding Fish's direction, asked Mata's endorsement of the check he (Mariscal) was carrying; for then it was evident that, after all, it was going to be Mariscal and not Mata who was to make the payment. Mata, relying on his instructions, could have at that moment refused to endorse the check and could have proceeded to consign the payment judicially. He did not do so, and there is not a documentary trace that he was reproached in any way because of it. In any case, he could have objected that, in accord with those same instructions, he should have made the payment "in the name of the government of Mexico," and that he complied if the receipt remained in his possession and was written in that form, as in fact occurred.

In any case, Vallarta, who does not appear to have been a man to use even sporadically the weapon of irony, never said to Foster, even in this sense, that if the United States was determined to consider the Lerdo government as the only legitimate one of Mexico, it should have expected to receive the payment of the claims from it. Far from this, one year afterwards, he paid the second installment as the first, that is to say, "in the name of the government of Mexico."

Even when both payments, and above all the first, did not bring the main fruit of recognition or even the accessory one of seriously exploring the possibilities of an arrangement leading to it, they remained as a demonstration of the capacity and desire of the Díaz government to comply with Mexico's international obligations. And in fact, in various documents of the United States Department of State they were mentioned in that regard, and in the instructions of William M. Evarts to John W. Foster to establish official relations, these two payments were again alluded to approvingly.

With these payments Vallarta pursued recognition above all; but, in default of it, he wished to have a direct channel of negotiation with the United States Department of State; in that way he would no longer be tied to Foster, who might not be able to transmit the opinion of the Mexican government to his government with equal fidelity and interest that a representative of its own would present them. Justifiable and advantageous as that purpose was, it does not seem that Vallarta was right in judging that the Department of State would receive Mata as minister plenipotentiary, for to have done so would have been equivalent to an unequivocal recognition of Díaz. However, it is difficult to appraise Vallarta's wisdom in taking that resolution. We know, of course, that the United States government did not receive Mata officially, and, from this point of view, it can be said that Vallarta failed; in reality, it was not a failure for him, for he had already foreseen this outcome. It was a failure for Vallarta in that the situation which every day became more discrediting to Mata should have been prolonged, and also in the way it ended, for neither Mata nor Vallarta expressed a protest over the rebuff in any form.

Nevertheless, one can hardly make Vallarta responsible for

the initial rebuff, for, as has already been said, Mata disobeyed his instructions: before ascertaining Evarts' intentions, he left in his hands a copy not only of his credentials but also of the proposal for a treaty for the pacification of the frontier. The most, perhaps, that can be said is that Vallarta did not recall Mata soon enough; neither did he attempt any reprisal, even though only external or verbal, against Foster; such, for example, as that of denying him the character of minister plenipotentiary and treating him simply as a confidential agent.

Vallarta did not succeed in controlling himself in his first important meeting with Foster, when Foster informed him that the Department of State was conditioning recognition on the prior resolution of the pending questions; but, even so, he obtained an important result. He succeeded in getting Foster to inform his government that its instructions to Brigadier General Edward O. C. Ord were repudiated by all Mexicans, without distinction of political alignments, and that Lieutenant Colonel W. R. Shafter was already considered as the symbol of United States enmity toward Mexico. His later negotiations always had the tone of a juridical brief; but when he conducted them in writing and calmly, as in his reply to the Foster memorandum, he achieved most brilliant results.

In time, nevertheless, he was to use many other diplomatic techniques, the bluff as well as deceit. One time he told the German minister that the Mexican government looked confidently toward the prospect of a war with the United States, because the country would come out of it victorious and united; and the German minister, as was expected, dashed off to tell Foster about it. At another time he consented to the latter's submitting memoranda on solutions to pending questions only in order to tell him, after having been informed of them, that as Foster seemed to lack instructions and Mata carried full ones to Washington, there was no reason to examine Foster's memoranda. It is true that the United States Department of State did not deal with Mata and that it immediately instructed Foster to re-initiate the negotiations with Vallarta; but when this occurred,

Vallarta was in a better position, now that he knew the opinions of his adversary, whom he now expected to find "more intractable." Therefore Foster rightly resolved to have an interview with President Díaz first.

In the basic negotiations, as has already been said, Foster moved with facility and intelligence, aggressive at times, conciliatory at other times; and the arguments that he used were ingenious, lucid and convincing. Vallarta, however, never lacked good replies, and in any case it was not he who cut off the conversations, but Foster; and it was Foster who found himself in dire straits to re-establish contacts, and he who had to call upon the good offices of Zamacona and Mata to do so.

Vallarta, nevertheless, has been criticized (by Zamacona in his own time and Valadés in ours) for his famous memorandum of September 10, 1877, which contained, in effect, the greatest concession that he would ever offer Foster for the pacification of the frontier. It is difficult, nonetheless, to reconcile that censure with an informed and impartial judgment. Aside from the fact that he did not give in on any of the other issues; aside from the fact that it was not possible to negotiate without yielding something; aside from the fact that in the inevitable give and take more is given when one is least able to resist; aside from the fact that the concession never reached the stage of execution; and aside from the fact that the adversary himself did not find it satisfactory because he desired more—apart from all that, the memorandum made only one important concession, and that was withdrawn immediately, not to be offered again and, of course, not to figure in the agreement finally signed. It was to consent to the reciprocal passage of troops across the international boundary when in pursuit of wild Indians and rustlers. Considered in the gloomiest manner possible, it was equivalent to the crossing being extended from Piedras Negras to Matamoros and to the pursuit being made not only against the Indians, that is the foreign ones, but also against the Mexicans engaged in rustling.

At the time that Vallarta offered that concession, cattle rustling was much more of a cause of the international conflicts than the incursions of wild Indians. Rustling, it hardly need be said, was a recognized crime and punishable by the laws of both countries; and the cattle thief was a criminal of common order. Rustling was thus a true, determinable crime that was not easily confused with acts that were not criminal or with crimes, such as political ones, that required more understanding and less rigorous treatment. Foster wanted the pursuit to be extended to any malefactor, which certainly would increase very much the frequency of the crossing of foreign troops and the possibility that this crossing might be arbitrary and unnecessary.

Thus, the memorandum was a unit, and as such it must be judged. Of course, many of the limitations on the crossing of troops that were proposed in it were maintained in all later negotiations, up to the time of their being accepted by the United States and incorporated finally into the treaty of 1882; such, for example, as the fixing of the limit of twenty leagues as a maximum for the penetration of the foreign forces in pursuit of criminals, no matter how near they might be to catching them; and also the prohibition of the crossing in populated areas in order to avoid conflicts with the civil or military authorities of the other country, and to avoid making ostentatious and insufferable the presence of foreign armies. Included, also, was the limitation that the pursuit should be abandoned and the return of the foreign troops begun when they met with Mexican troops that could continue the chase.

Finally, it must be taken into account in the very first place that Vallarta's memorandum presupposed that the Presidents of the two countries should agree on the duration of the authorization for the crossing and the places in which it would be permitted; that is to say, the possibilities of negotiating and of opposing were to be maintained during the execution of the agreement. And this was so much the key to Vallarta's supposed concession that Foster rejected the whole memorandum, because he foresaw that in the hands of one of the two Presidents—of Porfirio Díaz—would remain the possibility of paralyzing the agreement.

At the last Vallarta tarnished his most brilliant and patriotic diplomatic labor. On answering Foster's note informing him of recognition, he resolved not to restate his initial thesis that recognition would not be accepted as a prize for good conduct, but that the granting of it was an obligation. It is true, however it might have been, that the real victory rested on obtaining it unconditionally and on Evarts' confession that the United States and not Mexico was changing its position; it is true, no matter what, that recognition was a truce in a struggle that had already lasted a year and a half, and that Vallarta would have put an immediate end to the truce and stirred up the battle again if in his reply he had returned to that thesis. But it was no less true that the Lerdista press and the Roman Catholic press disapproved of his conduct, and that the approbation of the Porfirista press failed to be of any comfort or compensation.

THERE IS A LITTLE, or rather a great, mystery in appraising Foster's diplomatic conduct. It has already been said, and perhaps more than once, that he was an intelligent, serious, persistent man, sufficiently knowledgeable about the country and its men and that, in general, he was supported by his government. But it is not contradictory to affirm that he failed almost completely, since few of the agreements or solutions that he proposed were accepted either by his own government or by that of Mexico.

The explanation, as always, must be multiple. Of course, Foster had the misfortune of dealing, in the epoch of Sebastián Lerdo de Tejada, with José María Lafragua and in the first Presidency of Porfirio Díaz, with Ignacio Luis Vallarta—two of the best Secretaries of Foreign Relations that Mexico has had in all its independent history. He also had the bad luck of working during a period of nationalistic exaltation, of complete freedom of the press, of close and daily vigilance of official thought and conduct, so that the Díaz government, even if it wished, could not make great concessions without its enemies, and even its supporters, attacking Díaz and causing him real and great political damage. Furthermore, Porfirio Díaz came to power under very precarious circumstances, and one of his forms of strengthening his position was precisely to allow the phantom of foreign danger to spread over the country in order to unite the Mexicans, or to avoid open discord among them. Initially, therefore, it helped Díaz more for the pending problems with the United States to subsist than for their solution to cause them to disappear; that is to say, again, that Porfirio Díaz was gaining more by resisting than by giving in.

A good part of Foster's own failure must, nonetheless, be attributed wholly to himself. In the first place, he could not get away from the idea, uppermost to him, that because he was representing a strong, neighboring country, his demands would be accepted without any true resistance or with a resistance easy to overcome if he simply repeated his demands, and not because these demands were presented with intelligence and were both well founded and feasible. On various occasions he announced to the Department of State that soon he would report the progress and even the completion of his efforts; and in one dispatch made by telegraph, he was so sure of his own strength and the weakness of the Mexican authorities that he proclaimed that Vallarta "will give in completely." Also he was the victim of an error in perspective. None of the problems whose solution he demanded as a condition prior to the recognition of Díaz was new. He had been working on them with José María Lafragua since his arrival in Mexico during the Presidency of Lerdo. The cattle stealing was more frequent then, even though the incursions of wild Indians were not; the forced loans were levied on United States citizens and interests during the ten years of the Restored Republic and almost disappeared in the first Presidency of Díaz; smuggling into Texas from the Tamaulipan Free Zone—a greater problem at first than later—and the prohibition against the acquisition of real estate dated from the time of Ignacio Comonfort.

Foster was dealing with Lafragua on concrete cases that were arising, at times with success and at other times without it; in general, nonetheless, the solution was simply postponed because it could not be given immediately. But Foster became exasperated and agitated in dealing with Lafragua. Always a fact arose that Foster could never explain; but because of that the fact did not cease to exist and to be real. The problem was not peculiar to those men and to that period; on the contrary, it always had disturbed Mexico's diplomatic understanding with the United States. Lafragua—and Vallarta afterwards—a representative of a country where laws were scarcely respected or complied with, based and defended their position on law; while Foster, in the name of a nation in which law was respected, defended his on considerations of mere expediency, that is to say, on what was convenient or advantageous, on what would lead directly to the solution of a problem.

One time, for example, Foster, in the face of repeated incursions of wild Indians into Texas, proposed to Lafragua that the Mexican government should deliver them to the United States frontier authorities in order that they could be returned to their reservations. Foster's reasoning could not have been simpler or sounder. Those Indians were not of Mexican origin, nor would they have been assimilated into the country's population. They would continue living by their depredations, and as the Mexican government neither wished nor was able to watch them, much less prevent their incursions into Texas, it was better for Mexico to return them without worrying about their fortune in the United States, for Mexico, in every way, would rid itself of a burden and of an international responsibility.

Lafragua could not see the problem in that so simply practical form; rather, he replied to Foster with a long pathetic note in which he vividly revealed all his physical, intellectual and moral being. Most intelligently, supremely humanitarian, with astounding juridical erudition and the purest liberal inspiration, he went back and forth from the natural law to the written to conclude that there was not a single law in Mexico whose letter or whose spirit could impede the entrance and departure from Mexican territory of wild Indians; consequently, their entrance could not be prevented, nor could they be forced to leave.

All of this must have led Foster, himself a lawyer (and from Harvard University) to the idea that in the casuistic negotiation of these problems he would never find the quick solutions that he desired; on the contrary, he would always encounter eternal delay and, above all, interminable and exasperating juridical allegation. And therefore, on seeing the appearance of a revolutionary government needing recognition, he seized upon this circumstance as a providential opportunity to solve permanently all pending questions by making their solution a condition prior to granting it.

But in this tactic Foster committed one of his gravest errors—and the United States Department of State committed it also by making common cause with him—first, because the greater difficulty of resolving simultaneously five or six questions, instead of resolving them one by one, is evident. Then, the combination of all of them and their presentation in a block meant ignoring that some were more compelling and important than others; and that therefore the lesser should be sacrificed to solve the greater. To place on the same level, for example, the incursions of wild Indians and the prohibiting of the acquisition of real estate on the Mexican frontier was to violate the natural perspective of these problems. From the exclusively United States point of view, the former destroyed present riches, while the other, at most, delayed—for it did not prevent—future expansion at a time when Foster was convinced that Mexico lacked an immediate economic future and that American investments would not be lucrative. It was just as erroneous to claim reparations for damages already committed and therefore specific—such as the indemnification of those caused during the revolts of La Noria and Tuxtepec—as well as protection against future, and consequently uncertain, damages at the same time that he was asking for an international agreement that would exempt his countrymen from forced loans.

One of the decisive factors that made his mission fail was the fact that Foster and the Department of State not only did not agree on the time of granting recognition to Mexico, but they did not agree even on the motives that were obstacles to it or the manner of overcoming these obstacles. Foster began with a cautious and sensible attitude when at first he counseled the diplomatic corps to establish personal relations with the new authorities in Mexico City, to observe the development of events, to keep their respective governments informed and to await instructions from them. (In that same meeting, however, Foster did not fail to say that his own government recognized only that of Lerdo.) Afterwards, Secretary of State Hamilton Fish gave Foster discretionary powers to recognize Díaz, and Foster resolved not to wait longer but to introduce the solution of all pending questions. The Department of State then approved his decision and by so doing admitted the idea of a conditioned recognition.

A little while afterwards, Foster adopted the criterion of granting recognition as soon as Díaz should be transformed into a constitutional President through the elections, which had already been called, meanwhile continuing to negotiate the pending problems. He announced then that he would recognize at once that Díaz' was the only *de facto* government; but he resolved not to do it publicly and not even in writing, limiting himself to communicating it verbally to Vallarta. And having in mind a hardly applicable precedent, he recommended the sending of a personal letter from Díaz to the newly elected President of the United States.

While he was awaiting the result of that step, he continued reporting favorably on the Díaz government and came to accept Vallarta's thesis that recognition would bring with it a better atmosphere for negotiating differences; furthermore, he judged that if it were done thus, it would be easier for him to obtain an agreement among the military leaders for the reciprocal passing of troops over the international boundary. Foster insisted a short time later that that was the best solution, and in order to support it, he wrote a long confidential letter to Evarts in which he went so far as to meddle in the sacrosanct ground of the "traditional policy" of his country in the matter of recognition. He said, for example, that stability, one of the criteria for granting recognition, was a relative notion, as was demonstrated by the fact that the United States had begun relations with almost all of the sixty governments that Mexico had had in the last fifty years. He added an argument that he had not used until then, and which was partially inaccurate, that the lack of relations obliged him to serve his government and its citizens in a less than effective manner.

It was already too late, for William M. Evarts, decidedly more than Fish, had resolved to settle on Foster's first criterion: before the United States would grants its friendship to Mexico, it needed to be sure that this friendship was mutual. Foster, as was logical, began now to work within those definitive instructions; nevertheless, from time to time he made observations with the intention of casting doubt on their efficacy and justification. Was not the indignation provoked by Shafter's last invasion natural? The orders given to Brigadier General Ord were a great obstacle that held up the negotiations. Would it not be wise for President Hayes to reconsider them? But in a short time he advised that the movement of United States troops should not be restrained; that there should always be United States ships of war in Mexican ports and that President Hayes should use energetic language in reference to the "Mexican question" in his message to Congress.

When Foster appeared for the first time before the Congress of his country, he gave an intelligent and just explanation of the obstacles that were limiting Mexico's cooperation in the pacification of the frontier, an explanation that he never had given so well substantiated and so resolutely to the Department of State. But when he appeared in company with Evarts, he agreed with the thinking of the latter that far from the lack of recognition having damaged Díaz' government, it had strengthened it.

Even in the matter of making their position known to the Mexican government there was little agreement between the Department of State and its minister in Mexico City. Evarts' instructions were always somewhat peremptory and they without fail used some expressions that might offend, as "if Díaz is honest about this"; but they were not of angry intent and it could even be said that, in view of the long antecedents of the subjects, they were cordial. Foster's accompanying note, as has been said, was quite dry, devoid of the feeling of satisfaction that, at last, an annoying period in the relations of the two countries had been concluded.

All of this does not mean that Foster's work lacked skill or that another representative of the United States might have succeeded better, because it should be repeated that a close and detailed study of his mission cannot fail to awaken a feeling of admiration, and so much the more so in comparison with all the diplomatic representatives that followed him down to Henry Lane Wilson, all of whom were without doubt his inferiors.

One of Foster's personal successes was the insistent recommendation that Mexico's first step in the task of cooperating in the pacification of the frontier should be to name a single commander of the federal forces, and that this nomination should fall to an officer of high rank, experience and prestige. The reasons that made this measure necessary were properly explained, and even when Porfirio Díaz could offer only the mediocre solution of Jerónimo Treviño, the situation undeniably improved with his designation. That measure was Foster's idea; it was never suggested by the Department of State and Foster did not even receive encouragement to persist in it. The fact is that the first limitation of the instructions to Ord was ordered as a reply to the designation of Treviño, for the Department of State as well as the United States Secretary of War took it as the first sign that the Mexican government had finally awakened to the gravity of the frontier problems.

Helping the government of Mexico "to awaken" to the seriousness of these problems was one of Foster's great successes; for if any defect, incredible as it may be, is to be found in the attitude of the Mexican government, it is the absolute lack of comprehension of the problem of the wild Indians. The attitude of an exceptional man like Lafragua has already been cited. Not a single opinion on the seriousness of this problem is to be found in the papers of Vallarta and Zamacona, a sign that it in itself did not worry them except as a cause of friction with the United States. On the other hand the excellent and experienced pedagogue Francisco Naranjo asserted that with a good education the wild Indians would become a part of the Mexican population and would be factors in a new prosperity. And Porfirio Díaz offered in one instance to send to the southeast of the country all the barbarous Indians captured in the military campaign against them; thus would be resolved, of course, the problem of their murdering and robbing Texans, not mattering that afterwards they might rob and murder the Mexicans in the southeast.

One thing more—and not an insignificant one—Foster secured. In spite of the zeal with which he carried out his mission, of the perseverance and even the rudeness with which he defended his point of view, and in spite of the fact that in the eyes of the Mexicans he was the embodiment of the war of aggression, he found out how to keep the respect of those with whom he was dealing. Private documents are not known in which the Secretaries of Foreign Relations or their associates who dealt with him—José María Lafragua, Ignacio L. Vallarta, José María Mata, Eleuterio Ávila, and Miguel Ruelas—passed adverse judgment on him. Vallarta, who suffered from him in his worst period, resolved to make official rectification to the effect that he did not hold the opinion that Foster was the greatest obstacle to recognition. Mata, in spite of his failure in Washington, sought him out and entertained him; Manuel María de Zamacona did the same, even though he seemed to have the impression that Foster was "more Papist than the Pope." With Ignacio Mariscal and with Matías Romero he had very close friendships, notwithstanding the fact that he publicly argued the economic conditions of Mexico with the latter. He established good relations with Jerónimo Treviño, Servando Canales and Francisco Naranjo. It cannot be doubted that Porfirio Díaz held him in esteem, nor that Foster prided himself on having had Díaz in his home and that in it Díaz became acquainted with Carmen Romero Rubio, his heart's delight. Foster, in fact, was the author of a theory that has been since adopted by more than one Mexican historian that that marriage was providential, because to the rude efficiency of the man was added the sweet refinement of the lady.

PORFIRIO DÍAZ WAS, of course, a principal actor in this drama, even though on few occasions is it possible to determine exactly the true nature and significance of his role. His *Archivo,* has revealed nothing up to now—or, searching for the negative interpretation, it would reveal that his predicaments did not interest him greatly, an absurdity, of course. His *Archivo* does not reveal anything because never, it seems, shall we know if everything in it is being published, or if the documentary pieces are being selected according to a preconceived image; but also it is silent because Porfirio Díaz was not an active correspondent but a passive one. He answered, when he would reply, what others asked him; but seldom, if ever, did he take the initiative of asking anything of interest of his fellows or of himself. That being the situation, who could write to him about this drama? Those who could do it, because of the character of their relations and of their political position, saw him in Mexico City, in the Cabinet, in the Chamber of Deputies, in the Senate, or in an account of some important daily newspaper. Such was the case of Vicente Riva Palacio or of Matías Romero. Both were close to him, in good political positions and active correspondents; but both were in the cabinet.

In the aide-mémoires of Vallarta and of Foster appear occasionally points of view or requests of Porfirio Díaz, and in such instances I have been very careful so to state in this account.

Unfortunately, too few of these cases have occured to make interpretation safe; but, and as far as the information goes, Porfirio Díaz seemed to have an attitude of energy greater even than Vallarta. The latter in a particular instance was inclined to ask the Mexican Senate for authorization to agree to the reciprocal passage of troops over the border if the United States revoked the instructions to Ord, while Porfirio Díaz wanted to add the condition that Mexico would furthermore require explanations and reparations for invasion into its territory. In the narrative parts of this work, other documents found in the archives of Vallarta and Matías Romero have been spoken of that inversely give the idea that the frictions with the United States profoundly preoccupied Porfirio Díaz, besides causing him great perplexity and real disgust, since they persisted and even grew worse in spite of his having the firm conviction that he had done everything possible to remedy them.

BE THAT AS IT MAY, there can be no doubt that in the diplomatic struggle Mexico was the conqueror and the United States was the conquered. In the more general and more permanent confrontation of the interest of one country with the other, there can be little doubt that the United States was the winner, since on succeeding in taking from Porfirio Díaz his vigilance and his anti-imperialistic convictions, the United States was able to exercise in Mexico an unrestricted influence. Nevertheless, the United States lost something much more important and more permanent than the expansion of its economic interests and its political influence: it lost the admiration and the trust of the Mexicans. A day will come when a history of the ideas of the Mexicans about the United States will be written, and then it will be seen that, in spite of the War of 1847, that that country was held in great esteem and in great admiration. It represented for the Mexicans the most advanced country in the world in its political organization and the only one that undertook with success the gigantic task of creating a limitless richness that was spread over all and not over only a small aristocracy or a few oligarchs. That esteem and that admiration were transformed into very different ideas and feelings: the negative ones of distrust, suspicion and even hate. When the Department of State ordered its diplomats and consuls in Mexico to make an inquiry in order to find out if the United States and its citizens were popular, and the result of it showed an openly expressed unpopularity, the question should have arisen of whether obtaining economic preponderance at the price of losing esteem and admiration was worth the price.

Big stick diplomacy was in style, but from it one can draw the moral that this book seems to present: threat and compulsion are like playing with fire, and contrary to common belief, the fire sometimes burns.

NOTES

Chapter I. NAW RG59 DI, Oct. 21, Nov. 23, Dec. 6, 1866; NAW RG59 DD, Dec. 24, 1866; June 25, 1867; Dec. 1, 13, 24, 1866; March 6, June 10, 11, 12, 15, 21, 22, 1867; July 1, 10, 1867; ARE III/364 (72-73) /2, pages 1-7; Hicks, *The American Nation*, II, 14-43; ARE/ 364 (72-73) /2, pages 9-12, 13, 17, 21-22, 26-27, 31-32; DL, X, 585-88; DL, XII, 498-99; DL, XIII, 73-75; DL, XI, 471-72.

Chapter II. MR, Nov. 28, 1876; NAW RG59 DD, Nov. 28, 1876; MR, Dec. 1, 1876; MH 77, pp. 251-52; NAW RG59 DD, Dec. 9, 1876; DL, XIII, 123-26, 69-72, 90-91; MH 77, pp. 24-25; AIV, no. 530; PV, Nov. 30, 1876, Dec. 1, 4, 1876; NAW RG59 DD, Nov. 28, Dec. 19, 1876; DL, XIII, 92; NAW RG59 DD, Dec. 8, 1876.

Chapter III. NAW RG59 DD, Dec. 1, 4, 1876; ARE III/242 (73-72) /44, pp. 15-17, 18-21; NAW RG59 DD, Dec. 29, 1876; NAW RG59 DI, Dec. 20, 1876; APD, XVI, 188; ARE III/242 (73-72) /44, pp. 23-27; AIV, no. 530; NAW RG59 DI, Jan. 19, 1877; NAW RG59 DD, Jan. 16, 1877; ARE III/242 (73-72) /44, pp. 39, 43; NAW RG59 DD, Jan. 20, 1877; ARE III/242 (73-72) /44, pp. 43-44, 48-52, 55, 57-60, 93-101; NAW RG59 DD, Feb. 12, 1877; MR, March 7, 13, 1877; DO, March 8, 14, 16, 1877; NAW RG59 DI, Feb. 12, 1877; VM, Feb. 6, 1877; NAW RG59 DD, Jan. 20, Feb. 19, March 3, 1877; ARE LE (libro especial) 1293, pp. 10-13, 15-19, 43, 48, 50, 56, 59; ARE LE 1293, II, pp. 15, 59, 77, 80, 83, 88, 98, 103, 110, 114, 118, 119, 122, 126; NAW RG59 DD, March 4, April 28, May 8, June 16, July 30, 1877; AMR PV1878, XI.

Chapter IV. Webb, *The Texas Rangers*, 311-20; HR 45th Congress, 1st Session, *Ex. Doc.* 13, p. 128; Morison, *The Growth of the American Republic*, II, 5, 79-80; Webb, *The Great Plains*, 61, 169; Morison, *op.*

cit., 83, 81; Webb, *op. cit.,* 207-59; Morison, *op. cit.,* 91; Webb, *The Texas Rangers,* 322; Rippy, *The United States and Mexico,* 282; Callahan, *American Foreign Policy in Mexican Relations,* 354; Webb, *op. cit.,* 233-39, 242, 287-89; HR 45th Congress, 1st Session, *Ex. Doc.* 13, pp. 9-10; Webb, *op. cit.,* 298, 293; Rippy, *op. cit.,* 286; *Informe de la comisión pesquisadora . . . ,* 119, 130, 124; Webb, *op. cit.,* 256, 261-62, 264-65; Callahan, *op. cit.,* 356; *Correspondencia diplomática relativa a las invasiones . . . ,* 4; HR 45th Congress, 1st Session *Ex. Doc.,* 13, pp. 4-5, 9-10; Rippy, *op. cit.,* 290; ARE 241.5 (73-72) /7, pp. 20-31.

Chapter V. NAW RG94 from Ord to the Minister of War, Feb. 16, 1877; Morison, *op. cit.,* 56-74; Bowers, *The Tragic Era, passim* and especially pp. 522-40; Morison, *op. cit.,* 76-78; NAW RG59 DD, March 19, 1877; MR, March 14, 17, 1877; S, March 22, 1877; NAW RG59 DI, Dec. 26, 1876; NAW RG59 DD, Dec. 9, 1876; NAW RG59 DI, Feb. 12, March 3, 4, 1877; NAW RG59 DI, March 27, 31, 1877; HR 45th Congress, 1st Session, *Ex. Doc.,* 13, pp. 4-5; NAW RG94, Ord to Sherman, Jan. 3, 1877; NAW RG94, Dedin to Sherman, Jan. 25, 1877; NAW RG94, May 27, 1877; NAW RG59 DD, April 24, 1877; NAW RG59, Confidential letter of April 28, 1877; NAW RG59 DD, April 25, May 7, 8, 24, 28, 1877.

Chapter VI. NAW RG59 DI, May 16, 27, 1877; NAW RG94, McCraig to Sherman, June 1, 1877; Rippy, *op. cit.,* 296; *A Compilation of the Messages and Papers of the Presidents of the United States,* X, 4419-20; ARE LE, 396, pp. 72-80; AIV, 564; NAW RG59 DD, May 28, June 18, 1877; ARE LE, 396, pp. 88-91; NAW RG59 DD, August 2, 1877; ARE LE, 396, pp. 92-93; AIV, no. 537; ARE LE, 396, pp. 90-103, 105-07; *Correspondencia diplomática . . . ,* 42-46, 54, 56; NAW RG59 DD, May 28, 1877; MT, June 20, 1877; *Correspondencia diplomática . . . ,* 61-62, 67; NAW RG59 DD, June 18, 20, 22, 28, 29, 1877.

Chapter VII. VM, June 20, 1877; Co, July 17, 1877; F, July 6, 1877; MR, April 8, May 22, 1877; PV, April 19, 1877; MR, April 4, 1877; F, June 28, 1877; Pt, April 27, May 16, 1877; S, May 2, 1877; F, May 29, 1877, July 18, 1877; HT, May 17, 1877; Pt, April 27, 1877; MR, May 18, 1877; Pt, June 17, 1877; Mt, May 23, 1877; MR, April 8, June 19, 1877; F, July 14, 1877; Pt, July 8, 1877; F, May 30, June 23, 1877; DO, June 23, 1877; F, June 27, 1877; Mt, June 26, 1877; F, June 20, 22, 1877; MR, June 19, 20, 1877; Pt, June 21, July 20, 1877; F, July 2, 24, 26, Sept. 13, Nov. 15, 1877; Pt, July 25, 1877; DO, July 20, 1877; Mt, Sept. 2, 1877; Pt, Oct. 19, 1877; BN, Oct. 20, 1877; M, Nov. 9, 1877;

DO, Nov. 12, 1877; F, July 18, August 23, Sept. 16, 1877; BN, Oct. 20, Nov. 15, 16, 20, 1877; F, Nov. 24, 1877; BN, Dec. 6, 1877; VM, Dec. 12, 18, 1877; PA, Dec. 27, 1877; F, Feb. 2, 1877.

Chapter VIII. DL, VIII, 95; NAW RG94, Sherman to Sheridan, June 9, 1877, Sheridan to Townsend, June 12, 1877; HR 45th Congress, 1st Session, *Ex. Doc.,* 13, p. 17; Mt, June 20, 1877; Pt, June 29, 1877; Mt, July 12, 1877; NAW RG94, Sheridan to Townsend, June 29, 1877, Dedin to Ord, June 25, 1877, Ord to Sheridan, June 27, 1877; Mt, July 13, 1877; NAW RG94, Ord to Sheridan, July 6, 1877, Ord to Townsend, July 13, 1877, McCraig to Ord, July 14, 1877, Ord to Mc-Craig, July 16, 1877, Commandant of Fort Duncan to Ord, July 24, 1877, Williams to Ord, July 21, 1877, Naranjo to Ord, August 2, 1877; Pt, August 12, July 25, 1877; F, July 28, 1877; Pt, July 31, 1877; Mt, Sept. 1, 1877; NAW RG59 DI, August 15, 1877; NAW RG59 DD, August 23, 1877; F, Sept. 1, Oct. 7, 12, 1877; BN, Nov. 20, 1877; VM, Dec. 1, 1877; MR, Jan. 2, 1878; VM, Jan. 15, 1878.

Chapter IX. NAW RG59 DD, June 23, 28, 1877; *Correspondencia diplomática* . . . , pp. 66-67; NAW RG59 DD, June 30 (confidential letter), July 8, August 12, Sept. 4, August 31, Sept. 4, 1877; DL, II, 19; NAW RG59 DD, Sept. 4, 1877; ARE LE 1712, pp. 11-15; DL, II, 456; NAW RG59 DD, Sept. 4, 1877; ARE LE 1712, pp. 15-57.

Chapter X. NAW RG59 DD, confidential letter of August 31, 1877; *ibid.,* Sept. 11, 1877 (confidential letter) ; *ibid.,* Sept. 15, 1877; NAW RG59 DI, Oct. 6, 1877; *ibid.,* DD, Oct. 30 (confidential letter), Nov. 8, 10, 12, 16, 17, 28 (telegram), 28, 1877; ARE LE 1712, pp. 85-92; NAW RG59 DD, Nov. 28, 1877; ARE LE 1712, pp. 102-10, 112-30.

Chapter XI. NYT, Dec. 9, 1877; ARE 2-1-1781, pp. 3-9; MR, Jan. 6, 1878; NAW RG59 DD, personal letter, Dec. 14, 1877; Pt, April 23, 1878; NAW RG59 DD, Dec. 14, 1877; MR, Jan. 6, 19, 1878; M, March 24, 1878; Pt. March 24, 1878; ARE 26-23-68, pp. 116-53, 16-34; MR, Jan. 18, 1878; ARE 1-1-115, pp. 1-8; ARE 2-1-17-80, pp. 76-82; MR, Jan. 6, 1878; ARE LE 1712, pp. 39-41; NAW RG59 DD, Feb. 9, 1878; Pt, Jan. 23, 1878; NAW RG59 DD, Sept. 5, 9, 1878; BN, March 19, Feb. 28, 1878; LI, March 5, 6, 1878; BN, March 19, 22, 1878; NAW RG59 DD, March 14, 1878; NAW RG59 DI, March 23, 1878; NAW RG59 DD, April 8, 11, 1878; BN, April 10, 1878; MR, April 12, 1878; F, April 11, 12, 1878; Rno, Sept. 7, 1879; BN, April 13, 1878; M, April 11, 1878; Pt, April 12, 1878.

Chapter XII. Li, April 12, 1878; BN, April 13, 1878; Li, April 13,

1878; NAW RG59 DD, May 2, 1878; ARE LE 1712, pp. 152-54; NAW RG59 DD, May 2, 1878; ARE LE 1712, pp. 154-74; AIV, no. 135; NAW RG59 DD, May 2, 15, 1878; AIV, no. 534-140; AMR PV78; AMR PV76-77; IM, I, 165; AMR PV1876; AMR PV78; ARE 26-23-68, pp. 61-91, 100-01, 106, 116-53, 113-15, 155-62; MR, August 30, 1878; M, Sept. 19, 1878; MR, Sept. 20, 1878; VM, August 30, 1878; MR, Sept. 21, 24, 1878; ARE 26-23-68, pp. 164, 168, 171-82, 183-85, 188-89; F, June 4, 6, 1878; MR, June 25, August 21, June 11, August 31, Sept. 4, 1878; PA, July 18, 1878; F, June 12, 13, 1878; MR, June 20, 1878; NAW RG59 DD, April 22, 1878; NAW RG59 DI, June 31, 1878; VM, June 22, 1878; *Memoria* A78, pp. 21-32; MR, July 19, 28, August 27, 28, Sept. 12, 1878.

Chapter XIII. AMR PV78; NAW RG94, Ord to Sherman, Sept. 30, 1878; NAW RG94, Sheridan to Sherman, June 24, 1878; NAW RG94, McCrary to Sherman, Sheridan and Ord, June 29, 1878; *ibid.*, Ord to Sherman, July, 1878; *ibid.*, Sheridan to Sherman, July 2, 1878; *ibid.*, Sherman to McCrary, July 6, 1878; HR 45th Congress, 2nd Session. *Index to the Reports of Committees of the House of Representatives. Report no. 701*, p. x; NAW RG94, Thomas M. Vincent to the commandant of Fort Clark, June 29, 1878; NAW RG94, Ford and Storms to Ord, and the latter to the former, August 17, 19, 1878; *ibid.*, McCrary to Sherman, August 19, 1878.

Chapter XIV. NAW RG59 DD, May 23, June 17, 1878; NAW RG59 DI, July 24, 1878; NAW RG59 DD, June 27, 1878; ARE LE 1712, pp. 198-213; NAW RG59 DD, July 15, 1878; NAW RG59 DI, August 13, 1878, Jan. 15, June 23, 1879; NAW RG59 DD, Oct. 14, 1878; NAW RG59 DI, August 9, Nov. 15, 1878; NAW RG59 DD, Dec. 26, 1879; ARE LE 1712, pp. 198-213; NAW RG59 DD, August 24, Oct. 30, 1878; NAW RG59 DI, Dec. 2, 20, 1878; ARE LE 1712, pp. 226, 215-19, 214-15; NAW RG59 DD, August 30, Sept. 19, 21, 7, 23, Oct. 13, 15, 1878; ARE LE 1712, pp. 215-19; NAW RG59 DI, Sept. 20, 28, Oct. 1, Nov. 1, 1878, Feb. 20, 1879; NAW RG59 DD, March 15, April 30, July 23, Sept. 11, 1878; NAW RG94, Ord to Sheridan, June 21, 1878; NAW RG59 DI, Nov. 29, 1878, Jan. 22, 1879; NAW RG59 DD, Jan. 22, 1879; NAW RG59 DI, Sept. 14, 20, 1878; NAW RG59 DD, Oct. 5, 16, Dec. 10, 14, 23, 1878, March 1, April 8, Sept. 21, Dec. 18, 1879; NAW RG59 DD, Nov. 29, 1878; NAW RG59 DD, Dec. 22, 1879; NAW RG59 DI, Feb. 10, March 1, 1880; NAW RG59 DD, Feb. 2, March 2, 1880; NAW RG59 DD, personal letter of Dec. 13, 1879; NAW RG59 DD, April 17,

22, 1880; NAW RG59 DI, March 1, April 22, 1880; NAW RG59 DD, May 4, 10, 1880; NAW RG59 DI, June 13, 18, 1880; NAW RG59 DD, June 20, 28, 1880; NAW RG59 DI, June 26, 1880; NAW RG59 DD, July 23, 1880; NAW RG59 DI, coded telegram of Sept. 14, 1880; NAW RG59 DI, Sept. 14, 15, 1880; NAW RG59 DD, Sept. 21, 22, 25, 30, Oct. 17, Nov. 3, 1880; *Memoria* 81, pp. 6-7; ARE 7-9-15 (1) ; ARE 11-95, pp. 1-16; Li, May 25, 1881; S, August 26, 1882; VM, August 27, 1882; Li, August 27, Sept. 21, 1882; Ponl, August 7, 1880; MR, Jan. 5, 1882; Li, March 1, 1881; MR, March 6, 8, 1881; Li, March 9, 1881; Na, March 22, 1881; HT, March 20, 1881; Rp, Dec. 2, 1881; Li, March 2, 1881; S, Feb. 7, 1882; Li, Oct. 11, 1882; *Memorias,* pp. 84, 98, 90, VII; Pt, March 1, Feb. 28, 1883; Li, March 15, 1883; S, March 12, 1883; VM, March 15, 1883; Pt, March 17, 1883; S, March 21, 26, 27, 1883; Li, March 17, April 28, May 5, 1883.

BIBLIOGRAPHY AND KEY
TO ABBREVIATIONS

Two well-known works on Mexican-United States relations are those by J. Fred Rippy and James Morton Callahan. The latter is an extreme example of traditional diplomatic history—namely, a work that is built solely and exclusively on diplomatic correspondence. But although Callahan is to be admired for his skillful use of United States diplomatic documents, it must be pointed out that he does not use even so much as one single Mexican document—an astonishing omission in a serious work whose subject is the foreign policy of the United States in Mexico. How is it possible to explain the origins, purposes, and results of this policy if one ignores the part played by the country which, actively or passively, experienced it?

Rippy's book, besides being free to some extent of this inexplicable fault, is more sensitive (or more intelligent) insofar as one not infrequently finds attempts to explain the adverse reactions to, and even condemnation of, United States Policy, as well as the historical occurrences. There is nothing of this sort in Callahan's work, and for this very reason it smacks strongly of the State Department.

Incidentally, for a modest Mexican historian needing sorely to know all that has been written on the theme he proposes to explore, particularly if the subject has been treated by great scholars, a scrutiny of North American bibliography does not fail to be disconcerting. Rippy, who published the first edition of his book in 1926, ignored Hackett's work on the recognition of Díaz, which came out in 1924; and Callahan, whose book appeared in 1932, ignored the existence of both the 1926 and 1931 editions of Rippy's book.

In any case, for the purposes of the present study it has not been possible to make much use of the classic works by Rippy and Callahan. In large measure they identify the Mexican-United States relations of this period with the "peaceful penetration" that occurred, in effect, during a good part of the Porfirista period, whereas here I study the political effects that such penetration produced in Mexico.

Of the books used bearing on United States relations with Mexico, the two really outstanding ones are those by Walter Prescott Webb. A rare mixture of knowledge, talent, imagination, and lofty love for the subject, they may be read for the simple pleasure of seeing the play of Webb's great intellectual and emotive gifts. For my purposes, however, their usefulness was limited to clarification of some factors that might explain the background of frontier frictions. Similarly, the usefulness of works by Bowers, Hicks, and Morison and Commager was limited to proving certain facts about United States life.

It will be seen that, except for the work of Valadés, the Mexican historians have contributed nothing to the study of United States-Mexican relations during the period to which this book is confined.

In contrast to the paucity of printed works is the truly overwhelming wealth of documentary sources. Of these sources, the Mexican are less abundant and less carefully preserved, less readily available for consultation or even frankly inaccessible; but, even so, in the archives of the Mexican embassy in Paris (rich, important, intact, and now very well catalogued and described by Luis Weckmann), of the Mexican embassy in Washington (less rich and ill preserved), and, above all, in the holdings of the Minister of Foreign Relations, there is a real store of documentary materials from which one can derive, except in a few instances, a very solidly based diplomatic history. At the other extreme are the sources of the National Archives of the United States, impressively rich, magnificently well preserved and classified, of an ease of access for consultation so generous and effective that it is unequaled anywhere else in the world.

In addition to this enormous horde of official documentation, other manuscript sources have been consulted: in the United States, the private archive of John W. Foster, deposited in the Manuscript Division of the Library of Congress—but unfortunately it contained not a single document of interest for this work; and in Mexico, the personal archives of Ignacio L. Vallarta and Matías Romero.

AIV: MS Archivo de Ignacio Luis Vallarta. (In the hands of his grandsons, Ignacio and José Vallarta Bustos. The number that follows is that of a classification made by Vallarta's son.)

AMR PV: MS Archivo de Matías Romero (in the Banco de Mexico). Papeles varios. (The number that follows the initials PV corresponds to the year.)

AP: *El Amigo del Pueblo*. Mexico City.

APD: *Archivo del general Porfirio Díaz. Memorias y documentos.* (Prólogo y notas de Alberto María Carreño.) 19 vols. Mexico: Editorial "Elede," 1947-55.

ARE: MS Archivo de la Secretaría de Relaciones Exteriores de México. (The initials LE indicate that the number of the expediente corresponds to its topographical location; otherwise the number refers to the decimal classification. The letter *f* corresponds to the folio of the respective document.)

Bancroft, Hubert Howe. *Vida de Porfirio Díaz*. San Francisco: The History Co., 1887.

BN: *La Bandera nacional*. Mexico City, September 12, 1877-May 12, 1878.

Bowers, Claude G. *The Tragic Era. The Revolution after Lincoln.* Boston: Houghton Mifflin, 1929.

Callahan, James Morton. *American Foreign Policy in Mexican Relations*. New York: Macmillan, 1932.

———. *The Evolution of Seward's Mexican Policy*. Morgantown, West Virginia University Studies in American History, Series I, Nos. 4-6.

Co: *El Combate*. Mexico City, January 30, 1876-October 3, 1880.

Correspondencia diplomática relativa a las invasiones de territorio mexicano por fuerzas de Estados Unidos de 1873 a 1877. Mexico: Cumplido, 1878.

DL: Dublán y Lozano. *Legislación mejicana*. 44 vols. Mexico, Imprenta del Gobierno, 1876-1913.

DO: *Diario oficial del gobierno supremo de la República*. Mexico, 1876-1915.

F: *El Federalista*. Mexico City, January 2, 1871-1878.

Foster, John Watson. *Las memorias diplomáticas de Mr. Foster sobre México, con un prólogo de Genaro Estrada. (Archivo histórico diplomático mexicano*, no. 29) Mexico, 1929.

Gregg, Robert D. *The Influence of Border Troubles on Relations between the United States and Mexico*. Baltimore: The Johns Hopkins Press, 1937.

Hackett, Charles Wilson, "The Recognition of the Díaz Government by the United States," *Southwestern Historical Quarterly*, XXVIII (July, 1924), 34-35.

Hicks, John D. *The American Nation*. 2nd edition. Boston: Houghton Mifflin, 1949.

HR: United States. 45th Congress, 1st Session. *Index to the Executive Documents of the House of Representatives of the United States . . .* vol. I. Washington: Government Printing Office, 1877.

HR: United States. 45th Congress. 2nd Session. *Index to the Reports of Committees of the House of Representatives. Report no. 701. Report and Accompanying documents of the Committee on Foreign Affairs on the Relations of the United States with Mexico.* Washington: Government Printing Office, 1878.

HT: *El Hijo del trabajo.* Mexico City, 1877-1881.

Iglesias, José María. *La cuestión presidencial en 1876.* Mexico: Tipografía Literaria de Filomena Mata, 1892.

IM: *Informes y manifiestos de los poderes ejecutivo y legislativo.* 3 vols. Mexico: Imprenta del Gobierno Federal, 1905.

Informe de la Comisión pesquisadora de la frontera norte al ejecutivo de la Unión sobre las depredaciones de los indios y otros males que sufre la frontera mexicana. Mexico: Díaz de León, 1874.

Lester, Edward. *The Mexican Republic.* An Historical Study. New York: The American News Co., 1878.

Li: *La Libertad.* Mexico City, January 5, 1878-December 31, 1884.

López Portillo y Rojas, José. *Elevación y caída de Porfirio Díaz.* Mexico, Librería Española, s.f.

M: *El Mensajero.* Mexico City, January 2, 1871-December 5, 1880.

M81: *Memoria que en cumplimiento del precepto constitucional presenta al décimo congreso de la union el C. Ignacio Mariscal, secretario de estado y del despacho de relaciones exteriores.* Mexico: Tipografía de Gonzalo A. Esteva, 1881. (It covers the period for 1878-Sept., 1881.)

MacCorkle, S. A. *American Policy of Recognition towards Mexico.* Baltimore: The Johns Hopkins Press, 1933.

Memoria A78: Memoria que en complimiento del precepto constitucional, presentó al congreso de la Union el C. Ignacio L. Vallarta, secretario de estado y del despacho de relaciones exteriores. Mexico: Imprenta de Gonzalo A. Esteva, 1878. (Covers years December 6, 1875 to December 10, 1877.)

MH77: *Memoria de hacienda y crédito público correspondiente al quincuagésimo segundo año económico trascurrido del 1 de julio de 1876 a 30 de junio de 1877, presentado por el secretario de hacienda y crédito público al congreso de la Unión el 10 de diciembre de 1877.* Mexico, 1877.

Morison, Samuel Elliot and Henry Steele Commager. *The Growth of the American Republic.* 2 vols. 4th ed. New York: Oxford University Press, 1952.

MR: *El Monitor republicano.* Mexico City, January, 1873-1890.

MT: *El Monitor Tuxtepecano.* Mexico City, 1876-1877.

Na: *El Nacional.* Mexico City, 1880-1894.

NAW RG59 DD: MS National Archives. Washington. Record Group 59. Dispatches of Foreign Agents to the Department of State.

NAW RG59 DI: MS National Archives. Washington. Record Group 59. Diplomatic Instructions.

NAW RG94: MS National Archives. Washington. Record Group 94. Papers of the Secretary of War of the United States.

NYT: *The New York Times.*

Ponl: *Periódico oficial del estado de Nuevo León.* Monterrey, 1876-1880.

Pt: *La Patria.* Mexico City, 1877-1913.

PV: *El Pájaro verde.* Mexico City, 1861-1875.

Richardson, James D. *A Compilation of the Messages and Papers of the Presidents.* 11 vols. New York: Bureau of National Literature, 1908.

Rippy, J. Fred. The United States and Mexico. 1st ed., New York, 1926; 2nd ed., 1931.

Rno: *El Republicano.* Mexico City, January 1, 1879-1881.

Rp: *La Republica.* Mexico City, 1880-1885.

S: *El Siglo XIX.* Mexico City, 1841-1896.

Valadés, José C. *El Porfirismo. Historia de un régimen.* 3 vols. Mexico: José Porrúa and Editorial Patria, 1941-47.

VM: *La Voz de México.* Mexico City, April, 1870-1909.

Webb, Walter Prescott. *The Great Plains.* Boston: Ginn & Co., 1931.

———. *The Texas Rangers. A Century of Frontier Defense.* Boston: Houghton Mifflin, 1935.

INDEX

Abilene, Kansas, 44
abbreviations, key to, 245
Acapulco, Mexico, United States consul at, 64, 110, 183
Ackley, steamboat, 104
Alatorre, Ignacio R., 179
"Alcestes," pseudonym of newspaper-man, 57
Alfonso, king of Spain, 34
American News Co. (The), 148
American debt, 15, 18, 22
Antillón, Florencio, General, 27, 51
Arbeu Theater (Mexico City), 196
Arriola, border bandit, 198-199
Arthur, Chester A., President of the United States, 215
Aubert, J., et Cie, French firm in Mexico City, 16
Austin, Texas, 215
Austrian; *see* military forces
Ávalos, Ceferino, Mexican soldier, 200
Ávila, Eleuterio, Mexican agent on Joint Claims Commission, 24, 25, 29, 170-172, 176, 192, 195, 199, 205; chief clerk in Mexican Department of Foreign Relations, 235
Ayutla, revolution of, 148

Baghdad, Tamaulipas, Mexico, 193
Baja California; *see* Lower California
Bancroft, Hubert Howe, 14 n., 247
bandits in Texas, 45, 179
Bank of London and South America, 18
Banning, Henry B. (United States Senator), Chairman of Committee on Military Affairs, 139, 146-147
Barron and Forbes, English firm in Mexico, xi, xii, 13, 16
Bavaria, steamship, 31
Baz, Juan José, 5
Béistegui, Félix, estate of, 16

Belgium, officers and troops of, 3, 156
Benavides, Rafael, General, 51, 90
Beneke, Esteban, German merchant in Mexico City, 14
Benítez, Justo, 17, 174
Benson, Nettie Lee, viii, xii
Bibiano; *see* Villarreal
bibliography, 245
Blanco, Miguel, General, 61, 149
Blaine, James G., United States Secretary of State, 207, 208
Bowers, Claude G., 52, 240, 246, 247
Bravo, Río; *see* Rio Grande
Brazil, emperor of, 215
Bringas, Jesús, wealthy Mexican, 15
Brownsville, Texas, 45, 76, 187
Bryan, Guy M., adviser of President Hayes, 67
Bullis, John L., Lieutenant, 59, 96, 161, 186
Bureau of Indian Affairs, 42
Burdel, Ernest, of the French legation in Mexico, 63

cable, of the Atlantic Coast of the United States, 196
Cacahuamilpa, Mexican caves, 211
California, 140; legislature, 142
Callahan, James Morton, 5, 240, 245, 247
Camacho, Sebastián, 16
Camargo, Tamaulipas, Mexico, 94, 104-107
Campbell, Lewis D., United States minister to Mexico, 5-6
Canales, Servando, 50-51, 90, 93, 101-102, 105-107, 149, 200, 203, 236; death, 217
Canales Division, 217
Carbó, José Guillermo, General, 217
Carlota, empress of Mexico, 3
Carmelita; *see* Carmen Romero Rubio

[251]

Carreño, Alberto María, 247
Casimiro Collado, stagecoach firm in Mexico, 16
Catholic Church, 5, 93
Catholic newspapers, 109, 153, 156, 158, 208, 228
cattle industry, in Texas, 40, 42-44, 66, 218; in Chihuahua, 218
Ceballos, José, 27
Central Rail Road of Mexico, 212, 219
Cervantes, Manuel C. de, 16
Charles, Hipólito, 90
Chiapas (state), government of, 122
Chicago, Illinois, meat packing center, 43, 215
Chihuahua (state) Mexico, 84, 92, 103, 129, 133, 135, 201, 203, 217-218
Cimatario Hill, 4
Ciudad Juárez, Chihuahua, 219
Coahuila, Mexico, 51, 76, 84, 86, 92, 103, 129, 133, 175, 191, 194, 196, 200-201, 210, 217
El Combate (Mexico City) newspaper, 81
Coke, Richard, governor of Texas, 47-8; United States Senator, 96
Colegio de Mexico (Mexico City), v
Collado, Casimiro, 16
Colorado, state of, 43
Commercial relations, between United States and Mexico, 193-194, 202
Comonfort, Ignacio, President of Mexico, 122, 229
Commager, Henry Steele, 246, 248
Confederate States of the South, 7, 10, 38, 218
Convention of 1868 between the United States and Mexico, 26, 114, 126
Corona, Ramón, republican forces of, 4
Corpus Christi, Texas, 45
Cortina, Juan N., Mexican general, 28, 35, 51, 59, 76, 108, 156
Cosío Villegas, Daniel, v, vi, vii, viii; Minister Plenipotentiary of Mexico, vi; delegate to the United Nations, vi; works of, v-viii
Credit Mobilier, 53
Cuba, shipment of cattle to, 44
Cuellar, José T. de, secretary of the Mexican legation in Washington, 69-70, 74
Cuellar, Rómulo, Mexican general, 217

Daran, Martin, French merchant in Mexico, 14
Darven and Co., banking firm in Mexico, 18
Dávila, Narciso, 51; Lerdo partisan in Nuevo León, 86
Diario Oficial (Mexico City) official newspaper, 87-88, 111-112, 114, 116, 133, 247
Díaz, Félix, Mexican general, 147
Díaz, Porfirio, anti-imperialist, vii-viii, xii, 19; archive of, 236, 247; cabinet, 131, 201, 236; change from anti-imperialist to supporter of economic imperialism, vii-viii, xii, 237; constitutional president, 35-36, 139, 149; economic measures, 14-18; election of, 33-35, 64, 149; Foster's appraisal of, 64-65; Jacobin liberal, xi-xii, 17, 45-46; non-recognition of, by Lerdo de Tejada, 85; recognition of, by Guatemala, El Salvador, Spain, 35-36, 221; by France, 156; by Belgium, 157; by the United States, 19-22, 27-28, 31-35, 51, 58, 61-65, 69-73, 82, 87, 91, 94-95, 119-120, 127-129, 136-138, 148-159, 166-168, 174, 221-225
Dickens, William C., claimant against Mexican government, 114
Durango (state), Mexico, 92

Eagle Pass, Texas, 45
England, 25, 38; interests in Mexico, xii; ships, 6; treaties, 9, 121
Epoca (La), Mexico City daily newspaper, 83
Escalante, Antonio, Mexican merchant, 13, 18, 221
Escobedo, Mariano, Mexican general, 4, 46, 86-88; Lerdista revolutionary, 104, 174-175
Espronceda, Rodolfo, Mexican bandit, 106
Estrada, Genaro, Secretary of Foreign Relations, 214, 247
Europe, 3, 164
European contraband, 194; goods, 193, 216; trade, 193
Evarts, William M., Secretary of

State, 58, 62-67, 72-77, 90-91, 118, 130-131, 139, 145-146, 150-159, 177, 179, 183, 196, 202, 207, 216, 219, 224-225, 228, 233-234; extradition policy of, 106-107, 159, 167, 200, 202

Far East, commerce, 140
Federalist (EL), Lerdista daily newspaper, 20, 87, 156, 247
Fish, Hamilton, Secretary of State, 25, 30-33, 48-49, 58, 62-63, 149, 213, 222-223, 232-233
Fisher, King, Texas outlaw, 45
Florida, 54-55
Fondo de Cultura Económica, v
Ford, John S., Texas Senator, 187, 242
Fort Brown, Texas, commandant of, 60, 101, 203
Fort Clark, Texas, 59, 242
Fort Craig, 203
Fort Duncan, Texas, 104, 198, 241
Fort San Juan de Ulúa, Mexico, 183-184
Foster, John W., United States minister in Mexico, xi-xii, 14, 16, 20-28, 30-36, 49, 51, 58-66, 69, 72, 74-86, 87-90, 98-99, 106-107, 110, 112-163, 168-171, 175-176, 189-200, 216, 222-236, 246-247
France, v, 38, 63; aid to Maximilian, 3; troops of, 3-4; foreign legion, 156
Free Zone on Mexican northern border, 32, 39-40, 73, 78, 98, 110, 123, 129, 133, 156, 183, 193-194, 202, 216-217, 229
Frisbie, John B., United States general, 147, 167
Fuero, Carlos, Mexican general, 217

Gadsden Treaty, 202
Galveston, Texas, 215
García, Fructuoso, Colonel, 198
García, Trinidad, Mexican Secretary of Government, 163-165
Garden City, Texas; see El Jardín
Garza, Segundo, Mexican bandit, 105
Garza Ayala, Lázaro, 51; Lerdo partisan in Nuevo León, 86
Garza Galán, José María, 198, 218
Germany, legation of in Mexico, 35, 38, 131, 225

Gómez del Palacio, Francisco, 170
González, Manuel, Secretary of War, 163, 165; President of Mexico, 207-208, 213, 217
Goríbar, Faustino de, wealthy Mexican, 15
Grant, Ulysses S., Candidate for President of the United States, 7-8; President of the United States, 11, 47, 52, 54, 56, 58, 211, 215
Great Plains, 41, 43
Guadalajara, Jalisco, Mexico, 26, 35
Guadalupe Hidalgo, Treaty of, 11, 202
Guanajuato (city), Mexico, 18, 22, 51
Guatemala, 208; chief of state, 35; legation of, 35; population, 122
Guaymas, Mexico, 4
Guerrero (state), Mexico, 64
Gulf of Mexico, 43, 135

Hackett, Charles W., 245, 248
Harding, John Wesley, Texas outlaw, 45
Harrison, John P., xii
Harvard University, 231
Havana, Cuba, 6
Hayes, Rutherford B., President of the United States, 50, 57-58, 63, 65-68, 70, 74, 80-82, 84, 86-87, 95, 97-98, 100-101, 106, 108-109, 111, 114, 119, 150, 167, 179, 183-184, 188, 190, 195, 202-203, 207, 213-214, 216, 219, 221, 233; election of, 52, 54-56, 139, 218; cabinet of, 84; message to Congress, 68
Hermosillo, Sonora, Mexico, 4
Hicks, John D., 239, 246, 248
Historia mexicana, vi
horse thieves, 103, 109
Hubbard, Richard, governor of Texas, 97, 106
Hunter, W., legal conselor of the Department of States, 34

Iglesias, José María, 92, 220, 248; enemy of Díaz, 13, 17, 20, 22, 30, 33, 50-51, 84-86; faction of, 25, 27, 51, 58
Independencia, warship, 29-30
Indians, 32-33, 40-42, 45-46, 48, 53, 59, 64, 66, 71, 78, 102, 104, 125, 129-130, 133, 137-138, 145, 160, 162-169, 178, 181-185, 189-191, 194-198,

201, 203, 205, 207, 218, 226-227, 229-231, 235; Apaches, 111; Comanches, 41, 181; Crow, 48; Kickapoo, 111, 181; Lipan, 103, 111, 181; Mezcaleros, 111; Plains Indians, 41-42; Seminoles, 111, 186; pursuit of, 41-42, 46, 111, 124-125, 189-190, 194, 196-197, 201, 226, 230-231
International law, 65, 212
International Review, 148
Investigating Committee of the Northern Frontier (Mexican), 46
Ireland, 38
Italy, chief of state, 35-36
Iturbe, José María, wealthy Mexican, 15; brothers, 16

Jalisco (state), Mexico, 27
Jardín (El), 198
Jiménez, Vicente, Mexican general, 64
Joint Claims Commission, 9-10, 12, 15, 19-20, 24-25, 29, 142-143, 199, 213, 221
Johnson, Andrew, President of the United States, 4, 7-8, 52
Journal, Indianapolis newspaper, 154
Juárez, Benito, President of Mexico, 4, 8, 11, 94, 142-143, 175, 220
"Juvenal," pseudonym of anti-Lerdo journalist, 14

Kansas (state), 43
Kelley, J. M., Captain, 175
Knights of Saint Patrick, 215

Lafragua, José María, Secretary of Foreign Relations, 28, 49, 84, 228-230, 235
Landero y Coss, Francisco, Secretary of the Treasury, 211
Laredo, Texas, 43
Las Cuevas Ranch, 47
Lascuráin, Ramón D. de, wealthy Mexican, 15
Lerdista faction, 25, 51, 76, 79-80, 83, 86, 88, 90, 100, 102, 105, 116, 150, 160, 175; invaders, 83, 104; press, 86, 105, 153, 156, 228; rebels, 198
Lerdo de Tejada, Sebastián, President of Mexico, xi, 13-14, 17, 19-22, 27-29, 32-34, 50-51, 58, 69, 75, 82, 84-89, 91, 92, 94-95, 114, 116, 133, 140, 142, 154, 159, 163, 174-175, 220-224, 228-229, 232; Secretary of Foreign Relations, 3, 8-10
Lester, Edward, journalist, 147-148, 248
Libertad (La), Mexico City newspaper, 153, 158-159, 209, 211-212, 215
Limantour, José Ives, 16
Lincoln, Abraham, 7, 52, 247
London, England, 30-31
Lloyd's of London, 31
loans, forced, 6, 60, 73, 82, 110, 119-121, 125-126, 129, 132-134, 138, 202, 216, 229, 232
López Portillo y Rojas, José, 14, 248
Louisiana, 8, 54-55
Lower California, 92

MacCorkle, S. A., 248
Machoro, Paulino, Lerdo partisan in Coahuila, 86
Maine, 207-208
Mariscal, Ignacio, exile in New York, 178, 222-223; head of Mexican legation in Washington, D.C., 22-25, 30-31, 64, 68, 70, 76-78, 212-213, 235, 248; minister of Mexico under Lerdo de Tejada, 31, 213; Morgan informant, 206; recall by Mexican government, 69, 72
Márquez, Leonardo, Mexican general, 3, 5
Martínez, Pedro, 51; Lerdo partisan in Nuevo León, 86
Martínez, Ignacio, 27, 31
Martínez Zorrilla, Juan, wealthy Spaniard in Mexico City, 13
Mata, Filomena, 85, 248
Mata, José María, magistrate of the Supreme Court of Mexico, 81; Mexican member of the Claims Commission of Mexico and the United States, 25-32; minister plenipotentiary for Mexico in Washington, 69-70, 72-75, 83-84, 89-91, 95, 106, 117-125, 129, 132-137, 142, 144, 147, 159, 169-171, 176, 178, 189, 190, 194, 196, 222-226, 235
Matamoros, Tamaulipas, Mexico, 24, 37, 44, 51, 101, 135, 149, 183-184, 187 226
Mathews, Stanley, United States Senator, 146
Maverick County, Texas, 45

Maximilian, 3, 5, 22; military forces of, Austrian, 3; French, 3-5, 156

Mazatlan, Mexico, detention of two United States schooners in, 110, 183

McCraig, George G., 241

McLane-Ocampo Treaty, 131

McCrary, George W., Secretary of War, 66, 140, 179, 183, 188, 201, 242

McKenzie, Richard S., United States Army Colonel, 48, 175-176, 187

McNelly, L. H., Captain of Texas Rangers, 45, 47

Mejía, Ignacion, General, return from exile, 175

Mendez, Juan N., General, 16, 18, 75, 220

Mexico: acquisition by foreigners of real estate on border of, 122, 192-193, 229, 231; agriculture, 91; army, 92, 96, 101, 103-104, 111, 114, 118, 125, 130, 132, 135, 137, 141, 146, 149, 163, 165, 175, 178-180, 185-187, 199, 201, 203-204, 206, 217, 227; citizens of, 37-39, 41, 45, 47, 52, 84, 87-89, 96, 100, 107, 114, 119-121, 124-127, 151-152, 166, 181-192, 201, 214, 235, 237; claims against the United States, 8, 10-12, 19, 85, 197-198; Congress of, xi, 11, 27, 34-36, 58, 64, 107, 111, 122-123, 131, 163, 174, 179, 192, 219, 249; Chamber of Deputies of, 75, 149, 174, 236; Senate of, 75, 144, 160, 162-165, 168, 171, 173, 189-190, 194-195, 204-205, 236-237; constitution, 86, 126, 134, 159, 163, 173, 205; debts of United States citizens in, 6, 85; Department of Foreign Relations, 18-19, 21, 24, 26, 32, 112, 168, 170-173, 189-190, 199, 209, 213, 220; foreign concessions in, xi; frontier problems in north: pacification, 29, 33, 35, 37, 42, 45-48, 51-52, 59-61, 66-67, 70-80, 82-83, 98-101, 106-110, 113-116, 123-124, 160-167, 178-188, 194-203, 225-235; criminal refugees from the United States, 28, 58-59, 64, 71, 77, 137, 141, 164; smuggling, 28, 33, 38-40, 46-47, 193-194, 217; industry, 91; invasions of the United States territory by, 100, 105-107, 120, 129, 160, 176, 198, 204, 206-207; Investigating Committee of the Northern Frontier, 46; investment of foreign capital in, xii, 87, 219; legation in Washington, D.C., 26, 68, 85, 90, 115, 144, 160, 172, 195, 212-213, 221; mines, 19; public opinion, 117, 131, 136, 195; railroads, 29, 212, 219, concessions for construction of, xi; Revolution of 1910, vi; Secretary of Foreign Relations, 32, 72-73, 84, 90, 112, 118, 123, 134, 143, 145-146, 161-164, 170, 189, 200, 203, 220, 235, 246; Secretary of the Treasury, vi, 211; Secretary of War, 76, 78, 113, 194, 203, 211, 217; Supreme Court, 119, 161, 174, 189, 215; threat of war with the United States, 168, 181, 197, 208, 225; treaties, 121, 124, 126, 205; United States claims against, payment of, 13-18, 26-32, 66, 221-224; Vice-president of, 220; withdrawal of French troops from, 3-4

Mexico City, xi, 4, 25, 29, 31, 35, 50, 88, 91, 116, 139-140, 149, 175, 201-202, 211-212, 218, 220, 232, 234, 236

Mier y Celis, Antonio, 15-16, 18

Mijares, Antonio, 13

Miramón, Miguel, General, 3-5

Missouri, commander of United States Army in, 60, 100; state of, 215

Monitor Republicano (El), Mexico City newspaper, 14, 57, 249

Monitor Tuxtepecano (El), Mexican newspaper, 249

Montana (state), 43

Monterrey, Nuevo León, Mexico, 4, 90, 211; United States consul in, 200

Montes, Ezequiel, magistrate, 121

Morgan, P. H., United States Minister to Mexico, 202-206

Morison, Samuel Elliot, 239-240, 246, 249

Mormons, 40

Mount Vernon, 215

Nacional (El), Mexico City newspaper, 249

Napoleon III, 4; United States agreement with, 4

Naranjo, Francisco, General, 104-105, 207, 217, 235-236, 241

National Bank of Mexico (Mexico City), vi

National Railroad (Mexico), 219

National School of Economics (Mexico City), director of, v

Nebraska, state of, 43

Negrete, Miguel, military commander of Mexico City, 175

Negroes, 55

Nevada, state of, 43

New Mexico, state of, 43, 203

New Orleans, Louisiana, 5-6, 28-30

New York (state), legislature, 53

New York City, 18-19, 23, 31, 54, 85-86, 148, 178, 215, 221; dailies, 31, 57, 84, 86-87, 90, 92, 153, 213, 215, 249; *Evening Post,* 213; *Herald Tribune,* 57, 86-87, 92, 153; *Times,* 57, 249; *World,* 31, 57, 86, 90

Niagara Falls, 215

Noria (La), Revolt of, 52, 78, 98, 129, 231

North Dakota, state of, 43

Northern Division (of Mexican Army), 76, 132, 217

Notes, 239

Nueces Valley of Texas, 43

Nuevo Laredo, Tamaulipas, Mexico, 183-184, 219

Nuevo León (state), Mexico, 51-52, 84, 86, 92, 100, 102, 200, 210; press in, 96, 249

Oaxaca (state), Mexico, xi, 17, 21, 147, 211, 215

Ogazón, Pedro, Secretary of War, 76-77

Ohio, state of, 54

Oklahoma, state of, 43

Olaguíbel y Artista, Carlos, director of *La Época,* 83

Ord, Edward O. C., Brigadier General of United States Army, 48, 60-64, 67-68, 70, 75-80, 84, 87-88, 91, 95-109, 113-117, 119, 124, 141, 146, 150, 160-161, 178-180, 184-188, 190, 194, 196-197, 201, 203, 209-214, 225, 233-234, 237, 240-241

Ord de Treviño, Roberta Augusta, daughter of Brigadier General Ord, 209-211

Oregon, governor of, 55; Democratic elector of, 55

Ortiz de la Huerta, Rafael, wealthy Mexican, 15

Otterbourg, Marcus, consul general for the United States in Mexico, 5; Minister of the United States in Mexico, 6

Pájaro Verde (El), Mexico City newspaper, 249

Palo Blanco enterprise, 90

Paris, 5; Mexican archives in, 246

Patria (La), Mexico City newspaper, 90, 249

Paz, Ireneo, 90

Peru, 121

Pesqueira, Ignacio, governor of Sonora, 120

Philadelphia, the *Press* of, 57

Piedras Negras, Coahuila, Mexico, 37, 48, 75-76, 100, 131, 183-184, 198-199, 226

Pimentel, Fernando, wealthy Mexican, 15

Plumb, Edward Lee, secretary to Lewis D. Campbell, 6; representative of United States companies, 87, 140

Plymouth, United States battleship, abondons Veracruz, 80

Poland, immigrants from, to Texas, 38

Porfirista faction, 20, 22, 58, 87-91, 100-101, 142, 145, 155, 175, 198, 223, 228, 246

Portilla, Anselmo de la, 57

Potomac River, 56

press (the), in Mexico, 14, 20, 32, 57, 81, 83, 86-87, 90, 93, 95, 105, 117, 131, 136, 145, 153, 156, 158, 176, 187, 195, 228, 247, 249; in the United States, 57, 147-148, 154, 248; Catholic, 109, 153, 156, 158, 208, 228

Press (The) of Philadelphia, 57

Price, William R., Captain, commander of the Ringgold Barracks, 105-106

Pritchard, William, explorer of oil deposits in Mexico, 147-148

Puebla (state), Mexico, 4, 50

Querétaro (state), Mexico, 4-5, 105

Quiroga, Julián, 51

Railroads, concessions for construction of, in Mexico, xi; in United States, 140; Mexican, 217, 219

Ramsey, Alexander, Secretary of War, 201

Remington rifle, 104

Remolino Ranch (Coahuila), 175

República (La), Mexico City newspaper, 249

Republicano (El), Mexico City newspaper, 249

Revueltas, Silvestre, General, 51, 60

Reyes, Bernardo, Colonel, 217

Richardson, D. S., United States chargé d'affaires in Mexico, 154-155

Richardson, James D., 249

Ringgold Barracks, 104-105

Rio Grande City, Texas, 47, 106, 125

Rio Grande River, 37, 42-44, 46, 67-68, 77, 89, 92, 99-100, 106, 109, 114-115, 129, 140, 164, 180-183, 189, 200

Rippy, J. Fred, 240, 245-246, 249

Riva Palacio, Vicente, Secretary of Public Works, 163, 236

Romero, Matías, Mexican Minister to the United States, 3, 6-8, 236; Secretary of the Treasury, 8-10, 112, 123, 129, 147, 163-165, 215, 236-237; archives of, 246

Romero Rubio, Carmen, wife of Porfirio Díaz, 215, 236

Romero Rubio, Manuel, 87

Ross, Stanley Robert, viii

Ruelas, Miguel, Secretary of Foreign Relations, 203-205, 235

Ruíz, Joaquín, 170

Russia, United States legation in, 201, 212

rustling, 28, 32-33, 42, 44, 46-47, 71, 102, 114-115, 120, 124-125, 130, 159, 175, 178, 180, 186, 189, 191, 199, 217-218, 226-227, 229

Saltillo, Coahuila, Mexico, 4

El Salvador, legation of, 35, Chief of State of, 35

San Antonio, Texas, 43, 175, 183, 186, 203, 209, 212

San Luis Potosí (city), 4

Santa Rosa, Coahuila, Mexico, mountain of, 194

Saxony, 121

Schleicher, Gustav, United States Congressman from Texas, 139-140, 153, 175; chairman of Committee on Mexican Affairs, 185, 209

Scotland, 38

Seward, Frederick W., First Undersecretary of State, 65-67, 69, 72, 75, 77-79, 106, 133-134, 149, 247

Seward, William H., Secretary of State, 4-11

Shafter, W. R., Lt. Col. in United States Army in Texas, 48, 58-61, 67, 75-76, 98, 100, 104, 131-132, 135, 161, 179, 186, 225, 233

Shelby Joe, general in the Civil War, 83-84

Sheridan, W. T., General in the United States, 8, 100; Commander in Chief of the United States Army, 141, 179-182, 184, 241-242

Sherman, W. T., General in the United States Army, 66-67, 99-100, 141, 161, 169, 182-184, 188, 240-242

Sierra Madre mountain range, 182

Siglo XIX (El), Mexico City newspaper, 57-58, 215, 249

Sinaloa (state), Mexico, 92

Sobrino, Vicente, wealthy Spaniard living in Mexico City, 13

Sonora (state), Mexico, 84, 92, 217

South (the), 54, 67

South Dakota, state of, 43

Southern States, 7-8, 39, 67, 218

South Carolina, state of, 54-55

Spain, chief of state, 35; citizens, 35; legation of, 35

Spencertown, New York, 148

Saint Louis, Missouri, 215

Saint Petersburg, Russia, 213

State University of New York, Stony Brook, New York, viii

Storms, P. R., United States Senator from Texas, 187, 242

Susquehanna, battleship, 5

Tagle, Ciro, Mexican commissioner sent to Washington, 25-30, 32; sent with money to pay first part of United States claims, 222

Tagle, Protasio, 26; Minister of Justice, 163-165, 174,

Tamaulipas (state), Mexico, 28, 46, 50, 76, 84, 86, 101, 106-108, 200, 210, 217

Tampico, Tamaulipas, Mexico, 44, 183, 196

Tecoac, victory of, by Díaz, 50

Teresa, Nicolás de, wealthy Mexican, 15

Terrazas, Luis, Colonel, 206, 218

Terrazas, Joaquín, 218

Texas, Republic of, 43

Texas (state), 8, 28, 37-40, 42-45, 48, 51-52, 59, 67-68, 76, 78, 100, 102-108, 114, 159, 179, 181-182, 185-187, 191-192, 198, 200, 203, 209-210, 217, 219, 229; authorities, 47, 60, 197; citizens, 46, 96-97, 141, 194; congressmen, 95; dragoons, 93; federal forces in, 59, 76, 100; governor, 188; merchants, 40, 60, 193-194; legislature, 215; ranchers, 60; rangers, ii, 45, 47, 249; troops of, 48, 141

Texas Pacific Railroad, 140

Thompson, Henry, correspondent of *Herald Tribune* of New York, 5

Thornton, Edward, English arbiter, 114-115, 126

Tilden, Samuel G., candidate for President of the United States, 54-55, 67

Treviño, Jerónimo, General, chief of Mexican federal forces on the northern frontier, 52, 76-77, 79-80, 89-108, 111, 113-114, 132, 166-167, 179, 194, 200-201, 209-211, 215, 234, 236; Secretary of War, 211, 215, 217

Treviño hierarchy, 51

Treviño y Ord, José Jerónimo, son of General Jerónimo Treviño, 211, 215

Trías, Ángel, General, 76

Trimestre ecónomico, vi

troops, reciprocal passing of border of, 71, 85, 100-105, 113, 115-120, 123-124, 130-138, 159-173, 178, 189-191, 194-196, 203-208, 226-227, 233, 237

Tuxtepec, Plan of, 14, 17, 19, 25; revolt of, 17, 24, 26, 45, 51-52, 76, 78, 82, 156, 231, vii; revolutionaries, 116

Tuxtepecan army, 45, 83

Tuxtepecan press, 88

United Nations, Economic and Social Council of, vi; Mexican delegation to, vi

Union Pacific Railroad, 53, 140

United States of America: attorney-general of, 48; citizens in Mexico, xi, 6, 9, 21, 29, 38-39, 43, 45, 47, 82, 84, 86, 90-91, 96, 98, 107, 122, 126-129, 132-134, 137-138, 145, 155, 159-160, 181-183, 191-193, 198, 202, 207-208, 216, 219, 229, 238; Civil War, 7-8, 38-40, 43, 45, 52, 54, 193; claims against Mexico, 6-12, 17-19, 22-27, 69, 98, 110, 126, 134, 137, 221-223; Congress, 7-8, 23, 39, 46, 52-53, 55, 56, 68, 108, 133, 139, 141-142, 147-148, 151-153, 162, 182, 184, 186, 188, 194-195, 233; House of Representatives, 53, 55, 85, 139, 185, 202; Senate, 10, 53, 77, 147; corruption in, 53-54; Department of Defense, xii, 49, 53, 99, 103, 186; Department of State, xii, 5-7, 10, 20, 24-25, 27, 29-32, 36, 58-59, 61, 66, 70, 72, 77-78, 99, 106, 117-118, 120, 127, 132-137, 140-144, 147, 150-154, 160-162, 168, 190-205, 222-225, 229-234, 238, 245; forced loans by Mexican government on citizens of, 119-121, 125-126, 137, 193; Homestead Act, 40; Morrill Act, 40; invasions into Mexican territory, 100, 160, 168-169, 175-176, 190-191; intervention in Mexico, xii, 4-5, 57-58, 61, 75-77, 86, 90-94, 96, 99, 102-103, 106, 108-109, 113, 115-120, 123-125, 129, 145, 160-162, 166, 169, 179-180, 186, 188, 190, 192, 195-198, 203-208, 231, 237, 247; legation in Mexico, 24, 87, 155, 213; Mexican claims against, 8, 10-12, 85, 197-198; Mexicans in, 37-39, 41, 45, 107, 127, 181; military forces of, 47-49, 52, 54, 59-60, 66-67, 76, 85, 92, 94, 96, 98, 100-102, 108-109, 114, 119, 125, 129-132, 135, 137, 140-141, 162-168, 178-188, 190, 192, 194, 198, 201-206, 212; political parties, 39, 54-56; public opinion in, 56, 81, 87, 90-91, 95, 141-142, 147, 153, 176, 215; presidential election in, 23, 52-56; railroads, 40-41, 43, 57, 217; Reconstruction, 7-8, 38, 54; Secretary of State, 75, 85, 150, 176, 184, 202, 207, 212; Secretary of War, 49, 54, 58, 102, 108-109, 140, 178, 184, 188, 201, 234; Supreme Court, 56; threat of war with Mexico, 84-89, 168, 181-183, 197, 225; treaties, 6, 9, 70-85, 124-126, 136, 200, 202, 227

Valadés, José C., 226, 246, 249
Valdés, Pedro W., alias "Winkar," Lerdo partisan in Tamaulipas, 86, 104-105
Vallarta, Ignacio Luis, archive of, 246; Secretary of Foreign Relations, xi, 14, 18-36, 60-80, 82-83, 90, 95, 97-99, 107, 110-139, 142, 144-150, 154-165, 169, 171, 175, 189, 206, 219-230, 232, 235-237, 248
Vallarta Bustos, Ignacio and José, 249
Valle, Adolfo T., Colonel, 206
Valle, Pedro, 13
Veracruz (city), 5-6, 20, 28-29, 39-40, 80, 135, 183-184, 196, 211, 215; Bay of, 5
Victorio, barbarous Indian, 205-206
Villa Jiménez, Mexico, attacked by armed forces, 175
Villarreal, Bibiano, 103; General Jerónimo Treviño's private secretary, 90
Voz de México, Mexico City newspaper, 81, 157, 249

Wales, Prince of, 215
War, of Intervention, 6, 37; of 1846-47, 168, 237; of Reform, 37
Ward, L. F., Lt. in United States Army, 109

Washington, D.C., 8-9, 22, 24-26, 28, 30, 72, 74-75, 77, 90, 95, 103, 106, 115, 117, 133, 137, 142, 144-145, 148, 150, 154, 158-160, 167-171, 195, 198, 212-213, 215, 221, 223, 225, 235; Library of Congress, 213, 246; Mexican Embassy in, 246; National Archives, xii, 5, 213, 246, 248
Washington *Republican*, 57, 153
Webb, Walter Prescott, ii, 38, 41, 44, 207, 239-240, 246, 249
Weckmann, Luis, 246
West Virginia, University of, 5
Western Union Telegraph, 55, 196
Wilhelm, emperor of Germany, 35
Williams, R. A., Lieutenant, 104
Wilson, Henry Lane, United States Ambassador, 234
World War I, 34
Wyke, Sir Charles, English minister, 143
Wyke-Zamacona Treaty, 88
Wyoming, state of, 43

Zacatecas (state), Mexico, 4; City, 4
Zacatecas quarters, 196
Zamacona, Manuel María de, 133-134, 138, 142-148; Secretary of Foreign Relations in 1861, 143; confidential agent to the United States, 144, 150; Mexican Minister Plenipotentiary in Washington, 167-173, 195, 202, 207-209, 216, 219, 235
Zaragoza, Ignacio, General, 94